Cultural Reverse II

The book proposes a new academic concept, "Cultural Reverse" (文化反哺), referring to the phenomenon beginning in China in the 1980s in which the older generation started to learn from the younger generation, and analyzes the multiple causes and social impacts of this trend.

Following on from the first volume, this second volume further analyzes the multiple causes of cultural reverse, including rapid social change, the influence of peer groups, and the impact of the media. Then, in a broader context, the author discusses the complex interdependence of and conflict among the State, society, and youth. He tells a story of the transformation of Chinese youth over the past hundred years, and names this "one-place" (fast-changing China) and "one-time only" (unrepeatable) phenomenon the "China feeling".

The innovative content of the book pushes the barriers of the academic field. Scholars of Chinese sociology and general readers interested in contemporary Chinese society will find this book to be essential.

Zhou Xiaohong served as dean of the School of Social and Behavioral Sciences at Nanjing University for 16 years; now he is a senior professor of Humanities and Social Sciences at Nanjing University. His main research fields are sociological theory, social psychology, and contemporary China studies.

China Perspectives

The *China Perspectives* series focuses on translating and publishing works by leading Chinese scholars, writing about both global topics and China-related themes. It covers Humanities & Social Sciences, Education, Media and Psychology, as well as many interdisciplinary themes.

This is the first time any of these books have been published in English for international readers. The series aims to put forward a Chinese perspective, give insights into cutting-edge academic thinking in China, and inspire researchers globally.

Titles in sociology currently include:

The Way to a Great Country
A Macroscopic View on Chinese Population in the 21st Century
Tian Xueyuan

Social Structure and Social Stratification in Contemporary China
Lu Xueyi

Social Construction and Social Development in Contemporary China
Lu Xueyi

Economic Transition and People's Livelihood: China Income Distribution Research
Zhao Renwei

Economic Transition and People's Livelihood: China Economic Transition Research
Zhao Renwei

Academic Experiences of International Students in Chinese Higher Education
Mei Tian, Fred Dervin and Genshu Lu

For more information, please visit www.routledge.com/series/CPH

Cultural Reverse II

The Multidimensional Motivation and Social Impact of Intergenerational Revolution

Zhou Xiaohong

LONDON AND NEW YORK

This book is published with financial support from the Chinese Fund for the Humanities and Social Sciences

First published 2021 by Routledge

2 Park Square, Milton Park, Abingdon, Oxon OX14 4RN
605 Third Avenue, New York, NY 10017

Routledge is an imprint of the Taylor & Francis Group, an informa business

First issued in paperback 2022

English Version by permission of The Commercial Press.

British Library Cataloguing-in-Publication Data
A catalogue record for this book is available from the British Library

Library of Congress Cataloging-in-Publication Data
A catalog record has been requested for this book

ISBN: 978-0-367-90415-9 (hbk)
ISBN: 978-1-03-233595-7 (pbk)
DOI: 10.4324/9781003024309

Typeset in Times New Roman
by Swales & Willis, Exeter, Devon, UK

Contents

Illustrations

Figures

Tables

1 Social transition as the impetus to refurbish history

China is crossing the river as fast as it can. And sometimes the process is more like the spawning run of salmons—hopefully jumping up rapids rather than taking carefully chosen steps. Salmons can cover a distance of 300 miles in about three weeks; China is packing the changes of decades into a few years. And what is true for China on a huge scale is true within the small scale of families; within one generation, prospects in life have changed dramatically. Parents have to adjust to new values and desires of their children at high speed. And Chinese children have to walk a tightrope between respecting their parents and neglecting their parents' wishes.

John Naisbitt

How is history refurbished?

"Man cannot step twice into the same river" is a famous saying of the ancient Greek philosopher Heraclitus. He wanted to tell us that nature is changing all the time. In fact, the same is true of human society. Today, when the changes triggered by globalization and social transformation are increasingly the most remarkable facts of our time, we can even say that one cannot step into the same river Once. Because "stepping in" is a process, and between the beginning and the end of this process, the changing society we live in may have changed beyond recognition.

Human society has been changing since ancient times, but transformation becoming a social fact concerned with human beings or a theme of human self-conscious thinking is, like sociology itself, the product of modernity (Giddens, 1982: 1). Anyone familiar with the history of social science in the West knows that the main achievements and fundamental rules in it basically come from the so-called great transition from tradition to modernity from the 18th century to the 20th century. To put it simply, the path of change and analysis of its motivation is the entire intellectual heritage of Western or modern social sciences. It is in this sense that we also propose that we should strive to understand in academia the great social changes that have taken place in China over the years from 1978 to 2020 of reform and opening-up to the outside world; otherwise, as Huang Wansheng said, "both China and the West will suffer a great loss"

(Huang & Liu, 2009; Zhou, 2010). In fact, the study of cultural reverse, through the changes in the intergenerational relationship, to see the great changes in Chinese society, is one of these systematic efforts.

Although human society is always in the process of change, there are only two great changes with real qualitative significance. The first is the transformation from primitive society to civilized society, namely the emergence of civilization itself (Huntington, 2010: 47) around 5,000 BC. Another is the so-called "modernization" that has been spreading all over the world since the beginning of the 18th century. As a transition from traditional to modern or agricultural society to industrial and post-industrial society, modernization is the most drastic, far-reaching, and apparently inevitable social change in human history (Rozman, 2003: 5), which includes industrialization, urbanization, and literacy, education, affluence, increased social mobilization, and more complex and diverse occupational structures (Huntington, 2010: 47). If, in 5,000 BC, neither the human mind nor the complexity of society allowed our ancestors to analyze and discuss the meaning of the emergence of civilization, then, as a child of modernity or change, social science, especially sociology, which has grown since the 18th century, has begun to consciously think about human social change in the face of increasingly frequent and complex social changes, relying on various empirical means obtained by the development of modern natural science. As early as the 18th century, the pioneers of what would become known as sociology, Battista Vico in Italy, Adam Ferguson in England, and Comte de Saint-Simon in France, were the first to contemplate the difference between past and present history, and to attempt a syllogistic division of human history.[1] One sign of the most successful of these attempts was the concept of an "industrial society" by Saint-Simon, who found the most appropriate connotation for the "modern" of modern society. Under their influence, the Frenchman Auguste Comte, the father of sociology, and the British Herbert Spencer, the second father of sociology, began to establish change as one of the basic contents of this new discipline. For this reason, Comte established the social dynamics with human social change as the theme, and, like the founders of sociology including Saint-Simon, used syllogism to express the process of social change as the theological, metaphysical, and positive stages. Spencer, on the other hand, takes it a step further by focusing on the changes that have occurred since the beginning of the Industrial Revolution, and thus naturally divides the history of human change into the history of the transition from a martial society to an industrial one. In Spencer's case, the essence of a martial society is its coercion, "while with the industrial type of society, organized on the principle of voluntary co-operation, there harmonizes that monogamic union which voluntary domestic co-operation presupposes" (Spencer, 1925: 569).

Since the transformation of European society from traditional agricultural society to modern industrial society directly gave birth to social science, it is quite natural, then, that discussions of tradition and modernity based originally on the unilinear evolution theory become what Weber calls the ideal type (Weber, 1949: 90), or Parsons's model variable (Parsons & Shils, 1951: 77).

Thus, the literature of the social sciences is full of variations of the binary traditional–modern pair, including Mann's identity–contract society, Spencer's warrior society–industrial society, Marx's feudalist society–capitalist society, Tonnies's community–society, Tocqueville's aristocracy–democracy, Durkheim's mechanical solidarity–organic unity, Weber's patriarchal traditional economy–rational capitalist economy, as well as Cooley's primary group–secondary group, Sorokin's intimate relationship–contractual relationship, Redfield's townsfolk society–civil society, Becker's sacred society–secular society, and Fei Xiaotong's etiquette society–legal society (Zhou, 2002: 139). Although no one today views the traditional–modern as absolutely opposite poles, and no longer insists on the development model of single-line evolution, and no longer simply thinks that the path that the Western countries have gone through must be the path that other countries will follow,[2] people are still accustomed to discussing the themes related to change under the conceptual framework of the traditional–modern, regarding its development as the basic path of modernization.

Since Comte and Spencer, various theories have been formed in the field of sociology in order to explain social changes, especially the social changes since industrialization. Among them, the influential or popular theories include the theory of evolution, the theory of circulation, the theory of function, the theory of conflict, and the theory of modernization. Influenced by Darwin's theory of evolution, evolution theory views social changes as the natural succession of different historical stages. According to cycle theory, society is a living organism, which concerns the process of birth, growth, maturity, and aging. Functional theory holds that each part of society is an interdependent whole, which plays its respective role in the overall equilibrium, while the excessive or insufficient exchange of information or energy between subsystems may lead to structural changes inside or outside the system. The conflict theory holds that the power inequality in social life is the main cause of social repression and conflict, while the ubiquitous social conflict is the basic root of human social change. Finally, on the basis of Parsons's structural function theory, in order to compete with the raging communism in the 1950s, and in addition to Marx's class struggle theory of conflict, the modernization theory was established as a road of development and change for the underdeveloped countries with the United States as the standard. Based on the development experience of European and American countries, the modernization theory regards the road they have taken as a linear process of social changes that will or must affect all countries in the world.[3]

Theory is gray, the tree of life is always green. In the process of the emergence, formation, and modification of various theories of social change which are contradictory to each other, the world has been changing more and more rapidly in the 20th century, especially after World War II. Daniel Bell, an American sociologist, argues that two salient facts distinguish our society today from past history. First, the speed of change. Because the world is developing at an accelerated speed, "no longer would any child be able to live in the same kind of world—sociologically and intellectually—as his parents and grandparents had inhabited" (Bell, 1999: 170). Second, the scale of change, which, including population, economy, and knowledge, is growing at an unprecedented rate. The growth of population alone, especially the growth of the urban population, makes the social relations among people become increasingly complicated and diversified. Just as Engels commented that London had a huge benefit because of the population, so this massive concentration of 2.5 million people gathered in one region increases the power of 2.5 million 100 times (Engels, 1957: 303), and now there are at least a dozen cities in the world with more than ten times the population of London.

Compared with the thousands of years that preceded it, the speed of change over the decades is often surprising. Eric Hobsbawm, a historian and sociologist, has written with keen observation and vivid prose that when a convict who was imprisoned in the 1950s came out of prison in Italy more than a decade later, he suddenly felt as if he had lived another life. In the late 1970s, vendors in a remote Mexican town, each with a Japanese calculator in his hand, settled accounts for tourists who had come from far away. Just a decade ago, no one in the area knew about calculators. Therefore, Hobsbawm says that by the 1960s, 80% of the world's population found themselves suddenly ending their medieval lives (Hobsbawm, 1999: 435). However surprising, Hobsbawm's exclamation was made over 50 years ago. In the last 50 years or so, the world has been moving forward with what Toffler calls "accelerating momentum" thanks to economic growth and technological advancement on a global scale (Toffler, 1970: 19). Electronic technology with the computer as the core, biotechnology, optical communication technology based on laser and optical fibers, marine engineering, space development, the utilization of new materials and new energy sources, as well as the biological genetic engineering symbolized by "cloning", which is becoming more and more popular, have changed the relationship between human beings and nature irreversibly in the past decades. It was this series of changes that led to the arrival of the "post-industrial society" centered on information technology, which Daniel Bell first anticipated in 1962 (Bell, 1999: ciii). Manuel Castells writes in *The Rise of the Network Society* that in a short few decades, the new information technology revolution swept over the whole world with lightning speed, and its characteristic is "the immediate application to its own development of technologies it generates, connecting the world through information technology" (Castells, 2010a: 32). All this has created a whole new world in which:

> chips and computers are new; ubiquitous, mobile telecommunications are new; genetic engineering is new; electronically integrated, global financial markets working in real time are new; an interlinked capitalist economy embracing the whole planet, and not only some of its segments, is new; a majority of the urban labor force in knowledge and information processing in advanced economies is new; a majority of urban population in the planet is new; the demise of the Soviet Empire, the fading away of communism, and the end of the Cold War are new; the rise of the Asian Pacific

as an equal partner in the global economy is new; the widespread challenge to patriarchalism is new; the universal consciousness on ecological preservation is new; and the emergence of a network society, based on a space of flows, and on timeless time, is historically new.

(Castells, 2010b: 372)

If, as Toffler says, we can divide 50,000 years of human history into 800 living generations (each divided into 62 years), it was six generations ago that we saw print, four generations ago that we were able to calculate time relatively accurately, two generations ago that we started using electric motors (Toffler, 1970: 14), and one generation ago that we started using television. So all of the new changes Castells is talking about happened in the second half of the last of the 800 generations, or 30 years.

If we go back before 1978, the description here, especially of the global social changes that followed the scientific and technological revolution after World War II, has little to do with China, which for thousands of years was called the "central state". At that time, China, using Castells's language, was in a state of being "switched off" in relation to the new technology system (Castells, 2010a: 38). At the height of the Great Leap Forward in 1958, according to Mao Zedong's vision, the Sixth Plenary Session of the Eighth CPC Central Committee pointed out that "the general feature of the current international situation is 'the enemy continues to rot day by day, and we get better day by day'", but for the next 20 years, the enemy did not rot, and we did not get better. We really got better after the reform and opening-up in 1978.

There were many factors that stimulated Deng Xiaoping, the "chief designer of reform and opening-up", to make his decisions, which include his belief of contributing to national rejuvenation from an early age, his early study in France, his painful experience in the unprecedented Cultural Revolution, his efforts to find the motivation for the "legalization" of socialism that was on the verge of collapse, and the "developed" reality of developed countries he witnessed later. In October 1978, during a visit to the Nissan factory in Japan, when Deng Xiaoping was informed that the labor productivity of Nissan was dozens of times that of China's then most advanced Changchun First Automobile Factory, this pragmatic old man who never gave up sighed, "Only after coming here did I understand what modernization is" (Wu, 2010). Thus, at the Third Plenary Session of the Eleventh Central Committee held at the end of this year, when this "clear-headed" old man was replaced as the protagonist of the political scene, China, an ancient civilization with a history of 5,000 years, once again kicked off the changes and began to take off in a real sense.

In different chapters of this book, we have described the changes in Chinese society since 1978. Although China's economic aggregate has been growing since the reform and opening-up, its GDP has risen from 364.5 billion CNY in 1978 to 99,086.5 billion CNY in 2019, and it became the world's second largest economic power after the United States in 2010, which serves as the most direct indicator of change in Chinese society, though the transformation of a country of 1.3 billion people over 1978–2020 is far from being represented by a single measure of GDP or economic growth. In 2009, John Naisbitt, the American futurologist best known for his book *Megatrend*, was inspired by the powerful influence of the rapid changes in Chinese society, and moved his research institute to Tianjin, China. He described eight changing trends in this land under the title of "China trend" (Naisbitt & Naisbitt, 1990), the narrative thread of which provides the most succinct account of a social transformation that has spanned more than 30 years:

(a) Emancipating the mind: The reform and opening-up allowed the Chinese people to abandon the shackles of ideology and see the reality of what China could be. With this in mind, the Chinese gave up class warfare, and while the economy grew, the structure of society changed dramatically. Meanwhile, the number of college graduates, a reserve force for the middle class, rose from 165,000 in 1978 to nearly 7 million in 2014.

(b) A combination of "top-down" and "bottom-up": The power of the former is based on more than 40 years of achievement, and most people believe that government can lead the country forward; the latter is based on the realization that the people must enjoy a fuller democracy. Therefore, while Yu Keping said "democracy is a good thing" (Yu, 2006), thousands of people in Xiamen and Shanghai expressed their democratic demands rationally and intelligently by a way of "walking", which led to the abandonment of the PX chemical project and the maglev project advocated by the local government.

(c) Planning the "forest" and letting "trees" grow freely: If the "forest" means country, society, and group, then "trees" mean the various individuals that grow in it. Today, people do have freedom of choice, from the nature of the organization they belong to, their occupation, their profession, their income, to what they wear, what they like, where they live, and how they live.

(d) Crossing the river by feeling the stones: This is a brilliant reform maxim in the same vein as Deng Xiaoping's "cat theory", whose core is to be bold and unconstrained by rules and regulations. From 1980 to 2020, Shenzhen, a small fishing village, became a metropolis second only to Shanghai and Beijing in terms of population and GDP. Wang Shi, who started by selling corn, built Wanke into one of the top three real estate companies in China.

(e) The budding of art and academia: Although "Qian Xuesen's question" still makes the Chinese government and academia embarrassed and uneasy, at least ten universities are aiming to be world class. In the free field of art, China not only inherits much classical art, but also is becoming an experimental field for all kinds of popular and avant-garde art. "From music, songs, films, media, fashion and hairstyle, the trend of popular culture starts to become 'the weathervane of social change', and also becomes the basic mode of the film system" (Cui, 2010: 183). Just a few years ago, in Nanjing in the autumn of 2010, I watched Taiwan drama director Lai Shengchuan's *The Treasure Island Family*. More importantly, I, who grew up in the "military compound" of the Communist Party, can now openly lament the fate of the "Kuomintang soldiers" and their descendants in the "military compound" in Taiwan.[4]

(f) Integration into the world: Before 1978, when the friends of China were said to be all over the world, I knew only the beacon of the Mediterranean—Albania, a tiny country of little more than a million people, and Prince Sihanouk, who was deposed and exiled to China. Thanks to Deng Xiaoping's policy of opening-up, the millions of people who have been abroad, including me, have really found out what "a distant land is near" or "global village" means. After China joined the WTO in 2001, people began to talk about the G20, G8, and even G2 when goods with the "Made in China" logo flowed around the world. For the first time, China became an important member of the world family.

(g) Freedom and fairness: For all the complaints about the fairness of reality in China, the freedom it has must be far greater than it was 42 years ago. By contrast, the Naisbitts, who know China well, have not embarrassed the Chinese government by their handling of the subject, and pointed to the latter's efforts to deal with the tension between the freedom of the few to achieve economic success and the fair demands of the many for social services. For example, with the high marketization and the rise of the wealth class,[5] the country in recent years has also been trying to change various unfair social management systems, including the household registration system, employment system, education system, and medical system, and striving to realize a universal social security system, including for the rural population.

(h) From Olympic gold medals to Nobel prizes: These are not limited to sports or technology; they are simply symbols of China's ability to catch up with the world in a certain field. Indeed, not only have the 2008 Beijing Olympics and the 2010 Shanghai World Expo surprised the world, but China has also led the world in a number of areas. In 2008, astronaut Zhai Zhigang became the first Chinese to walk in space when he stepped off the Shenzhou VII spacecraft; the ARJ21 is part of China's ambitious effort to develop large jets after its successful entry into the world regional jet market; on December 3, 2010, the test speed of the Beijing–Shanghai high-speed railway under construction reached 486 kilometers per hour, setting a new world record, and China became the world's leading advanced country in the field of high-speed railways with an operating mileage of 35,000 kilometers by 2019 (Xinhua News Agency, 2010a).

Since the birth of modern social science, countless scholars have devoted their lives to explaining social changes and their causes in the past 200 years. The forces of history are found to be manifold, ranging from the natural environment, economic growth, technological innovation, and cultural integration to the subjective efforts of individuals, especially elites. It can almost be said that there are as many ways of describing social change as there are ways of studying society (Chirot, 1986: 2).

Some people strongly believe that the disappearance of the great Mayan civilization, which had flourished for centuries, was more or less related to the drought caused by El Niño in the 8th and 9th centuries AD (Fagan, 2009: 128–147), just as the drought in Asia during the warm period of the Middle Ages reduced the grassland areas and killed a large number of livestock, resulting in nomads having to expand their search for pasture and water and then invading neighboring territories—thus the iron feet of Genghis Khan swept across the Asian continent (Fagan, 2008: 52). Some people are convinced that economic growth, especially the change of economic form, is the most serious subject of social change, because with the change of the economic base, all large superstructures change slowly or rapidly (Marx & Engels, 1973, Vol. 2: 83). It is also believed that "in the radical gap between the present and the past, technology has been one of the chief forces in the diremption of social time" (Bell, 1999: 188). Just as the steam engine represented the arrival of industrial society, electronic technology, especially computer technology, represented the arrival of post-industrial society or the information society. Even Lenin once thought, at the extreme, that communism is Soviet power plus the electrification of the whole country (Lenin, 1995: 363). Some also believe that change is caused by the clash and blending of cultures, including values, behavior patterns, and materials. Since Arnold Toynbee in "*Historical studies*" proposed that the challenge and response of civilizations brought about the cyclic development of society, Huntington further discussed the conflict between different civilizations in the modern world and its role in the reconstruction of the world order. The non-Western world responds to the dual challenges posed by modernization and Westernization in three ways: total rejection, total acceptance, and acceptance of the former and rejection of the latter (Huntington, 2010: 51). Finally, there is the conviction that great people, especially those with Weber's "charisma" (Weber, 1978: 245), drive history. Therefore, Pareto regarded human history as the history of the elite circle of the "lion" and the "fox" (Pareto, 1968). Thomas Carlyle also said that the history of the world is the history of the great men who lived in it (Diamond, 2006: 453). Although those of us who have been steeped in the materialism of "the masses make history" would be wary of the elitism or "heroic view of history" expressed in these discourses, it is also true that even the history of modern China after 1949 is closely related to the existence of Mao Zedong and Deng Xiaoping and their radically different styles of doing things.

For China after 1978, we can say that almost all of the above historical factors have been involved in the great changes of Chinese society. In view of the fact that China is an ancient land of 9.6 million square kilometers, with a population of 1.3 billion, with 5,000 years of civilized tradition, after 1840's precarious fate and the establishment of a rigid system after 1949, perhaps none of the single historical factors mentioned above are responsible for the huge changes in this ultra-stable society.

In fact, we are far from having a complete picture of what has happened to the country from 1978 to 2020, and why. But, as far as this argument is concerned, we believe that it is this unprecedented transformation that has created a huge gap between the generations now living in Chinese society and the theme we are now discussing—cultural reverse, the self-evident theme of our society.

Old habits and new rules

No sooner had I written this heading than I was reminded of an intergenerational conflict that occurred a few years ago among some acquaintances. Small as it is, it does illustrate the inherent logic of intergenerational tension and conflict at a time when rapid social change has made old habits and new rules coexist.

Doctor A has always been a good girl. Although she was born in a county in H province, which is not developed, she has always been cared for by her parents and teachers since childhood because of her excellent academic performance. She got her doctorate from a university in the south and taught there when she was only around twenty-seven years old. Before long, ambitious A married her high-powered classmate B, who had no doctorate. After graduating from the rural area of J province, B had successfully changed his profession to become a practicing lawyer in the same city and obtained the master of law degree. Although both of them had just started to work for a short time, and did not live a rich life, because of their good careers and their love for each other, their life was enviable.

The trouble came when A went back with B to his hometown in J province after marriage. Originally, B's parents were really happy beyond words, thinking of how they had brought up their son with all kinds of hardships over the past decades and sent him into a famous university, as well as how he has become a lawyer in the provincial capital and married a woman doctor whom people in the countryside had never seen. A, who was not used to the countryside, was surrounded by villagers on the third floor of B's house; although she felt a little uncomfortable, she was happy to meet her parents-in-law for the first time. However, after a short period of excitement, A and her parents-in-law encountered a problem: According to the custom in B's hometown, the new daughter-in-law should wash her mother-in-law's feet once to show her obedience to the seniors and filial piety. This was the first time well-educated A had ever heard of the custom of asking someone to wash the feet of a woman whom she had met for the first time at noon, and this made her almost cry. However, B's parents didn't offer any alternatives to this custom just because A was a doctor. In their eyes, A is in the first place their daughter-in-law, and then a doctor!

I really do not know if A washed her future mother-in-law's feet, and I do not need to know. But those of us who study sociology know that the conflict here would not have happened a hundred years ago or a hundred years from now. A hundred years ago, in that "where the needle goes, the thread follows" era for women, before a woman got married, her parents would have long ago told her to honor her in-laws, and washing feet is but a certain ritual of filial piety; one hundred years later, in an era when men and women are becoming more equal, at least in legal terms, and the supremacy of the older generation is gone, perhaps only parents whose brains have been run over by cars will want their new daughter-in-law to wash their feet. So the problem here is not with B's parents, and certainly not with A, but rather with the juxtaposition of old habits and new rules that comes with the passing of the old and the new—in this sense, both parents and children are somehow out of time.

At the beginning of Chapter 4 in the first volume of this book, we fully discussed how, in a transitional society with rapid changes, the coexistence of old habits and new rules is a common phenomenon. But the problem is that, because the pace of change is so rapid, so much has changed in the course of a generation—as Toffler puts it, it is like taking what should have happened in a 100 or 300-year period and bringing it all together in a compressed way in a single 10, 20, or 30- year period such that it cannot but cause some kind of "future shock" to two or three generations living at the same time. Indeed, a change at such a rate between the old and the new is sobering to the customs, beliefs, and self-images of millions of people. Never before in history has such a rapid change occurred at such a rate in such a short historical period (Toffler, 1970: 25–26).

Such a rapid change will inevitably lead to the endless emergence of new things and new rules, and the two interdependent results of it are, on the one hand, the parents' original knowledge, experience, and even value judgment lose their explanatory power and inheritance value, and, on the other hand, it gives the children their first chance to "give directions" to their parents. This is actually the external macro-background of the phenomenon of "cultural reverse" caused by social changes.

In all kinds of ball games, we often see this phenomenon, that is, the players who are very good and even hold the world championship title lose the game, because they cannot adapt to the new rules, while those unknown newcomers often stand out. Today's world is a vast arena where the real competition is between the older generation and the younger generation, and the reasons for the former's loss of dominance and the latter's emergence are often the same as those in ball games: there are new changes and new rules. In the face of these changes and new rules, the older generation, familiar with the old habits, is at a loss, while the younger generation, brought up with the new rules, is at ease with them.

Worldwide, these new changes occurred after World War II, especially after the increasingly rapid globalization that we have already talked about and will continue to talk about since the 1980s. It was the enormous social changes triggered by technological progress that allowed innovations, both tangible and intangible, to proliferate rapidly, thanks to the almost unimpeded flow of capital and culture across the globe that had followed the end of the Cold War. New things and changes like feminism, democracy, "dink" culture, single-parent families, supermarkets, Greenpeace, WTO, the white-collar class, and consumerism in the social life field accompanied by scientific and technological progress have not only deepened our understanding of the changing nature of society, but also changed many game rules previously regarded as natural. As a result, the older generation, like the immigrants who arrived in the New World on the Mayflower in 1620, suddenly found themselves in a completely foreign environment, and as Margaret Mead said, accidentally became "time migrants" (Mead, 1970: 73).

The changes in Chinese society from 1978 to 2020 have attracted worldwide attention. They are bringing the older generation from tradition into the modern age at a very fast speed, making their previously almost extravagant ideal into a reality. At the same time, the older generation also abandons much of the knowledge and experience they have acquired in the first half of their lives, and they feel that they are the first generation that cannot leave a spiritual "legacy" for their children. In our interviews, many parents feel that their youth has been delayed, that they have learned nothing when they should have studied, while their children have encountered the great era of reform and opening-up. Therefore, it is inevitable that their children surpass them. In addition, as a special case, China's rural areas are further away from modernization, so the changes, shocks, and setbacks experienced by the people there are the most intense in the current transition from tradition to modernity (Zhou, 1998).

In the interviews in Beijing, we found that in the two families of BV and BW in Zhejiang village, parents' dual immigrant status—they are, in the words of Margaret Mead, "time migrants" from tradition to modernity and "space migrants" from country to city—made their "spiritual backwardness" more obvious than in other parents. Specifically, while their children are already comfortable in Beijing, they are still struggling to adapt to modern city life. BWF simply said, "I wouldn't stay in Beijing for a day if it weren't for earning a few bucks" (BWF, 1995).

Almost 20 years later, similar stories are still being told, but the details have changed. SAF, 45, graduated from the College of Mining and Technology in Xiangtan, Hunan province. After graduation, he gave up his job as a mining engineer in his hometown to do business in Shanghai because he was passionately in love with his classmate SAM. He set up a company in Shanghai that did heating engineering, which was small but had dozens of employees. Since he was adopted as a son by his uncle at an early age, he had to support his biological and adoptive parents, as well as a large number of siblings. He had been staying in Shanghai and could not personally take care of his parents back home in Sichuan, so he was kind and guilty enough to help any sibling in trouble. As a result, his money was not only spent like water, but also his small business had become a "poverty relief" base for the members of his extended family, where more than 30% of the employees were his relatives. More relatives in the company means more trouble, and the SAF couple were exhausted by their relatives' various demands. The son that majored in economics in Shanghai Finance and Economics Institute could not stand it any more, and accused his father of having no modern ideas about business. Although SAF knew his son had a point, he could not follow this modern principle—"They are all children of my brothers and sisters. If I don't help them now, I won't have the face to pay New Year's greetings to their parents when I go back home during the Spring Festival" (SAF, 2012). But an accident later led SAF to admit that it was a mistake not to have accepted his son's advice earlier. His nephew who had not been working well was driving drunk, which caused big trouble. Finally, SAF made up his mind to fire his nephew.

If rapid social change is a major reason why older generations have lost the value of passing on their knowledge and experience, and are thus unable to cope with the changing times, then the next question is why children can "feel good" in the face of all these changes while their parents struggle to cope. Obviously, in the face of the same change, the two generations must have completely different reactions, or they would not form such a big difference in values, life attitudes, and social behavior patterns, and the cultural reverse we are discussing would not be formed. Therefore, there are differences between the two generations in understanding and accepting new things, which may be the internal micro-reason of the phenomenon of cultural reverse triggered by social changes.

Specifically, there are many reasons why the older generation is slow and backward in the face of the same social changes. Generally speaking, there are no more than the following aspects. First, according to the laws of biology, with the increase of age, one's values, life attitudes, and behavior patterns become fixed, and one pays less attention to new things and loses interest in many things. Next, for parents born in the particular period of history, from the 1950s to the 1970s, and for the grandparents before them, the conservative and closed social atmosphere and irregular school education before 1978 left many of them with a very low cultural foundation. They cannot read all 26 letters of the English language, let alone absorb new knowledge and cultures that keep emerging. Last but not least, almost all respondents said that the shackles of tradition and experience are often the main reason why the older generation is missing out on new things and trends. In a 1998 interview with NFF, a professor of sociology born in 1948 whom we have mentioned in many places in this book, we analyzed how tradition and experience shackled the thinking and action of the older generation.

> We usually deal with things according to the original experience, and only when the original knowledge and experience are not enough, we will think of learning new things. The reason for this is very simple. This knowledge and experience comes from your own practice, and not only is it familiar to you, but it even forms a part of you, or what you call your "self", so you can no more easily deny it than you can deny yourself. However, this "heritage", which is both proud and more poignant, is sometimes a historical burden, which makes you either indifferent or unprepared to face new things. Children are different, they do not have any experience, but therefore no burden, they learn and use everything new, so they have more new knowledge and are more adaptable than us. And, fortunately for the

children of my son NFB's generation, the two decades they have spent growing up have almost entirely overlapped with the changes in Chinese society. As they grow up, the constraints of society are gradually being relaxed, and they are hardly subjected to any spiritual restrictions. Therefore, all the deviant events that are new to us and sometimes subversive in these 20 years are the most natural for them.

(NFF, 1998)

The NFF interviews already touch on part of the reason why children form their own "cultural power" or "discourse power", that is, the younger generation is not hobbled by old habits and old knowledge or traditions. For the older generation, when new knowledge or rules appear that are inconsistent with old experiences and traditions, new knowledge or rules may be regarded as weird; but for the younger generation, who have no stereotypes in their heads, new knowledge or new rules are taken for granted. Not restricted by old traditions, coupled with a strong curiosity, quick absorption ability, and a solid foundation in today's formal education (in our interviews, almost all parents admitted that what they had learned in school was at least five years behind where their children are now),[7] today's younger generation is naturally more adaptable to new things than their parents and grandparents. This puts the old habits and the new rules in two different camps. On the side of the old habits stand three generations born before 1960 (Zhang & Cheng, 1988); on the other side of the new rules stand the post-1970s or post-1980s generation that grew up after the reform and opening-up, and the generation that grew up naturally in the course of our study for more than 20 years—the post-1990s or even post-2000s. In fact, there is only one stark divide between the five generations: the "great proletarian cultural revolution", which lasted for ten years from 1966 to 1976.

We have discussed in Chapter 2 of the first volume of this book that, although countless people with lofty ideals have fought hard to overthrow the old traditions of the feudal society that lasted for thousands of years since modern times, a violent revolution aimed at fighting against feudal and colonial culture has unexpectedly formed a stronger "new tradition" in the 30 years after its victory (Walder, 1986).[8] According to sociologist Edward Shils, "at a minimum, two transmissions over three generations are required for a pattern of belief or action to be considered a tradition" (Shils, 1981: 15). In this sense, the formation of the "new tradition" of Mao Zedong's revolution is the most economical cultural inheritance in human history, and it has become the guide for action of 1 billion Chinese people effected over the shortest time. In the 30 years after 1949, the rapid formation and spread of the new tradition was attributed to: the model set by the October Revolution of the Soviet Union, the devastating victory of the Chinese revolution and the extraordinary charisma of the great leader in the revolutionary process, the highly centralized political and economic system of omnipotence established after 1949, the nearly perfect social mobilization system established by modern bureaucracy (Zhou, 2005), the various political study and ideological reform movement determined to shape "new socialists" like Lei Feng and "the good eight company on the Nanjing Road" (Whyte, 1974), the mutually reinforcing social mindsets of hundreds of millions of people formed in the highly integrated social system and series of achievements in the early years of the founding of the People's Republic of China (Zhou, 2009b), and various punishment systems including "bathing" (Yang, 2004), decentralization, public criticism, and "re-education through labor". In this way, the victory of the revolution overthrew the imperial power, but did not remove the shadow of feudalism centered on high centralization and the personality cult. It promoted China's industrialization, but the Soviet-style planned economy also restricted the development of the commodity and market economy. It eradicated the rule of blood families, but the all-encompassing system of units and rural people's communes reduced people's creativity and competition consciousness after restricting their freedom of movement and migration. In the end, it destroyed the Confucian feudal ethics and the nascent bourgeois ideology, but the living, innovative Marxism finally became the dogma that restrained the creativity of the masses. Under the influence of this social atmosphere, the Chinese nation with a population of 1 billion developed a highly politicized and highly homogenized or "depersonalized" social mentality. It can be said that from the Great Leap Forward to the Cultural Revolution, a series of political manias, rarely seen in the world, existed and were all direct products of this social mentality. These new traditions include ideological dogmas that bind people, rigid systems, backward ideas, and far-left habits, which, like the old traditions left over from Chinese society in 1949, existed together in China before 1978, often with contradictions and conflicts, but sometimes with surprising similarities.

During the reform and opening-up from 1978, while abandoning the far-left line of "class struggle as the key", Chinese society underwent a great transformation or change step by step. It is this social transformation, which has lasted for more than 42 years and has not ended yet, coupled with the same huge wave of globalization after China's integration into the world, that has laid the foundation for the birth of all kinds of new rules when all kinds of old and new traditions are gradually turned into old habits that do not adapt to social progress. And millions of older generations, once suffering from old habits, are now facing a relentless challenge to the new rules.

Social transformation: who fumbles for stones and who crosses rivers?

As early as 1928, German sociologist Karl Mannheim put the hope of social change on natural generation replacement when he wrote his article "The generation problem" (Mannheim, 1952). More than 50 years later, American sociologist Edward Shils, in his book *On Tradition*, which took him 25 years to write, continues along Mannheim's lines:

Much has been made of the changes in culture and social organization which are made possible by the succession of generations. Each generation comes to its task with a fresh mind, unencumbered by the beliefs and attachments settled in the minds of the generation antecedent to it. … Each new generation seems to have the chance to begin again, to call a halt to the persistence of the past into the present and to make its society anew. It suffers from the handicap of weakness, isolation, and helplessness in the face of many others who have already fallen into the grip of the past.

(Shils, 1981: 35)

Changes in Chinese society before 1978 were also caused by generational changes. Autumn 1975 to autumn 1976 was an eventful historical period in contemporary China. First, in August 1975, Zhumadian district of Henan province was hit by a huge rainstorm. Within a few days, the maximum central rainfall reached 1,631 mm and the maximum 24-hour rainfall reached 1,060 mm, setting a record for the same index in China. Rainstorms caused dozens of reservoirs to collapse, devastating 11 million *mu* of farmland, affecting 11 million people, and killing 26,000 people. On March 8, the following year, a rare meteorite shower fell in Jilin, China. It was spread over 500 square kilometers and comprised more than 100 meteorites, with a total weight of 2,600 kilograms. Then, at 3:42 am on July 28, a 7.8-magnitude earthquake occurred in Tangshan, Hebei province, with an epicenter intensity of 11 degrees and a focal depth of 12 kilometers—an earthquake area of 47 square kilometers. The new heavy industry city of Tangshan was immediately reduced to ruins. According to the statistics released two decades later, the death toll in the earthquake was 242,000, with 164,000 seriously injured and countless minor injuries. Up until 2010, *Aftershock*, directed by Feng Xiaogang, set a box office record as it generated the tears of the Chinese people, indicating that this earthquake and the subsequent Wenchuan earthquake will continue to be a lingering pain in the hearts of Chinese people forever.

Many years later, the economist Zhao Haijun talked about the "turbulence" in 1976 and said with a mysterious tone, "Every time something unusual happens in nature, it is a sign of something human" (Zhao, 2009: 285). Believe it or not, Premier Zhou Enlai died on January 8, 1976, five months after the heavy rains in Zhumadian; on July 6, 1976, three months after the Jilin meteor shower, Zhu De, chairman of the standing committee of the National People's Congress, died; more than a month after the Tangshan earthquake, Mao Zedong, the Communist Party chairman who defeated Chiang Kai-shek and launched the Cultural Revolution, died on September 9, 1976. This means that three of China's four first major Communist Party leaders died in 1976, with the exception of Chairman Liu Shaoqi, who was "knocked down" by Mao Zedong at the start of the Cultural Revolution and died in Kaifeng, Henan province, in 1969. Generational shifts can be placid but eerie.

Deng Xiaoping is the kind of person who was knocked down by the "fists" of history several times, but jumped out of its "clutches" every time. In July 1977, the year after Mao Zedong's death, Deng Xiaoping, after a lifetime of "three ups and downs", finally regained his breakthrough, and became the de facto leader of China, a country of 1 billion people. Thus, the Communist Party's power shifted to a second generation of leaders represented by this pragmatic little man, and, most important of all, this generational change of leadership brought with it an opportunity for change in Chinese society as a whole. It was also the Third Plenary Session of the Eleventh Central Committee of the Communist Party of China (CPC) that identified three epochal changes affecting the following decades: from "class struggle as the key" to economic construction as the center; from closed and semi-closed to being open to the outside world; from conformism to comprehensive reform in all areas of social and economic life. Thus the curtain of social transformation was officially opened at the end of 1978.

Centering on the great social transformation starting from 1978, it has been proposed to establish a distinctive sociology of transformation according to the characteristics of Chinese society. For example, Ambrose King proposed that there are at least two aspects worth considering when talking about the transformation of Chinese society: social transformation, that is, the transformation from one social form to another; and the transitional society, that is, the society in transition, holding that China may be such a society for quite a long time (King, 2009). Qin Xiao proposed that economic development and "market-oriented reform are part of the transformation of modernity", but "the miracle of economic growth can only be called the 'China story', and the formation of the 'China model' must be marked by social transformation" (Qin, 2009: 21, 27). Sun Liping, whom we mentioned in Chapter 1 of the first volume of this book, proposed that

> the communist civilization and its transformation, including China, the former Soviet Union and eastern Europe, are of great significance to the development of sociology. The study of the characteristics, operational logic and transformation of this civilization should become a new source of inspiration and power for the development of contemporary sociology and even the whole social science.
>
> (Sun, 2005)

It can be said that from the construction of the "four modernizations" proposed in the late Mao Zedong era to the "economic system reform" in the Deng Xiaoping era to the overall transformation of the whole society, the fields and contents involved are very broad, and the exploration of the sociology of transformation requires a high degree of abstraction and theoretical generalization of reality. However, everyone who has come all the way from 1978 to 2020 will never forget the landmark changes that have taken place in every field of social life since 1978. It is these changes that combine into a spectacular transformation picture:

The first milestone was the establishment of four special economic zones in Shenzhen, Zhuhai, Shantou and Xiamen in August 1980. The construction of the zone began with Yuan Geng, the venerable reform-minded old man we repeatedly referred to in our account of the Shekou incident of 1988. In June 1978, appointed by Ye Fei, Yuan Geng, then director of the Foreign Affairs Bureau of the Ministry of Communications, went to Hong Kong to investigate the business situation of the China Merchants Bureau established in 1872. As a result, compared with other enterprises in Hong Kong, the dismal business of China Merchants Bureau made Yuan Geng, who later became the 29th "leader" of China Merchants Bureau, have the idea of reform. In 1979, with the approval of the central government, the Shekou industrial zone, which China Merchants Bureau was responsible for organizing and implementing, was established, which laid the foundation for the central government's idea of developing special economic zones. In April, Deng Xiaoping supported the idea of Xi Zhongxun, the party secretary of Guangdong province, to set up processing zones in Shenzhen, Zhuhai and Shantou, adjacent to Hong Kong and Macao. The following year, the state council approved the establishment of four special economic zones, including the above-mentioned three cities and Xiamen. Then, in early 1984, 14 coastal cities, including Shanghai, Tianjin, Dalian, Qingdao, Guangzhou, Wenzhou and Beihai, opened up to the outside world and set up economic and technological development zones. In 1988, Hainan special zone was established; in 1990, Shanghai Pudong development zone was established ... More than 40 years have passed. Today, the development of special economic zones, especially Shenzhen, has demonstrated its exemplary and guiding role in China's social transformation.

The second milestone was the pilot program of "production quotas to households" in Xiaogang village, Fengyang county, Anhui province in 1978. Since the land reform in 1949, Mao Zedong had been determined to realize the collectivization of Chinese agriculture and eradicate the disadvantages of the small-scale peasant economy, which had triggered fierce struggles within the party many times (Zhou, 1998). But collectivization and the people's communes did not solve the problem of feeding Chinese peasants, and the 30 million people who starved to death in 1960–1962 still haunt those who grew up in those days. Then it happened in Xiaogang village that year.

On the night of November 24, 18 ordinary farmers risked their jail time by pressing their handprints and signing an agreement of "production quotas to households". The following year, an unprecedented harvest gave Wan Li, then the party secretary of the province, the confidence to support Xiaogang's "deviation". In September 1980, the central government issued a document affirming for the first time the reform action of "production quotas to households", which triggered the reform of China's rural areas.

At the end of that year, farmers in Guanghan county in Sichuan took the lead in removing the brand of the people's commune. Three years later, in October, the people's commune system, which had been implemented for 25 years, officially came to an end (Ling, 1996; Zhang, 1998).

The third milestone was the creation of a Sino-foreign joint venture, while also vitalizing the "red capitalists". After the victory of the Chinese revolution in 1949, although capitalists did not suffer from the same catastrophe as the landlord class, after the socialist transformation of industry and commerce in 1956, China's national capitalists and small capitalists had completely retired from the field of economic production, and were severely criticized as a representative of the exploiting class in the Cultural Revolution in 1966. On January 17, 1979, in the midst of spring in Beijing, Deng Xiaoping invited Rong Yiren, "king of flour", Gu Yanxiu, "king of bristles", Hu Zi'ang, "king of steel", Hu Juewen, "king of machinery", and Zhou Shitao, "king of cement"— the famous "five masters of industry and commerce"—to the Great Hall of the People for a discussion and a hotpot dinner. Several of them asked the central government to remove their "capitalist" title, but Deng Xiaoping seemed more interested in putting it back. Soon after, the China International Trust and Investment Corporation, in which Rong Yiren invested shares and served as President, was set up, not long after the Sino-foreign Joint Venture Law was passed. In the following decades, China has become a vital place for entrepreneurship with capital investment from all over the world. Thousands of Sino-foreign joint ventures and even wholly foreign-owned companies have not only brought capital, but also brought market concepts, talents, and technologies, making their own contributions to China's economic revitalization.

The fourth milestone is the development of the individual economy and private economy, while encouraging "some people to get rich first". Shortly after the above hot pot banquet, the central government announced their intention to "encourage and support the proper development of the individual economy, and all law-abiding individual workers should be respected by the society" (Zhao, 2009: 328), firstly because of the change of the concept of individual economy, and secondly because of the employment pressure brought by the return of 8 million educated youth to the city. Soon, Rong Zhiren, a young man in Huicheng, Guangzhou, opened a small restaurant. Nian Guangjiu, a native of Wuhu, Anhui province, established the famous Fool's Melon Seeds. In 1979 alone, the number of individual businesses approved to open reached 100,000. Since then, despite several twists and turns, China's private and individual economies have been booming. Article 11 of the 1999 Amendment to the Constitution states: "The individual economy, the private economy and other non-public sectors within the scope prescribed by law are important components of the socialist market economy" (Amendment to the Constitution of the People's Republic of China, 1999). Several of my friends, Jiang Xipei, a native of Yixing, Jiangsu province, who set up stalls in Hefei in the 1980s, later became a cable king and a representative of the 16th CPC National Congress. Chen Guangbiao, a Huaiyin man who set up stalls in Nanjing in the 1990s, later became the king of renewable resources and the national "best man" and moral model for his years of continuous and unremitting "social donations" and his selfless and fearless behavior during the Wenchuan earthquake.

Although many scholars, including Qin Xiao, have pointed out that no single economic or market transformation can replace the modern transformation of Chinese society—"The transformation of modernity refers to the transformation from traditional society to the modern civilized order supported by modern core values (freedom, rationality and individual rights), with market economy, democratic constitutionalism and nation-state as the basic system" (Qin, 2009: 18)—we can still believe that it is these changes in economic life that have laid the foundation for the comprehensive transformation of Chinese society that has made this country of 1.3 billion people begin to shift in the following directions.

First, along the path of industrialization from 1949 to 1978, it continued to realize the transformation from an agriculture-oriented society to an industry-oriented and service-oriented society. In the 30 years from 1978 to 2008, the number of employees in primary industry decreased from 70.5 to 39.56%, the number of employees in secondary industry increased from 17.3 to 27.24%, and the number of employees in tertiary industry increased from 12.2 to 33.17%. The change of industrial structure not only promotes the growth of new economic forms, but also promotes the differentiation of China's social structure, giving birth to the growing Chinese middle class (Zhou, 2005).

Second, and most important, is the transition from a command planned economy to a modern market economy. This transition has gone through many complicated processes. First, the transition was from one "based on planned economy, supplemented by market regulation" to a planned commodity economy; then in 1992, the 14th National Congress of the Communist Party of China explicitly established the socialist market economy system, "making the market play a fundamental role in the allocation of resources under the macro-control of a socialist country" (CPC Central Committee, 1993); finally, at the Third Plenary Session of the 18th CPC Central Committee held in 2013, not only was the adverbial "under the macro-control of country" deleted (actually further withdrawing state intervention in the market), but the basic role of the market in the allocation of resources was revised to "decisive role" (CPC Central Committee, 2013: 21). So far, though, China has yet to truly embrace the two basic prerequisites of a market economy, both hard and soft: There is neither a perfect constitution and private property protection system as a "soft indicator" nor a social security system as a "hard constraint", though the push to the market laid the groundwork for China's economic take-off.

Thirdly, there is the change from the highly ideological monistic culture to the ideological secular multi-culture. As we have already stated in the first volume of this book, the changes in Chinese culture, or Chinese values, attitudes, and patterns of behavior, over the years from 1978 to 2020, while often overlooked, are, like China's economic growth, one of the most dynamic and colorful areas of social transformation in the country. In a series of papers I have published, I proposed that while paying attention to a series of experiences accumulated in China's socio-economic development and structural transformation, namely the "Chinese experience", we should also pay attention to the great changes of Chinese people's values and social mentality in these years. I call this transmutation the "Chinese feeling" (Zhou, 2009b, 2010), and believe that it is possible to "provide a social or psychological model for developing countries around the world to learn from the transition from tradition to modernity because of its uniqueness" (Zhou & Qin, 2010a).

Fourthly, there is the transition from a highly centralized political system to a socialist democratic political system. Although this transformation was the most delayed and caused the most controversy, the economic growth was accompanied by a considerable degree of "suspension of the political system reform" (Qin, 2009: 21); since the abolition of the lifelong leadership system in the 1980s, the implementation of "villagers' autonomy", and the strengthening of grassroots democracy, the transformation has not stopped completely, and is causing further concern.

The rapid transformation has brought great changes to Chinese society, and inevitably brought contradictions and conflicts to the whole society. Against the background of changes and transformation, "profound changes in the economic system, profound changes in the social structure, profound adjustments in the pattern of interests and profound changes in ideology" (CPC Central Committee, 2006: 3) have become the basic characteristics of our complex times. And from what we are talking about, it is clear that different generations of people born and raised in different times of this society, due to their different life experiences, different educational backgrounds, different constraints from tradition and experience, and different interests and concerns in today's social structure, naturally have a different identification and adaptation to change and transformation.

> What bothers parents is that the new generation doesn't know the past. They don't know the "new youth" of the 1920s, the "red brat" of the 1930s, the "eighth route army" of the 1940s, the "builders" of the 1950s, the "red guards" of the 1960s, the "educated youth" of the 1970s, or the "fourth generation" of the 1980s. They are a generation without history and have nothing to do with everything that has happened in the last 80 years. They were born at the end of all tragedies, but they still have experienced more change than their peers in other countries, because they grow up in the country that changes the most. No difference in the lives of two generations in the world is as great as that of the Chinese ... They believe that the world has changed, that it will no longer belong to the meek, but to the independent will; no longer to belong to "two fears", but to new technology; no longer to belong to power, but to wisdom; no longer to belong to the honest, but to the ambitious; no longer to belong to their parents, but to themselves. Mao Zedong is in grandpa's heart, grandpa is in dad's heart, and they have themselves in their hearts.
>
> (Ling, 2008: 334)

Ling Zhijun, a political writer, offers a glimpse of the differences between the two living generations today. Perhaps the biggest difference, of course, is that the older generation is one with a history, connected to the last 60 or 80 years, while the younger generation is one without a history, but they are connected with the changed present and a future that will continue to change. In fact, it is this difference that leads to the two generations' different attitudes towards change or transformation. Because the older generation views the changing present and future as uncertain and even dangerous, they naturally rely on cautious attempts to "cross the river by feeling the stones" in the face of this change. The younger generation, on the other hand, sees the changing present and the future as a natural journey, and while their parents and grandparents "feel the stones", they have waded across the river, leaving behind them the mighty river. Over the past 42 years, countless young people have weathered the vicissitudes of the times and achieved magnificent lives. In fact, "You feel the stones and I cross the river" is not treachery or self-interest or unfilialness. From the experience of human history, the predecessors of each generation accumulate experience and explore risks through their own actions of "feeling the stones" for the next generation, while the ease of the younger generation in "crossing the river" depends on that older generation having felt the stones.

Globalization and the consumer storm

Social transformation is only one aspect of the process of social change that China have gone through since 1978. From the very beginning we have affirmed that our discussion of the intergenerational relationship of Chinese society marked by the phenomenon of cultural reverse will take place against the background of globalization. In other words, we are clearly aware that social transformation and globalization are two interwoven basic issues here, which are so closely intertwined, first of all, because they are both changes that have occurred in Chinese society since the 1980s. As a synchronic social transformation process, globalization, by virtue of the flow of capital, technology, goods, services, and labor across countries and regions, enables the mode of production, lifestyle, and even cultural expression represented by the United States and other Western developed countries to be expanded or popularized globally. As a diachronic process, social transformation is led by market transformation, which then triggers the huge changes in various fields of Chinese society. In fact, social transformation is not so much an inevitable result of globalization as the great transformation of China, the Soviet Union, Eastern Europe, and other former socialist camps, paving the way for the true "globalization".

In the field of daily life, one of the most direct effects of globalization on Chinese society is the wave of consumerism that has spread—in a country that had previously advocated thrift or hard work since 1949—and which has ever since become increasingly vigorous. From our discussion of cultural reverse or changes in intergenerational relationships, China's rapid economic growth in 1978–2020 and the changes in the material living conditions of different generations brought about by this growth, especially the changes in the consumption environment, are the biggest social and environmental differences encountered by two or three generations living today. Therefore, it is one of the most important reasons for their different values, life attitudes, and social behaviors. In a presentation on the growth of China's middle class at the Brookings Institution in Washington in the fall of 2009, I proposed that in the 30 years of China's social reform and opening-up, consumption reflecting lifestyle changes is a micro-mechanism or psychological mechanism for Chinese middle-class groups to construct a self-identity or to win a social identity (Zhou & Qin, 2010b). Considering that the 1949 revolution put an end to the former middle class, the real Chinese middle class is basically the first generation, which is the social darling created by the reform and opening-up over the past few decades (Zhou, 2002). It can be said that the growth history of China's middle class overlaps with the growth history of contemporary Chinese youth to some extent. This overlap makes the narrative of the growth of Chinese youth, especially young urban intellectuals, strikingly similar to the narrative of the growth of the middle class. In this way, we can also discuss how consumption constructs the self-identity of Chinese young people from the economic and social perspectives, and how it produces their values and lifestyles that are totally different from those of their parents and grandparents.

From the perspective of economic factors, the reason why consumption has become the main way for Chinese young people to construct their self-identity is not only that their growth trajectories go hand in hand with the economic development of society over the past 42 years, and the rapid rise of China's social GDP and a series of market-oriented transformations that have changed the quality of their daily life, but also that the educated young are therefore able to navigate the market economy and increasingly benefit from the reform and opening-up, globalization, and the shift towards markets. We have seen that in the process of continuous GDP growth and market transformation, the income of urban residents continues to increase. At the time of reform and opening-up in 1978, the average annual income of urban non-private enterprise employees was only 615 CNY. Since then, this figure has been increasing: 1,148 CNY in 1985; 2,140 CNY in 1990; 5,500 CNY in 1995; 9,371 CNY in 2000; 18,364 CNY in 2005; and 37,147 CNY in 2010; and 67,569 CNY in 2016 (National Bureau of Statistics). Average incomes almost double or more every five years. As incomes rise, people's consumption behavior, especially among the younger generation, is encouraged by the state, which varies from time to time. Before 1997, the government adopted a series of policies to improve people's living standards, such as increasing wages, adjusting the industrial structure, and reducing the annual accumulation rate, in order to reverse the disastrous impact of the Revolution in the Mao Zedong era on people's lives and to "overcome the crisis of legal resources" (Wang, 2009: 235). After 1997, the country encouraged consumption because the economic crisis in Southeast Asia and the insufficient consumption demand in the domestic market had become the bottleneck restricting the further development of China's economy. In order to promote its further development, the state explicitly proposed that "we should actively cultivate new consumption hotspots such as housing, so that housing construction truly becomes an important industry. We will actively develop services such as telecommunications, tourism, culture, entertainment, health care and sports" (Zhu, 2001: 1174). Thanks to the active advocacy of the state and various policy encouragements, after 2000, the consumption of the Chinese middle class, whose core is the younger, began to upgrade from durable consumer goods such as televisions, washing machines, and refrigerators to more prominent and explicit housing, private cars, and luxury consumer goods. In less than ten years after 2000, housing prices in China have generally increased by one or two times, even several times in coastal areas. When China joined the WTO in 2001, it was the first year when automobiles entered Chinese families. In the ten years after that, the production and sales of domestic sedans continued to achieve double-digit "blowout" growth, from 820,000 in 2001 to 5.32 million in 2007, and then to 18 million in 2010, which was a world first in growth. Moreover, the consumption of houses, cars, and luxury goods has not only become the main consumer markers that the young middle class and their children use to obtain recognition, but has also become the main testing ground for them to change their consumption ideas.[9]

From the perspective of social factors, the state's advocacy has not only led the consumption of the Chinese middle class, especially the younger generation, into the fast lane, but more importantly, thanks to the promotion of the state, coupled with the increasingly powerful wave of globalization after the 1990s, the values and lifestyles associated with consumerism began to take shape, especially the powerful and wealthy elites who got rich first and the increasingly large and younger middle class. This is especially important for the identity construction of the middle class, especially the younger generation. As we all know, consumption was the symbol of a bourgeois lifestyle in the propaganda of state ideology during the Mao Zedong era. To some extent, it was synonymous with waste, extravagance, and decadence. After the reform and opening-up, especially after the 1990s, the concept of consumption itself has undergone a "transformation" in mainstream discourse, and even the state has realized the driving role of consumption in the national economy. The market's natural demand for consumption coincides with the national will, which naturally makes all kinds of advertisements and market behaviors advocating consumption popular. Moreover, as time goes by, China's advertising demands begin to shift from a functional consumption value to a symbolic consumption value (Chen Sheng, 2003), and the emphasis on the symbolic meaning of commodities has become a sign of consumerism's ascendancy in China (Chen & Huang, 2000). These changes in the public interpretive framework around consumption provide legitimacy for the affluent class, including the middle class, and their children to improve their quality of life and even to distinguish themselves from the grassroots masses through consumption. Take various housing sales advertisements that have been popular in China for more than ten years as an example. The basic appeal theme is often not the comfort of the house itself, but the demonstration and improvement of personal status (Fraser, 2000). In the sales advertisements of housing in China, "Birds of a feather flock together", "Buy a new house, be a boss", "This is the common choice of professors, entrepreneurs and bankers", and other similar advertising slogans are everywhere, which are unabashedly outspoken about the role that buying a house plays in the construction of a person's class or social status. Also, the popularity of luxury brands like Louis Vuitton, Gucci, Hermes, Chanel, Rolex, Vacheron-Constantin, and Rolls-Royce in China reflects the importance of consumption, especially the symbolic consumption, for the young Chinese middle class to obtain self-identity.[10]

The improvement of Chinese people's material living conditions, or the transformation of consumption patterns, is of great benefit to the growth of the younger generation. They don't have to live frugally like their parents or grandparents, eating porridge with pickled vegetables every day, wearing the patchwork clothes of older siblings, sharing a small, dark room with siblings or even parents, or even using the money they would have spent on a Popsicle to buy a pencil. The progress of Chinese society after 1978 has created a material living environment totally different from that of their parents and grandparents. Children, especially those of the urban middle class, live in increasingly rich material conditions from the moment they are born. This not only makes their physical growth and development more robust, but also allows their spiritual or psychological world to grow freely without constraint. It also makes their choice of career and life path more arbitrary, more likely to go beyond the rigid restriction of simply being a "breadwinner", and to reach the peak experience of human self-realization, as Maslow said, or the free and comprehensive development of the human, as Marx and Engels said.

During the interviews, we felt again and again that the younger generation's ability to feed back culturally was closely related to the great improvement of society's material living conditions. Take the M family in Guangzhou as an example. GMF was the head of a research institution, and GMM was the financial director of an enterprise. Born in 1984, GMB had his parents' tall and slim figure, but not the roughness of people from northwest Shanxi province, so he looked more like those elegant and white lads in Guangzhou. Because of his good family, GMB was also very intelligent. He went to key schools all the way, even visiting the United States with his parents when he was only 15 years old. In the words of GMM:

> Although we had a decent family when we were little, we never dreamed of being like GMB. We often say, "All your wishes come true", but for the GMB generation, it's often done without a thought. My neighbors say GMB is very versatile, and he often asked me, "Mom, why can't you do anything?" I told him that if his father and I had lived like him when we were little, we would have done anything. Don't you think so? He knows everything in addition to those taught in textbooks: astronomy, geography, history, science, and many others, because he read a lot of books. He can

get whatever books he wants, while we had nothing but the textbooks when we were young. He is also good at English, not only because he began to learn English in the third grade of primary school, but he has several drawers of tapes and CDs bought for him at home. In 1999, his father GMF had the opportunity to visit the United States, and one of his main considerations for the trip was whether GMB could go to school in the United States. He is in good health and loves playing football and sports. Now we have all kinds of balls in our home. Unlike his father; although he also liked to play basketball when he was young, he either didn't have the ball or couldn't find the court. GMB also likes music, and practiced the violin for a period of time when he was a child. Later he thought the violin was not expressive enough, so he changed to the piano. Now, the college entrance examination is coming, but GMB said that the education mode in China is nothing but indoctrination and suppression, which he did not like, so GMF told me that we should respect the child's wishes and let him go abroad to study. I have no objection. I also know that with the prosperity of our country, this generation of children will really "fly high and far away" in the future as the song says, so I also support him to study abroad. Which parent now does not want to do all he can to satisfy his children's wishes? Besides, living conditions are good these years, even studying abroad is affordable. In the words of GMF, "Let's sell a suite for our son to study abroad".

(GMM, 2003)

Stories like the GMB family have been heard a lot over the years. Like GMB who later realized his wish to study abroad, more and more Chinese children are now going abroad to go to university or even secondary school. Unlike their parents, who went abroad in the 1980s and 1990s, they do not have to apply for scholarships abroad, wait for state grants, or eat instant noodles with only 20 USD on hand. Often with dozens of dollars in their pockets, they rent comfortable apartments in upscale neighborhoods in London, Boston, New York, Paris, Vancouver, or Sydney, and sometimes their mothers fly in to accompany them. According to statistics, during the 39 years from 1978 to 2017, a total of 5.19 million Chinese students studied abroad, and this number has been growing steadily, reaching 662,100 in 2018, 90% of whom studied abroad at their own expense (*China Education News*, 2018, 2019). The growing number of self-funded students is some of the clearest evidence of the growing influence of globalization and consumerism in China. And when you understand that reality, you really get a sense that the whole world at least in the eyes of the younger generation has become extremely flat, as Thomas Friedman said. The ten forces that "flatten" the world in the process of globalization—the advent of the era of innovation, the Internet, workflow software, uploading, manufacturing and service outsourcing, offshore business, the global supply chain, express delivery (FedEx and UPS), search services (Google or Yahoo), as well as a variety of digital, mobile, personal, and virtual steroids[11]—coupled with the rapid growth of GDP and private wealth brought by the reform and opening-up, have really given our children a completely different perspective and life experience from their parents. The material means they are able to rely on are becoming more and more abundant, which not only changes the image of a poor and weak Chinese society for nearly a century, but also changes the future and destiny of the younger generation, so that Friedman would say to his daughter:

> I don't care to have that conversation with my girls, so my advice to them in this flat world is very brief and very blunt: "Girls, when I was growing up, my parents used to say to me, 'Tom, finish your dinner—people in China and India are starving.' My advice to you is: Girls, finish your home-work—people in China and India are starving for your jobs." And in a flat world, they can have them, because in a flat world there is no such thing as an American job. There is just a job, and in more cases than ever before it will go to the best, smartest, most productive, or cheapest worker—wherever he or she resides.
>
> (Friedman, 2006: 279)

Although we mentioned in Chapter 1 of the first volume of this book that Ronald Inglehart argues that the younger generation that grow up during the boom years will develop a "post-materialistic value system" that focuses more on personal development and spiritual pursuits, in the era of globalization this unique value is likely to spread from developed countries to developing countries (Inglehart, 1997; Wu, 2008; Zheng, 2007), in fact, the improvement of material living conditions does not necessarily lead to a positive life. The rapid growth of GDP may lead to both wasteful consumerism and money worship. In fact, there is a natural connection between consumerism and worship of money.[12] It is when consumption becomes the most important activity and the most important value of human beings that people become ever more passionate about money and regard it as the main or even the only purpose of life's struggle.

The prevalence of consumerism certainly requires a material basis, but wealth and material goods do not automatically lead to consumerism. The emergence of consumerism or a consumer society as Baudrillard said is closely related to the following two factors: the mass production and diversification of products resulting from the global spread of the Industrial Revolution, and the emergence of egalitarian democracy also resulting from the Industrial Revolution. The democratic principles advocated by the democratic system are transformed from the real equality, such as the equality of ability, responsibility, social opportunity, and happiness, to a superficial equality and other obvious signs of social achievement and happiness (Baudrillard, 2006: 34). In other words, the Industrial Revolution broke the rigid hierarchical system of feudal society that restricted the possession and consumption of certain goods by ordinary people. And in the micro-technical context, the emergence of consumerism, as Daniel Bell puts it, was aided by three social inventions: mass production on an assembly line, which made a cheap automobile possible; the development of marketing, which rationalized the art of identifying different kinds of buying groups and whetting consumer appetites; and the spread of installment buying, which, more than any other social device, broke down the old Protestant fear of debt.

(Bell, 1996: 66)

In fact, there is one other role that is largely responsible for the prevalence of consumerism in modern society that is absent from this discussion: modern advertising, which is based on sophisticated communication technologies. If you can agree with Daniel Bell that advertising "is the mark of material goods, the exemplar of new styles of life, the herald of new values" (Bell, 1996: 68), then you would agree that advertising is essentially the twin of consumerism and has contributed to the promotion and penetration of consumerist values throughout society. Advertisements not only show the charm of commodities, but also reveal the symbolic meaning of them—in this way, houses and cars are not only places to live or means of transportation, but also symbols of status.[13] Advertising not only keenly captures consumers' social psychology, making them accept its propositions and propaganda through leading words, and by shortening the time interval from preference to action, namely consumption, but it also makes consumers believe that here is their life's value and hope, and that the advertised lifestyle is the one they want to have. Because of this,

advertising has replaced political propaganda as the largest discourse hegemony in modern society. ... Advertising, together with several other factors—convenience of goods (both for use and access), the manipulation of the society (especially the government and some experts) by business-men, the psychology of the public to show off and prove themselves by objects, and the unpredictable and never-ending fashion—constitutes the mechanism of producing a consumer society.

(Zheng, 2007: 47–48)

In the last 100 years, consumerism has become popular in Western society, but it has also been mercilessly criticized and ridiculed by social scientists, including at least the following aspects.

First, consumerism advocates naked materialism and hedonism, basing all human needs on the desire, pursuit, possession, and consumption of materials. It is this endless and insatiable pursuit of things that destroys the Protestant ethic on which modern capitalism depends for survival and development, and makes today's world an arena full of materialistic desires. There is no doubt that consumerism and its promotion of materialism and hedonism is one of the inherent characteristics of capitalist culture. In his article "Die protestantische Ethik und der Geist des Kapitalismus", Max Weber emphasizes that Calvinism—thrift and the legal pursuit of wealth—are the basic principles that promote the rise of Western civilization characterized by rational production and exchange (Weber, 2005); however, capitalism, as Bell says, has a double origin: It is based both on the "asceticism" that Weber emphasizes and the "acquisitiveness" that Werner Sombart discussed in *The Jews and Modern Capitalism* (Bell, 1996: xviii), which constitute the irreconcilable cultural contradictions of capitalism. If the former's emphasis on hard work, thrift, and moderation promoted the development of early capitalism, the latter's emphasis on consumption fostered hedonism, which became the intrinsic driving force of late capitalism or what Bell called "the new capitalism". In this new capitalist or consumer society, consumption takes the place of production, and the order of production is maintained by massive consumption or constant waste. In the abundance of things and the endless consumption of things, "just as the wolf-child became a wolf by living among wolves, so we too are slowly becoming functional" (Baudrillard, 1998: 25).

Second, consumerism holds that people do not consume for their own survival and development, and the real valuable purpose of consumption is to pursue the symbolic meaning of goods, which is the symbol of social evaluation. In other words, in a consumer society, consumption is a dynamic carrier that shows a person's wealth, status, class, identity, taste, and even personality characteristics. The level of consumption reflects the level of a person's social status and value realization. In Baudrillard's words, "in order to become object of consumption, the object must become sign", because "it is never consumed in its materiality, but in its difference" (Baudrillard, 1988: 22). Just because people's consumption objects have symbolic significance, they will naturally show or show off their wealth, status, or taste through their consumption items. As early as 1899, the American sociologist Veblen noted that, for tycoons who are created by a culture of money but have no benefit for the purpose of collective living, since consumption, especially the conspicuous consumption, is a proof of wealth and then ability or honor, "conspicuous consumption of valuable goods is a means of reputability to the gentleman of leisure" (Veblen, 1967: 47). Since the advent of the consumer society in the 20th century, the new middle class with its other-directed personality began to form "an 'abundance psychology' capable of 'wasteful' luxury consumption of leisure and of the surplus product" (Riesman et al., 2001: 18). At the same time, the inherent "status panic" caused more and more middle-class men and women to compete for consumption and put more effort into acquiring prestige symbols (Mills, 1979: 254).

Third, consumerism advocates that consumption is the ultimate goal of life; in other words, the value and significance of people's existence is reflected in what you can possess or consume and how much you can possess or consume, while labor and creation are just ways or means for us to obtain consumption materials. Under the guidance of such consumption values, people will naturally translate Descartes' "I think, therefore I am" into "I consume, therefore I am", advocated by consumer society; hence consumption has become a realistic way for people to obtain self-identity. Under the guidance of such values, it is natural to see the phenomenon that Marx ridiculed in his day: What people always thought they couldn't sell is now exchanged and bought. Even virtues, love, faith, knowledge and conscience are finally bought and sold. It is a time of widespread bribery, widespread buying and selling, or, to use the term of political economy, it is the period when everything spiritual or material becomes exchange value and goes to the market to find the evaluation that best matches its true value (Marx & Engels, 1973: 79–80). Unfortunately, these 100 years of economic and social development have not reversed the commodity fetishism that Marx attacked; on the contrary, with the rapid growth of GDP in the whole world, shopping and consumption have become the highest principles of the consumption society and of the trend of global spread.

If China's development is nearly a century later than that of the developed countries in the world, then in the decades after the reform and opening-up, when the growth of GDP made "some people get rich first" in the Chinese population, all the phenomena criticized and ridiculed by the above-mentioned thinkers were also prevalent in China. It is said that in China, a country with a per capita GDP of just over 4,000 USD and ranking more than 90 in the world, the consumption of luxury goods in 2009 has surpassed that of the United States, becoming the world's second largest luxury goods market after Japan. In 2018, Chinese people spent 770 billion CNY on luxury goods both at home and abroad, accounting for one third of the global total (McKinsey & Company, 2019). But consumerism in China is more problematic than that. If we say that the background of consumerism in Western society is homogeneous, that consumers as the main body of consumption are basically the same, and that there is no obvious group differentiation phenomenon in the consumption of the whole society, then the operational background of consumerism in China is extremely complex, facing the problem of consumption class differentiation and urban–rural division. As far as the former is concerned, the consumerism in Chinese society is mainly supported by a few high-income groups. The globalization expansion of multinational companies occupies the consumption capacity of these people and transfers the market of China, a developing country, from the internal state of the nation to a part of the world market (Chen et al., 2009). In the case of the latter, in the more populous rural areas, where food and clothing are mostly available, there is little prospect of further consumer satisfaction. This has not only led to the rise of the "knock-off products" characterized by piracy, cloning, and imitation, but also often trapped the Chinese economy in the dilemma of rampant consumerism on the one hand and insufficient domestic demand on the other (Duan, 2009). Therefore, while we sing the praises of the social prosperity and affluence brought by a growth of GDP, we have to reflect on and guard against the spread of consumerism.

It should be acknowledged that in general, from the perspective of intergenerational differences, the older generation is the adherent of the traditional consumption ethics of thrift and diligence, while the younger generation is the advocate and spokesman of consumerism. The younger generation in question is relative to the older generation, and may include the under-50s. Of these three generations, those born or brought up after the reform and opening-up, the post-70s, post-80s, and post-90s generations, needless to say, have grown up with the increase and accumulation of wealth. Although the 45–60-year-old generation experienced the extreme material shortage of the Mao Zedong era, some of them, the so-called middle class, are also the beneficiaries of this new era, the actual owners of wealth. This contradictory historical experience has given them a dual attitude towards material comforts and consumption. On the one hand, they feel that their children do not cherish money enough or understand hard-won happiness; on the other hand, they are vainer than their children, and their consumption may be more ostentatious.[14] In the interview, 11-year-old SKG and 22-year-old SMG complained about the excessive consumption desire of their mother. SKG even said it bluntly, "I think the reason why my mother is 'greedy' is she was frightened by her past poverty" (SKG, 2014). Thus, I believe that it may be impossible to form what Inglehart called "post-materialism" (Inglehart, 1997), or to enter what Zheng Yefu called a "post-materialistic era" (Zheng, 2007) in our generation. But the younger generation, who grew up in a truly affluent environment, is very likely to take a hard look at the meaning of consumption and, as Madsen put it, resist some of the negative effects of the consumption revolution in a more systematic way (Madsen, 2000: 318). Given that both SHG and SNG know how to arrange their parents' self-guided trips in Europe or the United States for minimal cost, and that SNG has taught parents how to shop online for inexpensive groceries—in the words of SNF, the largest online shopping experience has included a Simmons mattress (SNF, 2014)—this is not a wild guess. If so, it may be safe to say that there will not be a whole new cultural reverse movement about consumption and even the meaning of life in China in the future.

Intergenerational tilt, or the descending of the family orthocenter

If the rapid changes brought by social transformation and globalization are only the macro-background of the changes in the intergenerational relationship and the phenomenon of cultural reverse in Chinese society, then the changes within the families in this society triggered by this great change are the micro-environment.

In Chapter 2 of the first volume of this book, we discussed the traditional family system in Chinese society and the family ethics principle with its tradition of filial piety and seniority at the core. In his research on the Chinese family system, Fei Xiaotong quoted the British anthropologist Raymond Firth as saying:

> The triangle on stage or screen is the love conflict between two men and a woman (and more recently, two women and a man); but from the anthropologist's point of view, the real triangle in the social structure is the sons and daughters and their parents united by a common sentiment.
>
> (Firth, 2009)

Fei Xiaotong went on to write:

> The meaning of marriage lies in the establishment of the basic triangle in the social structure. A couple is not just a sexual relationship between a man and a woman, but a responsible partnership. In the contract of marriage two connected social relations are formed at the same time—husband–wife and parent–child. These two kinds of relations cannot be independent, as the relationship between the couple takes the parent–child relationship as the premise, and the parent–child relationship also takes the husband–wife relationship as the necessary condition. It is the three sides of a triangle and any side is indispensable .
>
> (Fei, 1998: 159)

Fei realized that although the husband–wife relationship and the parent–child relationship are interdependent, it is clear that in traditional Chinese society, the parent–child relationship is more important than the relationship between husband and wife and is the focus of the family structure.

But the parent–child relationship is not always sentimental. As children grow up, parents are responsible for transforming a biological person into a social one, and have to impose social norms on their children with some force, so that "it is no more difficult for people to live under the most despotic monarch than it is for a child to live under the parents who love him most" (Fei, 1998: 191). The difficulty of living under the parents is that they often hand over their unfinished "ideal" to their children, while they themselves face the "reality" and muddle through. But this is only a mild dislocation at a time when social change is painfully slow. In modern times, with the acceleration of social changes, the ideal itself has become an uncertain thing, or the ideal of the parents may become "rubbish" in the eyes of children. "The judgment of the previous generation is hardly suitable for the new environment of the second generation" (Fei, 1998: 155), so the imposition of this "rubbish" cannot but cause the tension of intergenerational relations, thus "the phenomenon of 'father not father, son not son' will occur" (Fei, 1998: 76).

The phenomenon of generational changes caused by social changes discussed by Fei Xiaotong became more obvious in China after 1978, when the family relationship in Chinese society shows a trend of intergenerational tilt or downward center of gravity (Liu, 2005). In other words, the importance of the younger generation in the parent–child relationship begins to increase. Although Schurmann argued that paternalism had fallen apart after the 1949 revolution (Schurmann, 1971: 7), and Stacey gently suggested that the so-called democratic patriarchy and patriarchal socialism had emerged in the Chinese family (Stacey, 1983), in fact "communism has not completely dismantled patriarchy" (Shen, 2009). The real factors leading to the collapse of patriarchy are the large-scale urbanization and marketization brought by the reform and opening-up and the family planning policy implemented in the 1980s. It is this series of continuous changes in social life that leads to the decline of patriarchy (Jin,

2000; Yan, 2006) and also leads to the inversion of the traditional parent–child relationship and the increase of the status and importance of the younger generation. Specifically, the above-mentioned intergenerational tilt phenomenon is related to the following three changes.

First, the intergenerational tilt or downward shift in family relations in Chinese society is related to the large-scale urbanization since the 1980s and the increase of social mobility associated with urbanization. As we all know, in the 30 years before the reform and opening-up, China's economy also made considerable progress, with an average annual growth rate of 6.1%. However, because of the "anti-urbanization" strategy adopted in the large-scale industrialization process (Murphey, 1980; Zhou, 2010), while highlighting the production function of cities and inhibiting their consumption and cultural functions, the urbanization rate in China has been below the average annual rate of 0.6%. At the beginning of the reform and opening-up, the urbanization rate was only 17.92%, which is far behind that of industrialization.[15] After the reform and opening-up, especially after 1996, China's urbanization made considerable progress, according to the sixth census, reaching 49.68% (Ma, 2011); that is to say, the average annual growth rate of urbanization in the 32 years after the reform and opening-up was 0.99%, while in the five years from 2005 to 2010 it was as high as 1.376% (by the end of 2019, China's urbanization rate had reached 60.60%). The significant changes brought about by the growth of the urban population, coupled with the impact of the one-child policy, which we will discuss later, led to the development of small and core families. The average size of each family is only 3.1 people, that is to say, the current Chinese family is mainly composed of an adult couple and their minor children. These new changes naturally place the child at the center of the family in what we call an intergenerational tilt or the descending of the family orthocenter.

Associated with urbanization, the increase of China's floating population also further promotes the miniaturization and centralization of family structure. Since the reform and opening-up, the mobility rate of the population has been increasing, and now it has reached 260 million people, among whom the majority are migrant workers (Ma, 2011). Jin Yihong confirms that this "de-regionalized" flow in terms of geographical boundaries and old relationships "greatly weakens the control ability of fathers over individuals, especially the younger generation" (Jin, 2010; Pan, 2007; Zhu, 2008). Thus, while the younger generation of minors has become the center of the family, the younger generation of adults has become more autonomous than ever before. For example, many studies on "working girls" have found that migrant work or employment mobility have formed an unprecedented impact on the traditional patriarchal family system. In terms of migration, work choice, love, marriage, birth, and social communication, female migrant workers have shown a challenge to their parents' authority (Tan, 2004). "No longer the master of the young" has also become a common lament of the parents' generation, including in our interviews.

Second, the intergenerational tilt or the descending of the family orthocenter in family relations in Chinese society is related to the change of marketization and various economic orders and distribution patterns associated with it. As we know, before 1978, the state-dominated redistribution system in Chinese society was based on people's social status (including political and professional status) and seniority in the system. In such a distributive system, the weakness of young people was not only reflected in their income, but also in the welfare system such as housing and health care, which made them rely on the older generation. However, as we discussed in Chapter 1 of the first volume of this book, after the reform and opening-up, the transformation of Chinese society towards marketization made the economic return of human capital become clear at least in the intergenerational field. This phenomenon of marketization leading to higher economic status of children, thus reducing the power of fathers over families, is now common in both urban and rural families. In urban families, as Liu Jingming's research confirms, the employment opportunities and levels of children with higher education have been much higher than those of their parents, let alone their grandparents (Liu, 2006a), while the growth of economic income has improved their intergenerational status in the family. In rural families, young people's income from migrant work is far greater than that from their parents' or grandparents' farming, which also accelerates the transfer of family economic power from the old to the young (Jin, 2010). Given that the younger generation often have an innate understanding of the market economy and its rules, like the BV families in Zhejiang village mentioned in Chapter 3 of the first volume of this book, this accelerates the intergenerational succession of many families—decision-making power in family matters is clearly beginning to tilt downward: the parents are not yet old physically, but the children have taken over spiritually.

> When we came to Beijing in 1993, BVB was only 16 years old. Of course, it was me and her mother who started the clothing business and he helped us. But it wasn't long before I realized that he had more brains than we did. Because BVB had contacts with Beijing young people nearby, unlike us who only associated with Wenzhou people, he spoke Beijing dialect well and had many more sources. For example, two years earlier, the government often rectified the "Zhejiang village", but because we knew few local people and had little information, we didn't know when to close up to "shun trouble", and often suffered losses. Then he told us when to close up. For another example, he often brought back some popular clothing styles. At first, I could not accept some of them, but tried to make some and sold well. Gradually, I simply let him decide.
>
> (BVF, 1995)

Third, the intergenerational tilt or the descending of the family orthocenter is also related to the impact and transformation of family form and parenting concept brought about by the implementation of family planning and the one-child policy since the 1980s. In the 1970s, China began to promote family planning. In 1980, it further implemented the one-child policy, which not only led to the decline of China's family fertility rate and population growth rate, but also created a special generation—the only children, and a new group of social cells, the one-child families (Wu, 2008: 263). Feng Xiaotian's research found that the "family of three", consisting of a couple and one child, has a different lifestyle from the previous extended family, among which the most important are: the living pattern in which the young live apart from their elders, yet take care of each other; the shift of the family center from fathers to children; and the increasing equality of the parent–child relationship (Feng, 1994). The shift of the family center from parents to children is determined by the importance of the only child in a family. It is obvious that one child will inevitably be the focus of the parents' attention and emotional concentration. Family emotions, consumption, education, leisure, and communication will all focus on this child. The equality of the parent–child relationship is also determined by the import-ance of the only child in a family. Since there is only one child, parents will naturally make concessions to their children when encountering problems. The frequent social communication and interaction between parents and children makes parents become "collaborators and big partners" of children on many occasions, forming relatively equal communication relations—games, for example, are more likely to take place in only-child households. Also, the pat-tern of only children living apart from their parents, with the two generations looking after each other, can not only achieve intergenerational care of grand-children, but also meet the emotional adhesion between grandparents and grand-children. The phenomenon of family members two generations apart being closer to each other in traditional Chinese society is often most fully expressed in the one-child families—because there is only one child, grandparents can put all their heart and soul into this child and realize their emotional attachment through taking care of him. In fact, the older generation often tolerates, appreci-ates, and even connives at the challenge of their grandchildren unlike the same kind of behavior in their children. The short essay "Go home and ask my grand-son" written by the late Mr. Fan Jingyi, the famous newspaper man we men-tioned in Chapter 1 of the first volume of this book, expresses this special emotion vividly.

> Recently, I often have meetings with my old comrades to discuss some new fields, subjects and knowledge, like the knowledge economy, intellectual property, the information superhighway, the use and management of com-puter software. Sometimes when faced with difficulties, some old comrades will naturally say "wait until I go home to ask my son" or "wait until I go home to ask my grandson".
>
> At first I was not used to hearing these words: After a lifetime of being an intellectual, even an intellectual of some fame, how can one even "go home and ask his grandson"? Later, when I thought more about it, I suddenly felt that this is not a disorder, but a reflection of the historical change we are experiencing.
>
> "Go home and ask my grandson" first shows that science and technology are developing rapidly in today's world, and our knowledge is increasingly

falling behind the wheel of the times. Our children and grandchildren are, or have been, far ahead of us. If you think about it, the science and technology we learned in elementary school, middle school and college is much naiver and superficial than what today's teenagers learn. Today, in many families, it is the case that a grandfather or a father is far less skilled at using a computer than a child who is still in elementary school. This is the progress of the society.

"Go home and ask my grandson" also illustrates a change in social attitudes. In the past, old people used to scold their children and grandchildren with such words as, "what do you know?" or "I have walked over more bridges than you have!" Now it is rare to hear such old-fashioned words, which are gradually replaced by "asking questions". This is because old people have admitted that their knowledge of modern science and technology is behind the times, so they are eager to catch up, and no longer consider it a loss of face to ask younger people. This is also the progress of the times.

In fact, even in western countries with highly developed science and technology, it is normal to "go home and ask my grandson". It is said that because of the rapid development of science and technology, judges often encounter professional knowledge that they do not know. Under such circumstances, judges often have to announce a temporary adjournment to consult experts or ask their sons or grandchildren. This is what a legal problem expert told me, so I think it can not be false.

This, of course, is not to disparage the elderly. The old have their merits and have much valuable experience for the young to learn. I just want to emphasize that in the face of ever-changing science and technology, the urgency of knowledge renewal is becoming more and more prominent for the old generation. This has become a worldwide issue. In the United States, some old doctors in their 50s and 60s have gone to study for new doctorates in order to rearm themselves. Therefore, in order to better keep up with the pace of the times, we must study hard and humbly, including learning from our second and third generations; otherwise, even if we want to "let ourselves play our part", the surplus value is increasingly limited. In this sense, the willingness to "go home and ask my grandchildren" is a good phenomenon worthy of praise, which is much more positive and valuable than constantly lamenting the "declining generations" or "feeling sorry for the current situation".

(Fan, 1998)

In an interview with the *Wall Street Journal* in 2003, I also said, "Parents used to obey the old order, and now they listen to their children" (Chang, 2003). The intergenerational relationship involved is not just between grandparents and parents living today, but between fathers and grandchildren, as well as grandparents and grandchildren. In other words, it has become one of the regular sights of our time that the older generation is beginning to listen to the younger generation.

No matter whether it is globalization, social transformation, or the inter-generational inclination brought about by the change of the family structure, in a word, all the forces of social change are working together to change the intergenerational relationship that has lasted for thousands of years in Chinese society. For it was the great changes that began in the second half of the 20th century that created the great rift in Chinese society that we have repeatedly highlighted between generations. In the following Chapters 2 and 3, we will also discuss the influence of the peer group of young people known as the "knowledge reservoir" or "extended memory" and the broader mass media on the intergenerational relationship of Chinese society, especially the phenomenon of "cultural reverse" we are talking about here. We will further confirm to our readers that the subversive revolution in intergenerational relations has also benefited from the interaction between young people, from the wave of information and knowledge brought by the media, and that cultural reverse is one of the most valuable life experiences brought to us by the intergenerational revolution.

Notes

1 Giambattista Vico tried to divide human history in the way of the ancient Egyptians into three ages: the age of gods, the age of heroes, and the age of mortals; Ferguson divided the development of society into three stages: primitive society, savage society, and refined society; Saint-Simon, on the other hand, believed that these three stages were the theological stage, the metaphysical stage, and the empirical stage (Zhou, 2002: 11–15).

2 Although we do not generally consider Marx's concept of development to be a linear evolutionary theory, in *Das Kapital* Marx did say that the more developed industrial countries showed the less developed industrial countries only a vision of the future of the latter (Marx & Engels, 1973: 8). The five-stage theory of human social development, which was later widely spread in China, came from Stalin's *On Dialectical Materialism and Historical Materialism* (1938). In this work, Stalin clearly proposed the single-line development scheme of five modes of production from a primitive commune system, to slavery, a feudal system, capitalism, and socialism (Stalin, 1962: 199).

3 To some extent, the theory of modernization was born out of the McCarthyism of the Cold War era of the 1950s, and thus naturally had an ideological tendency to justify America's post-war international policy (Peck, 1969), or to become what Michael E. Latham called the "non-communist manifesto" (Latham, 2003). Therefore, as Webster said, the fiercest criticism of the modernization theory is to accuse it of completely ignoring the influence of colonialism and imperialism on the third world countries (Webster, 1984: 37).

4 Although generally speaking, the artistic life of Nanjing, the "abandoned capital", is far less colorful than that of Beijing and Shanghai, it is only because of its historical association with the national government that the Chinese on the island of Taiwan have a special attachment to it. Taking Lai's plays as an example, Nanjing seems to have been his main experimental theater on the mainland. Thanks to my friend, Miss Zheng Sihua, who is the promoter of Lai Shengchuan's drama in the Nanjing area, I also had the honor to watch two other dramas directed by Lai in recent years: *Peach Blossom Land* and *Love on a Two Way Street*.

5 As China's middle class grows rapidly, so does its wealthy or economic elite. According to statistics, by the end of 2008, there were just 1.6 million wealthy

households in China, but that number is now growing at 16% a year. According to a 2009 report by McKinsey & Company, China will be the world's fourth richest country after the United States, Japan, and the United Kingdom. In 2018, excluding Hong Kong, Macao and Taiwan, the number of "wealthy families" on the Chinese mainland with assets of 6 million CNY reached 3.87 million, 250,000 more than the previous year or 7% growth, ranking third in the world after the United States and Japan (Global Consulting Group, 2018). I have discussed, using the views of Hungarian sociologists such as Szelenyi, the curious mixture of Communist Party, socialism, capitalists (now collectively referred to as "private entrepreneurs"), and capitalism in a rapidly developing socialist market economy. "In the sense of the market, China can be figuratively described as 'having both capitalists and capitalism' in contrast to Russia's 'having capitalists without capitalism' and central Europe's 'having capitalism without capitalists'." And, of course, the consistent leadership of the Communist Party (Zhou & Chen, 2010b).

6 By the end of 2013 when I revised this chapter, the operating mileage of China's high-speed railway had reached 11,028 kilometers, accounting for half of the world's total mileage, and another 4,883 kilometers were under construction.

7 It is reported that in 2009, students from Shanghai, China, ranked first in the Organisation for International Economic Co-operation and Development (OECD)'s assessment of the reading ability of 15-year-olds in 65 countries and regions, including the United States, the United Kingdom, Japan, Brazil, Hong Kong, and China. Shanghai scored 556, followed by South Korea (539), Finland (536), and Hong Kong (533) (Xinhua News Agency, 2010b). It also shows that the academic performance of Chinese children has improved remarkably compared with that of their parents.

8 Anyone who has read Walters's *New Traditionalism in Communist Society* knows that the author uses the concept of "new traditionalism" to show that the old traditions before 1949 did not die, but continued in various ways in the state, society, and factory system of new China. For example, the decision-makers of the state and the Party originally wanted to set up a set of impersonal and somewhat universalist "system of political incentives" aimed at motivating political beliefs and moral values in state-owned factories, but in specific factory practice, the leader of the unit as an agent starts from the pursuit of self-interest and transforms it into a personalized reward system aiming at encouraging workers and leaders to establish a long-term and close cooperative relationship. In this way, the original incentive system is changed and become a "principled particularism".

9 For example, in 2002, China's housing loan balance accounted for less than 2% of the total loan balance of financial institutions, but only one year later, in 2003, China's housing loan balance had risen to 1.2 trillion RMB, accounting for 10% of the total loan balance of financial institutions. According to the latest statistics, China's outstanding housing loans reached 25.8 trillion CNY in 2018.

10 During a visit to Paris in November 2008, I visited the Lafayette department store at 40 Rue Haussmann, next to the Paris Opera House. As soon as I walked out of the subway and into the shopping lobby, I thought I was back in China, because there were so many Chinese people everywhere, and there were signs on all the counters that said, "We offer Chinese service". I went up to the second floor and saw dozens of Chinese people lined up at the Louis Vuitton store, where bags were sold. As soon as I appeared, a man in his 40s, already carrying three Louis Vuitton bags, rushed up to me and asked me if I wanted to buy bags. After knowing that I wasn't going to buy one, he asked me if I could give him my passport, because in France, only one Louis Vuitton bag could be bought per passport. When I asked him why he bought so many Louis Vuitton bags, the man replied, "Only 500 euros for a Louis Vuitton bag! It's so cheap!" (Zhou, 2008a).

11 Friedman calls some of the new technologies "steroids," in his words, mainly because they amplify the effects of all the other flattening forces. Specifically, it is done in a variety of digital, mobile, virtual, and personal ways, which in turn flattens the world (Friedman, 2006: 145).

12 We used to criticize capitalism as pure money worship, but it is money worship in Chinese society that is truly jaw-dropping. According to a survey of 23 countries released by Ipsos in 2010, 69% of Chinese people agreed that "money is the best symbol of personal success", higher than the average of 57%. Close to China was South Korea, followed by India and Japan, while the U.S., which we have long regarded as a symbol of money worship, was only 33%. Ipsos thus concluded that: (a) easterners value money more than westerners; (b) people in transition countries value money more than those in developed countries, and China combines these two factors (Ipsos, 2010).

13 Interestingly, not only did I study advertising, but I also ran an organization called the Jiuge Advertising Company from 1995 to 1998, which didn't close until I went to Harvard University in the United States in early 1999 to do research. Although it has been a long time since I left advertising, I still remember the famous words of Claude Hopkins, an American advertising man, who said that advertising is to commodities what drama is to life (Zhou, 1994b: 1). No matter how negative advertising is to modern society, you must admit that it is advertising that makes the modern promotion of goods so wonderful.

14 When I visited Canada in the summer of 2010, on a cruise ship from Vancouver to British Columbia, I ran into more than 200 summer tour groups of high school students from Wenzhou, China. The middle-class children, bright and confident, all attended the top local high schools and had excellent interpersonal skills. They told me it cost almost everyone more than 100,000 RMB to come out once. I was surprised why they spent so much money. They replied that in addition to their own expenses, which would cost 40,000 to 50,000 RMB, they would also buy all kinds of expensive luxuries for their parents, especially their mothers. In their words: "Who doesn't have a shopping order from mom?" I asked for a copy of the shopping list, which covered everything from watches and handbags to cosmetics and clothes.

15 Under Preston's law, for every 1% increase in the industrial share of the workforce, the urban share grows by 2%, but in fact, not only did China's urbanization lag behind the industrialization in the 30 years before the reform and opening-up, but even after, urbanization still lags behind Preston's law. For example, during the period of reform and opening-up from 1978 to 2000, the proportion of industrial workers in the total workforce increased by 28.2%, while the proportion of the urban population increased by only 18.3% (Li, 2005b).

2 The peer group as knowledge reservoir and extended memory

> The parents in the era dominated by other-direction lose their once undisputed role; the old man is no longer "the governor"—and the installer of governors. Other adult authorities such as the governess and grandmother either almost disappear or, like the teacher, take on the new role of peer-group facilitator and mediator—a role not too different perhaps from that of many clergymen who, in the adult congregation, move from morality to morale ... It will be possible to put him into school and playground, and camp in the summer, with other children of virtually the same age and social position. If the adults are the judge, these peers are the jury. And, as in America the judge is hemmed in by rules which give the jury a power it has in no other common-law land, so the American peer group, too, cannot be matched for power throughout the middle-class world.
>
> David Riesman et al., 1961

The peer group and generational identity

Just as the wheels of the second half of the 20th century were beginning to slide into history, David Riesman, one of the best-known postwar American sociologists, in *The Lonely Crowd: A Study of the Changing Character of the American People*, was quick to note that with the increasingly rapid changes of modern society, the elders who used to occupy the supreme position in the socialization of teenagers begin to lose their supreme influence and give way to increasingly colorful and diverse peer groups. For this reason, Riesman points out that to explain personality changes in modern society, it is necessary to emphasize "the role of the peer group and the school in adolescence in the formation of character", although "perhaps itself underestimates the possibility of change as the result of the experiences of adulthood" (Riesman et al., 2001: xxxvii).

In Riesman's analysis framework, the "S-curve", which represents the changing trend of population growth, is regarded as an indicator of social change. The horizontal line at the bottom of the S-curve indicates that the population is not increasing, or is increasing very slowly, when the birth and death rates are very high; since a population explosion can be achieved simply by reducing mortality, Riesman calls this the incubation period for rapid growth. Then, as the West entered industrial society, the population began to increase rapidly because of increased grain production, improved sanitary conditions, and improved measures to prevent and control diseases. The middle section of the S-curve shows this upward trend, which is demographically called the transitional growth period. Finally, after World War II, with the transition of the United States from the era of production to the era of consumption, the decline of the birth rate, and the already reduced death rate, the population change began to enter the flat or even declining section at the top of the S-curve: society entered the so-called initial period of population decline.

Riesman's interest lies not in explaining the simple population growth and its trend in modern times, but in the influence of social changes on people's personality changes. In this sociologist's eyes, "each of these three different phases on the population curve appears to be occupied by a society that enforces conformity and molds social character in a definably different way" (Riesman et al., 2001: 8). To be specific, when society is in the farming stage, in the "incubation period of rapid growth" of population mentioned by Riesman, because of the slow social change, people's behavior patterns are subject to the influence of tradition formed over hundreds of years or even thousands of years. Society basically relies on tradition to achieve its members' compliance. In the 17th century, or after the Industrial Revolution, society entered the transitional growth period of population. The so-called "modern factors" of population mobility, technological innovation, rapid accumulation of capital, sustained commodity production, and colonial and imperialist expansion gave people greater choice and freedom, and they were no longer constrained by a traditional orientation, and society begins to rely on an "inner direction" or self-orientation for its members to comply with it. Finally, in the post-industrial era, with its emphasis on production and consumption, society began to enter an "initial period of population decline", when fewer and fewer people were engaged in agricultural production or raw material industry and manufacturing, and the working hours were beginning to shorten. In addition to material comforts, people had leisure. In these new conditions, the hardy and enterprising spirit of internally oriented persons became superfluous. Others, rather than circumstances, became the problem (Riesman et al., 2001: 18). At this point, society began to rely on the "other direction" to ensure that its members complied with it.

In Riesman et al.'s argument, others, beyond tradition and self, gradually become decisive factors affecting people's behavior. The most important modern component of this "other" for the younger generation is the peer group, "an informal group composed of people with similar status, age, interests, hobbies, values and behaviors" (Zhou, 1997: 136). Here, although age is a key variable, the influence of socioeconomic status, race, and gender differences cannot be ignored (Ennett & Bauman, 1996). Many sociological studies have confirmed that peer groups are increasingly influencing individual socialization in modern society: Not only do American and European high school students spend twice as much time per week with their peers as with their parents or other adults (Bronfenbrenner, 1970; Larson & Verma, 1999), but American teenagers report better moods when they are together with their peers (Larson, 1983). Similarly,

Chinese children are more likely to tell their peers what's on their minds, and even among Chinese students, the peer group is fairly homogeneous in terms of academic achievement (Chen, et al., 2003).

It was Theodore Newcomb, an American social psychologist, who first sensed and empirically studied the influence of peer groups. Newcomb spent several years from 1939 investigating the relationship between women's college experience and sociopolitical attitudes at Bennington Women's College in the United States. In LeVine's words, interaction with peer groups at this progressive university in Vermont changes the political and economic attitudes of female college students from conservative families (LeVine, 1966: 114). Specifically, Newcomb found that young students who had strong ties to conservative families tended to be more conservative when they entered college, but the college experience of interacting in peer groups over the following few years liberalized them in their political leanings and personal life styles (Newcomb, 1943: 274). Newcomb's work was not only the first to confirm the power of peer groups, but also provides practical support for the "reference group" theory proposed by the sociologist H. Hyman (1942).

Although Newcomb's genius led to the Bennington study later becoming a diverse guide to the hypothesis of peer group influence (LeVine, 1966: 122), the study itself is only one of the symbols of the rise of youth culture in the United States in the 1940s. There are many other events that also serve as symbols, but some of the most important are the following. First, American sociologist Talcott Parsons put forward the concept of "youth culture" for the first time in his article "Age and sex in the social structure of the United States" (Parsons, 1942), which later became the starting point for a series of studies and discussions on youth (Berger, 1972: 176). Second, the more popular concept of "teenage" or "teenager" is based on the term "adolescence" originally coined by the psychologist Stanley Hall. The shift from "adolescence" to "teenager" not only confirms Hall's prediction that there is a clear disconnect between childhood and adulthood, but more importantly, this period is no longer regarded as one of unrest and rebellion, but a period of consumption more acceptable to modern society. Third, in September 1944, a young fashion magazine called *Seventeen* was released for the first time. It inspired the "purest manifestations of American youth's desire for novelty, excitement, and self-identification", and "pulled together the strands of democracy, national identity, peer culture, target marketing, and youth consumerism into an irresistible package" (Savage, 2007: 450). Finally, around the time of *Seventeen*, a singer named Frank Sinatra became an icon for young people, especially young women, on Broadway in New York City. In addition to the thousands of girls at the Paramount Theater who attended five shows from dawn to dusk, Times Square outside was packed with tens of thousands of crazy girls who couldn't get tickets. Sinatra's voice was accompanied by their stomping, shouting, clapping, and screaming, and a rain of roses, underpants, and bras. This is "a phenomenon of mass hysteria that is only seen two or three times in a century" (Savage, 2007: 442).

Although the sentimentality of *Seventeen* and the commotion inside and outside the Paramount Theater gave Parsons, an old-school and somewhat conservative scholar, reason to think that American youth culture was more or less irresponsible (Parsons, 1942), his concept of this culture confirmed a new fact: Because of the needs of war and industry, "American adolescents had succeeded in creating a world quite distinct from both adults and children" (Savage, 2007: 453). There is no need to explain the fact that industry and consumption were dependent on teenagers, but it is curious that war put teenagers onto the history stage: Because the 18–30 age group was among the 7 million applicants, the remaining teenagers played a bigger role in daily life and the public sphere.

After the end of World War II, with the promotion of industrialization, especially post-industrialization, teenagers, peer groups, and youth culture began to spread all over the world (Larson & Wilson, 2004). Since then, as Eisenstadt puts it, almost all modern social development and social movements in developed countries such as the United States and Europe had their origins in diverse youth groups, peer groups, and youth movements, and what was called youth culture (Eisenstadt, 1972: 10).

China's youth culture in a completely independent sense emerged in the reform and opening-up era in 1978, and was shaped by the increasingly powerful market forces emphasizing consumption after 1992. But, as we have already described in Chapter 2 of the first volume of this book, the rampage of the Red Guard movement and the subsequent movement of intellectual youth into the countryside began, in Chinese fashion, to lay the foundations for the subsequent youth culture based around peer groups. Although both movements affecting tens of millions of people were manipulated and controlled by the Great Leader, the "rebellious" experience of defeating all the "feudalist, capitalist and revisionist" authorities all composed of elders, and the "honing" of leaving their parents and families and going to the countryside, made the power of the peer group more or less reflected in this generation of young people. Whether it is the Red Guard movement or the "movement to go to the countryside", some embryonic forms of peer groups and even youth subculture can be revealed, which we can discuss in at least two ways. First, in these two movements, a group of peers with distinct characteristics of intergenerational identity had been formed around the two iconic titles of the Red Guard or "educated youth". Whoever participated in the "chains" of the Red Guards, or had been to the countryside as educated youth, can clearly remember that, in the "chains" or countryside, no matter where you went, no matter whether you knew each other or not, as long as you reported that you were a Red Guard or an educated youth then other Red Guards or educated youth of the same age as you would put the rice bowl into your hand, or would give you their own bed to sleep in.[1] In the later stage of the movement, "all educated youth considered themselves to be part of the same group", and even farm youth, people married to local farmers, or non-agricultural workers required the administrative departments to identify them as "educated youth" (Bonnin, 2004: 380).

Second, in these two movements, the embryonic form of the youth subculture was formed, and the most distinctive sign was the emergence of "underground literature" and "educated youth literature", which are inextricably linked: Not only did the hostess of the earliest "underground art salon", such as Li Li and Xu Haoyuan, experience the transformation from Red Guard to educated youth, but the authors of the novels *Ruin* and *Escape* and the three core figures of the Baiyangdian School of Poetry, Mang Ke, Yue Zhong, and Duo Duo, were all educated youth (Yang, 1993).[2] In addition to poems and novels, many "songs of the educated youth", including the "The song of the educated youth in Nanjing",[3] constituted the main theme of the youth subculture in that special age. Although the culture of educated youth did not have the general "counter-culture" characteristics at this time, it did start to think independently and, as Pan Mingxiao said, gained its own expressive space in the countryside where social control was relatively weak (Bonnin, 2004: 344).

Compared with their parents, who used to be Red Guards and educated youth, the young Chinese who grew up after the reform and opening-up really formed their own relatively independent youth subculture, and correspondingly, the influence of their peer groups began to rise further. From the perspective of the reform and opening-up process from 1978–2020, there are many macro-institutional backgrounds that lead to the rise of peer group influence. First, the tolerance of politics, the popularization of university education, and the liberalization and diversification of career choice provided the post-70s, post-80s, post-90s, and even post-00s, who had grown up in the past four decades, with a stage to display their talents and a possibility for them to challenge adult authority, including parents. Second, the increasing frequency and rate of social mobility, the mainstreaming of two social mobility modes—"study in different places–employment in different places" and "leave the countryside to work" (Lu, 2004)—as Jin Yihong, a scholar quoted in the previous chapter, put it, form a "delocalization" of youth groups in terms of geographical boundaries and old relationships, and thus weaken parental control over offspring. Also, the influence of young people who study, live, and work together in foreign countries continues to grow, forming a kind of "culture of union" similar to what Margaret Mead called "co-figurative culture" (Mead, 1970: 25)—young people growing up began to model themselves on their early companions. Third, as the older children went out into the world, the one-child policy put into effect in the 1980s contributed to a large extent to the lonely only-child teenager with keys hanging around their necks leaving their families to seek friendship, understanding, and warmth among their peers. In those families where both parents went out to work, the peer group even became the main psychological comfort for children. Finally, as we shall discuss in Chapter 3, the development of the mass media, especially the electronic media from the 1990s, makes it possible for the younger generation to exchange, share, or vent their thoughts on the essence of life, scientific knowledge, life tips, emotional understanding, and even social resentment absent of the traditional sources of information or knowledge such as parents or teachers. In this way, in the socialization process of children, those students or peers who are slightly older or who are better-informed become the spiritual leaders or life mentors instead of parents or teachers.

When we first studied the social psychology and evolution of farmers from Jiangsu and Zhejiang provinces in Zhejiang village, my interviewees BH and BI mentioned that interacting with peers of similar age was the main way for them to understand society, observe the market, and acquire the Beijing dialect. Almost all the children of the families interviewed later mentioned without exception that the communication with classmates or peers was one of the main sources for them to obtain a lot of knowledge and information. In Zhejiang village, the people who had the most say about the market and the economic situation were often not the elders, but the young people who came to Beijing first. The experience they gained from exploring the Beijing market was a missing link in their parents' original knowledge stock, so they became entrepreneurial mentors and life models for others to follow.

The children of the urban families interviewed later, no matter how old they were or what their major was, in addition to academic knowledge coming mainly from the classroom and teachers, their social knowledge, science and technology news, fashion trends, and life experiences came from two main sources. One was the mass media, including the Internet, which will be discussed later, and the other was the peer group discussed here.

Considering that 8 million (2019) young people are now enrolled in universities every year, along with young people pursuing master's and doctoral degrees in universities, China has formed a rolling university student population of more than 38 million (2019). Among peers, classmates, especially those in college, have become a prominent peer group and an important social force shaping the younger generation. These 38 million college students participate in class discussions, academic reports, panel discussions, and teacher–student conversations; in addition, through self-organized academic salons, college student clubs, various association activities, and "bedtime talk" in their spare time, they are free to express their views and opinions on scholarship, on life, on society, and even on politics, which is more or less considered "off limits". Peer group communication is an important source of spiritual growth for these older children:

> College life is basically a collective life, and because we live in the collectivity, inevitably we will be affected by all aspects of it. For example, although everyone who enters our university is excellent, after all, personal vision and source of information is limited. But when we communicate with each other, our vision and information can be greatly expanded or broken through. Anyone who has had college experience knows that universities are information hubs. Take the "bedtime talk" after the dormitory lights are turned off every night as an example. This kind of informal communication, which is mixed with banter, ridicule and absurdity, is often the most intensive information exchange among students. At night, when it is time to go to bed, everyone is full of energy. From scientific discoveries to life lessons, to political gossip and even erotic news, there seems to be

nothing to be afraid to say. And the speaker is often full of ostentation, feeling his vanity has been greatly satisfied. I sometimes went home for a week or two, and by the time I got back to school, I didn't know a lot of things. For this reason, roommates often burst into laughter.

(NFB, 1998)

The claim of the NFB generation was borne out by the parents. NG's son and daughter are both in college, so their coming home on weekends is like giving a press conference about things parents have never heard of. NGM said, "Some of their knowledge and information comes from university professors, but more from their own classmates and unrestrained communication between classmates, which is what our generation lacks now" (NGM, 1998). Indeed, for these young people, who are intelligent and thirst for knowledge, the arithmetical progression of communication with each other has given them a geometric progression of knowledge and information. This is such a situation that the parent generation is actually dealing not only with their own children, but with their group or whole generation. Thus, behind every humble child may stand a closely connected group of peers, who become the knowledge "reservoir" or "expanding memory" for children to influence or "backfeed" their parents.

Like the modern rise of the peer group we discussed at the beginning of this chapter, special "others" in modern society may be the spiritual idols and identity objects of the younger generation, and further become the knowledge reservoir or expanding memory for that generation to backfeed to the older generation, not only because of the changes in the macro-factors in modern society, but also by having a profound and subtle personality and social psychology foundation. Here, there are two important links that cannot be ignored. First, how does the psychological process of identification or intergenerational identification occur in peer groups of similar biological ages? Second, how does the identification of such a pure psychological force translate into a real social existence, so that peer groups can replace parents and teachers as role models or life models for the younger generation?

The first part of the discussion starts with the conceptual definition of "identity" or "social identity". The word "identity" is directly related to the reflective understanding of who I am or who we are, where I am or where we are, and "recognition of a thing as different from all other things, and including in its unity all its inner changes and other diversities. Such a thing is said to remain the same or to have sameness" (Baldwin, 1998: 504). For a long time, identity and its related issues have been the focus of attention of sociologists and psychologists, and social psychology, formed in the intersection of these two disciplines, takes it as one of its core concepts (Zhou, 2008b). For example, as early as 1950, psychologist Eric Erickson listed "identity" and "identity crisis" as the themes of his book *Childhood and Society*, and deeply explored the relationship between identity and early life experiences (Erikson, 1950).[4] In Erikson's view, identity or identification is a sense of familiarity with oneself, a sense of knowing one's future goals, and an inner confidence in obtaining the expected approval from people one trusts (Erikson, 1959: 118).

Although identity or identification is crucial to the psychosocial development of individuals, the issue of identity or identification is not innate. Before puberty, children's identity is like pieces of cloth that have not yet been woven together. But by the end of adolescence, these scraps will have been woven into a single piece of fabric unique to the individual (Steinberg, 2007: 347). The patchwork process of these "rags" is, of course, a process in which adolescents acquire identity or identification. This occurs during adolescence, when, in addition to the physical and nervous maturation of the individual, children begin to disengage from their parents and make contact with others or society. It is this touch or interaction, as George Mead puts it, that requires the individual to understand the other's posturing (Mead, 1934: 154) and to know himself according to the views of others—for this reason, Cooley calls others the "me in the mirror" (Cooley, 1992: 118), while Fei Xiaotong vividly compares this process to "I look at how others look at me" (Fei, 1993)—so a person's sense of self or self-identity is nothing more than a reflection of what he or she is aware of what others think of him or herself. Further, this reflection constitutes the identity of the self; then the identification of this identity constitutes the group identity. Although from the standpoint of sociology, group identity is not the same as individual identity, the formation motivation of group identity is the same as that of individual identity: They are both about confirming their place in a group or society, and all group identification involves, as Harold Isaacs put it, clinging to the "house of Muubi" mentally or spiritually. Although the term "house of Muubi", which symbolizes the womb or matrix, is borrowed from Kikuyus, the search for a spiritual "anchor", for the self, or for an "I group" is a global exercise (Isaacs, 2010: 16). Moreover, personal identity problems are often catalyzed by insecurity, so it is a universal phenomenon that unstable or transitional groups, such as youth, urgently seek identity, especially intergenerational identity.

The second part of the discussion involves how to combine the psychological process of identification with broader social forces, especially group forces. If we translate this thinking, which is similar to European social identity theory, into our discussion of intergenerational relations, a very practical issue is: Why are the younger generation more likely to accept the values, life attitudes, and social behavior patterns of their peers when they also interact and connect with their parents, teachers, or elders?

The minimal-group paradigm, proposed by British social psychologist Henry Tajfel, provides an excellent explanation. In the experiment, Tajfel first asked the subjects to conduct a point estimation experiment on a card. Based on this, the subjects were randomly divided into two groups: the "overestimate group" and the "underestimate group", who were then asked to work on resource allocation. The results showed that although participants did not know each other and had never met or actually interacted with members of the same group, they still allocated more resources to members of their own group (Tajfel et al.,

1971). In other words, even if there was no prior interaction, as long as the subjects simply perceived the categorization, they would allocate more resources and positive evaluations to their own group. This kind of perceptual classification will make us subjectively perceive that we belong to others, thus creating a sense of identity (Zhang & Zuo, 2006). If we say that the experiment of Sherif et al., as early as in the 1960s, revealed that the real conflict caused by the competition for objective resources would have some influence on group and inter-group behaviors (Sherif et al., 1961), Tajfel's experiment, then, further reveals that awareness of group membership is the minimum condition for group behavior. Thus, once people become members of a simple or even meaningless category, it is enough to produce group-oriented perceptions and behaviors, which shows that subjective group identification will produce objective behavioral consequences.

Because of this subjective intergenerational identity, the younger generation realize their similarity and consistency, their shared interests, preferences and interests, and the psychological and physical differences between them and other groups, especially adult groups, and eventually form peer groups and subcultures that are abler to constrain their consciousness and actions. The formation of a youth subculture or peer group is very similar to the formation of the British working class described by the British historian Edward Thompson: Just as the subjective "consciousness" plays an important role in the objective "existence" of the working class,[5] "intergenerational identity" is equally important in the formation of young peer groups. Further, and most importantly, this mutual identification and alienation from adult groups, including parents and teachers, is the result of industrialization or modernization, both physically and psychologically—because it is industrialization or modernization that makes it possible for the younger generation to think and act together in a "group" way, outside of the family, in school or society. In this sense, peer group or intergenerational identity is itself a kind of modernity, the result of the interaction between modern society and the biological stage of individual physiological maturity.

The family and the school: how do conventional institutions decline?

The rising influence of peer groups is not an isolated phenomenon. To a large extent, it is related to the declining influence of families and schools in modern society, especially in the electronic age. If the family has been regarded as the basic unit of social life and part of a vast social network since human beings evolved a civilized society, even as the American sociologist William Goode said, it is the only social system that transforms a biological organism into a human being (Goode, 1964: 8), and schools are the institutionalized organizations that appeared widely after human beings formed civilized society, especially in modern times, the first bridge that leads children from family to society; and as Parsons said, the school is the first socializing agency in the child's experience which institutionalizes a differentiation of status on nonbiological bases. Moreover, this is not an ascribed but an achieved status; it is the status "earned" by differential performance of the tasks set by the teacher, who is acting as an agent of the community's school system.

(Parsons, 1964: 133)

In this way, both families and schools play an important role in the formation of the traditions of human civilization and the process of intergenerational transmission, so the formation of youth culture and the improvement of peer group influence must be analyzed on the premise that the traditions represented by families and schools or parents and teachers are declining in contemporary social life.

The family is clearly an older social institution than the school. The family, the basic unit of social life formed by marriage, blood, or adoption, has the basic functions of production, emotional comfort, sexual satisfaction, and education or socialization. If childbirth, emotional comfort or sexual satisfaction can all occur, some can even only occur, between peer couples, the function of education or socialization is generally limited to parent-child or intergenerational relationship, which directly involves the inheritance of human group values and culture. What distinguishes humans from animals are the so-called "cultures", including values, attitudes, and social behavior, which need to be passed down from generation to generation. Such inheritance can not only bring a convenience to the individual human life, but also an accumulation of human group civilization, which is called "socialization" by sociologists. Through the process of socialization, the younger generation acquires the values and life knowledge of their own ethnic group, and learns the roles appropriate to their social status, thus becoming appropriate members of the social life of the group. The family plays the most important role in the socialization process (Goode, 1964: 10, 19–20).

The importance of the family to the socialization of human groups is that this primary group, with its large number of direct, face-to-face interactions, as Charles Cooley put it, is not only the starting point for the socialization of each individual, but also provides the space and time for the older generation, with varying degrees of mastery of human culture, to urge, educate, and admonish the babbling younger generation. It is clear that most of the experiences and teachings parents pass on to their children are not entirely the result of their own direct experience and perception, but come from the whole society outside the family, which itself is the product of individual socialization and the accumulation of human civilization. Children are exposed to past experiences and human culture through their families or through their parents and grandparents: "He first learns about the world beyond his immediate radius of experience from his parents" (Shils, 1981: 170), and this is actually the most straightforward and obvious tradition that ordinary people are exposed to. For this reason, Cooley argued that "the fact that the family and neighborhood groups are ascendant in the open and plastic time of childhood makes them even now incomparably more influential than all the rest" (Cooley, 1909: 26). Therefore, in terms of the basis of human sociality and human ideals, the family, like the neighborhood, is "clearly the nursery of human nature in the world about us" (Cooley, 1909: 26).

However, the influence of the family on human groups has changed dramatically since industrialization, particularly since the 20th century. The most important factor is the miniaturization or centralization of family size. In the words of Goode, this revolution in the family pattern has caused the traditional family system (whether or not the clan system is included), usually dominated by the extended family and the united family, to collapse along with industrialization for more than a century (Goode, 1964: 108). And the revolution of the family model is part of the great revolution sweeping the whole world in modern times, which gives millions of people the power of their own choice and gives rise to the desire to overthrow the old government, create a new society, and launch a new social movement (Goode, 1964: 380).

The revolutionary significance of the change of the family pattern is firstly reflected in the fact that individuals, especially young individuals, have gained more freedom in marriage and life, which is because the control of the older generation that has been in place for thousands of years starts to go wrong. In Chapter 2 of the first volume of this book, we spent a considerable amount of time discussing the traditional Chinese family system and the filial tradition and order formed around it. This traditional family system "has remained largely unchanged for thousands of years" (Sun, 2012: 93). Not only is it the product of thousands of years of Chinese society, but in fact it has also maintained the continuation of this traditional society from generation to generation. As Mark Hertel says, it serves as a general pattern of continuity over time to offset the variations that gradually take place in the basic structure of Chinese society. The absence of significant social change during this long period of history is at least partly due to a tradition rooted in parental authority and control (Hertel, 1981: 392).

Although later than the Western world, the traditional Chinese family system has undergone revolutionary changes in modern times. The first impetus for family reform came from the revolution of 1911 and the new culture movement of the May Fourth Movement with "science" and "democracy" as the banner, and then the Communist Revolution, which surged through the 20th century, especially after 1978. Before 1949, the main reasons for family changes in China can be attributed to ideological factors, institutional factors, political factors, social factors, and educational factors, as Sun Benwen has asserted (Sun, 2012: 93–94). As for the post-1949 period, as Hertel puts it, the following four major events in China all contributed to the liberation of women and accelerated the disintegration of traditional paternalism (Hertel, 1981: 408). These four major events include: the marriage law of 1950, the Great Leap Forward movement that started in 1958, the Cultural Revolution that began in 1966, and the "historic transformation" of the reform and opening-up after the death of Mao Zedong in 1978. However, in the previous chapter, we stressed through Shen

Yifei that, in fact, "communism has not completely dismantled patriarchy"; what really led to the collapse of patriarchy and the Chinese family revolution was the radical change that Hertel failed to see at the time of writing *The Changing Family* in the early 1980s: urbanization, marketization, and the one-child policy introduced after the 1980s.

The fundamental reason why China's large-scale industrialization, which began in the Mao Zedong era, failed to break down family traditions and lead the younger generation from families to schools, factories and society, as the West did, is that the social system of urban and rural separation implemented by the industrialization in the planned economy era limited population mobility to the greatest extent, and kept the younger generation under the control of the older generation even as adults, and that the distribution system, biased toward revolutionary experience and seniority, makes the younger generation dependent on the older generation. For example, Deborah Davis-Friedmann noted that not only did many young people have to live together with their parents after marriage because they did not have their own house, but "it is common for urban children to contribute only 50 or 60 percent of their wages to cover the joint living expenses and to keep the remainder for their own savings or personal expenses" (Davis-Friedmann, 1991: 50). Furthermore, young people depend on their parents for jobs when the state is unable to provide new work. Taking over the jobs of one's parents, a way of obtaining a job that subsisted before the Cultural Revolution, even became an "ordinary procedure" (Davis-Friedmann, 1991: 27) at the beginning of the reform and opening-up in 1978.[6] The high dependence of the younger generation on their parents or family for housing, living expenses, and occupation not only maintains the domination and educational power of the elders over the younger generation, but also fundamentally maintains the family tradition of patriarchy.

From the perspective of intergenerational relations, the real decline of family tradition in Chinese society really originated from the reform after 1978. In Chapter 1, we attributed the decline of the traditional patriarchy and the resulting inversion of the traditional parent–child relationship to urbanization, marketization, and the implementation of the one-child policy in the 1980s. We have demonstrated that urbanization promotes the centralization and miniaturization of Chinese families, and the "de-regionalization" of the population associated with urbanization, especially of the younger generation, which weakens the parental control over the offspring. Marketization increases the economic returns of the younger generation with human capital, thereby reducing the traditional dominance of the older generation over the family. Finally, the one-child policy has not only changed Chinese people's concept of parenting, but also changed the relative importance of parents and children in family life, making children more important than ever. It can be said that it is precisely these macro- and micro-economic and social changes that have broken the rigid Chinese family tradition that has persisted for thousands of years. At the same time, the influence of peer groups has become more and more powerful.

In the face of this disconnect, and in the hope that the child's peer group will play a more positive role, parents who want to give their children more rational decision-making power as the parent–child relationship changes are also trying to combine parent–child or family influence with peer group influence. During my visit to Shanghai, SKM, who teaches family sociology at the university, talked about the eye-opening self-study camp experiment called "Energy Fun" that she started promoting two years ago.

"Energy Fun" is a term invented by SKM. The new teaching method hopes to bring "positive energy"—the energy of knowledge—to children in a playful and humorous atmosphere. The original purpose of SKM was to expand her daughter SKG's extracurricular education, so she brought together the children of 14 families she knew and who volunteered to join, and had activities for two hours every Saturday. Well-designed teaching courses were rich in content, including question training, mock interviews (the most successful was having the children interview their grandmothers and draw "family trees" for their families), campus orientation (visiting Fudan University under the guidance of the teacher), ethical problem discussion, a logic competition, and Energy Fun lectures (a presentation at the end of the course), among which the most challenging were surveys of various social issues, including the Spring Festival, my family's dining table (what is green food?), class work, public toilets, and disabled people. SKM says:

> I first promoted this program to solve the exam-oriented education problem in my daughter's study, so it was mostly the children of friends and acquaintances, being my daughter's age. Because I had a course in family sociology in university, I had a good understanding of general social problems. At first I asked my children to do their own thinking or research exactly as I wanted them to, and I didn't think they would go beyond my imagination. But in fact, they often had unexpected imagination, which had a great impact on me. For example, in the toilet civilization survey we arranged, in addition to the toilets in Shanghai or China, we also asked children who had the opportunity to go abroad with their parents during the summer vacation to do cross-country comparative studies. As a result, some went to Italy, Japan, South Korea, and some went to Vietnam or the United States. (SKG interjected, "I found that the toilets in Italy have a lot of painting, full of artistic atmosphere, and in Japan, the toilets are very clean, while in China, the toilets are so dirty that you don't want to go in." SKM said, "There are also many clean ones." SKG replied, "They all come from fancy restaurants.") I was most inspired by research on people with disabilities. At first I was unwilling to do this kind of research, because so many people had done it in China that it wouldn't be original. However, after the research, the children pointed out a problem that was not expected by the adults. The problem they pointed out was: Disabled people don't go out for the sake of going out, so blind paths and so on can't solve the final problem. (SKG chimed in again, "Take the ATM machine in Shanghai for

example. Disabled people can't reach the height of the machine even if they enter the self-help bank. But in northern Europe, you can lift the machine up and down, so it's very human.") You could say the kids saw the problem, and they were amazing.

(SKM, 2014)

When discussing the continuation of the tradition of human civilization, the American sociologist Edward Hills regarded the church and school as the main maintenance system of tradition in Western society, following the family (Shils, 1981: 234). Although the Roman Catholic church has a longer history than any university—like the University of Bologna founded in 1088 in Italy or Paris University in France founded in 1292—in Western civilization,[7] considering the specific situation in China, our interest here is in the school. Although great changes have taken place in education since the 19th century, and universities have added to the task of discovery, ever since schools appeared in human history, conveying and explaining past achievements have been their recognized basic function (Shils, 1981: 240). That is why, like the family, schools, including universities, have been the inheritors of the traditions of human civilization and one of the oldest institutions of society, whose mission is to study and deliver the knowledge treasures of all carefully studied fields of knowledge (Ruegg, 2007, Vol. 1: 9).

The emergence of school as a social system, in both China and the West, was not a specialized or independent educational institution at the beginning. In China, the earliest "school" appeared in the Western Zhou dynasty, which was called *piyong*, the place where the slave owners studied. Later, it was successively named *xiang*, *xu*, *xue*, *xiao*, and *shu*, so the "ancient educators have *shu* at home, *xiang* in the community, *xu* in the town, and *xue* in the capital" (*Book of Rites*), which were not only places for reading, but also for shooting and retirement. The school reached its peak in the Tang dynasty, and its institutions became increasingly developed due to the promotion of the imperial examination system. At the end of the Qing dynasty, modern education was set up, which was called *xuetang* in the *Charter of the Imperial School* in the 28th year of Guangxu (1902). After the revolution of 1911, education institutions were called xuexiao when the ministry of education of the Republic of China announced the new school system (the Renzi School System) from 1912 to 1913.

In Western history, the broad sense of "school" dates back to the time of Socrates. At that time a number of wise men who were traveling about came to Athens and earned their living by teaching their citizens. Later, Plato opened his Academy in the woods near Athens, which would last for centuries. However, this academy was not primarily about teaching, but more similar to a "salon" in the modern sense. "Schools" with a "school system" in a real or narrow sense appeared in the Middle Ages, when, in addition to some law schools and liberal arts schools, there were more missionary schools that mainly taught religious knowledge. Then there was the Renaissance, followed by the Enlightenment, which promoted the development of education and the advancement of universities to the public and society. In particular, "the success of the program of the Enlightenment reduced the prominence of theology", promoted the secularization of universities and education, and "an end of scholasticism was decreed thereby, as was also a redirection of the sciences towards empiricism and practical application" (Ruegg, 2007, Vol. 2: 629, 637).

Just as Cooley said that the family is the nurturing place of humanity, the school we discuss here is not only the carrier of tradition, but also the "nurturer of 'youth'" in modern times (Chen, 2007: 154), because as a social category, and not just as a stage of physical development, "youth" is actually the product of modern school education, which has become more and more popular and prolonged since the Industrial Revolution. For example, in a traditional agricultural society like China, a child of 13 or 14 who has just entered the period of physiological development may join his parents in the labor force tomorrow. There is no long transition period between the child and the adult. In modern China, the emergence of "youth" is related to the continuous growth of the student group formed in modern education. Just four years after the abolition of the imperial examination system in 1909, 1.56 million students were enrolled in the new schools, some of whom went to "boarding schools" with reference to American and British ones. The number of students studying abroad was also expanding, with more than 10,000 students studying in Japan alone (Fei & Liu, 1993: 440, 406). This is how the student body began to break away from the constraints of family and parents to a precocious life called "youth" with a certain distance from society, and to place hope in the reforming of old China by Liang Qichao, Chen Duxiu, and Hu Shi.

Clearly, in industrial societies, especially post-industrial societies, the extension of formal schooling has changed the way we define "adolescence" and "youth". Not only in developed countries like Europe and America, but also in a rapidly changing developing country like China, in recent decades more and more young people have entered universities or colleges to continue their studies after finishing secondary education, and thus the transition to adult work and family roles was delayed (Furstenberg, 2000; Ma, 2011).[8] In this way, more and more schools and years of schooling not only produce more and more "young people", but also raise the upper limit of the age of "youth".

If schools, by pulling young people out of the home, have considerably disrupted family traditions and become increasingly influential, in a world of bigger schools, more crowded young people, and more diverse means of communication, including electronic media, as interactions between teachers and students decline in frequency and dominance,[9] the influence of peer groups that form around the school but extend beyond it is also on the rise, and will no doubt in turn undermine the school tradition. According to Edward Hills, if the influence of parents and teachers declines, children will have to set their own standards, which means that they accept the standards of their most influential contemporaries (Shils, 1981: 231).

When discussing peer culture and modern education, the American sociologist James Coleman said that youth culture represents a transition between young people and larger society (Coleman, 1966: 244). We have discussed that youth is the product of modern industrial society, so youth culture is also a unique social phenomenon in industrial and post-industrial society. Coleman has made it clear that youth culture is in fact a peer culture. If such theories of youth from the West have any kind of universal value or explanatory power in the different countries that have successively entered industrial society, China's experience in the field of intergenerational relations over the past 42 years, including cultural reverse, should also confirm that the formation of contemporary Chinese youth culture is based on the emergence of a large number of peer groups and the rise of their influence. If, as is said, learning among peer groups is greater than the sum of family and school (*New Weekly*, 2010: 191), with increasingly diversified peer groups, the traditional relationship among youth, family, and school will surely undergo a reconstruction, and the so-called tradition based on family and school will surely undergo a historic evolution.

Growing up in cyber culture

For most of the 20th century, the challenges to home and school from real youth peer groups were manageable. Parents and teachers, by virtue of their status advantages, economic means, or institutional educational power conferred by biological facts or social structures, can still, to a certain extent, instill mainstream social values into their children through families and schools, and maintain traditions that are lax but do not collapse. But the rise of cyber society after the 1990s has inexorably upset that balance. The virtual peer group formed around the electronic network, relying on network technology, especially the web2.0 network technology popularized after 2003, not only develops the rebellious, independent, interactive, and creative youth culture to the extreme, but also constructs a brand new youth culture—a network culture in fact. The rise of a network culture provides the younger generation with the realistic possibility of breaking away from the control of the elders and growing freely, which makes them become the leaders of the Internet era and the feeders of the older generation.

Network culture is a new way of human existence based on information technology and carried by the Internet, including all the cultural forms, cultural products derived from the network and its applications, and the human interaction or communication mode prevailing on the network. If culture is the product of human communication or contact, human cultural forms can be divided into oral culture, text culture, print culture, electronic culture, and the network culture we are talking about (Li & Chen, 2005). If the birth of language made it possible for human society to communicate and think, the birth of writing made it possible for the speaker or thinker to be separated from what he says or thinks, and the advent of printing increased the breadth of this separation. Further, the electronic or audio-visual culture constructed through film, radio, and television in the 20th century effectively destroyed the identity hierarchy established by writing or written culture, making it a true mass medium or mass culture, so that Friedrich Williams could say: After the war, there was an explosion or revolution in communication in the world led by television (Williams, 1982).

In a sense, the emergence of the Internet in the second half of the 20th century was an epoch-making revolution comparable to the emergence of the written word. The main feature of this revolution, in the words of sociologist Manuel Castells, is "the formation of a hypertext and a meta-language which, for the first time in history, integrate into the same system the written, oral, and audio-visual modalities of human communication" (Castells, 2010a: 356). Text, image, and sound are integrated into one system at the same time. Under the condition of open and readable paths, people in different places or spaces can interact on the network at a selected time, which is a new mode of communication indeed. The novelty of this mode of communication lies in its cyberspace, as the Canadian science fiction writer William Gibson once said. In the 1984 novel *Neuromancer*, cyberspace is a computer-generated space into which characters plug in. For Gibson, cyberspace is a sympathetic illusion which is not a real space, but an imaginary space (Kramarae, 1995: 38). For the sake of imagination, Gibson and Barlow describe it as the space where you talk on the phone (Gibson & Barlow, 1992: 78). In fact, whether on the phone or on the computer, if you have to communicate with others in a certain space, this space is called "cyberspace". So, you are sitting in a Newtonian physical space on one side of the screen, and interacting with the other side of the screen in a mysterious cyberspace. Although cyberspace is virtual, the interactions that take place there and their consequences can be real.

Because cyberspace is virtual, so are the peer groups of young people who meet and interact in it. The virtuality of the peer group formed in cyberspace is fully reflected in the title of "net friends", just as "no one knows you are a dog on the Internet", people interacting with each other are just an anonymous symbol on the Internet. However, because people can engage in more convenient, frequent, diversified, and in-depth interaction on the Internet through various kinds of common media or new media than in real life, its impact on the virtual peer group is not only real but also powerful. It will play a role in "a larger social space scale than ever before, and form a power to deconstruct and reconstruct the existing social structure" (Chen, 1998).

There are all kinds of shared media that interact through the web, including email lists, discussion groups (its common form is Usenet newsgroup, BBS, and Forum), chats, web logs, podcasting, the Wiki Model, social software and virtual community, synergy and publishing, XML (extensible markup language), peer-to-peer communication, video sharing, and massively multiplayer role-playing games (Hu, 2008: 90–113). Take the extremely popular BBS and Forum in China. They are basically electronic communities based on discussions about politics, society, economics, sports, technology, and almost everything, including dating. The former includes Shuimu Tsinghua (Tsinghua University BBS), Lily (Nanjing University BBS), Weiming (Peking University BBS), and Riyue Guanghua (Fudan University BBS). At present, almost every university in China has a BBS. As long as you follow some basic rules, you are free to register and enter, choose your favorite sections, and make personal comments on relevant issues. The latter includes "Tianya", "Xici.net",

"Qiangguo BBS", and "Baidu tieba", which open up a simple interactive communication environment and attract a large number of people to gather, providing electronic commons for the dissemination and discussion of public topics. Although both BBS and Forum are free to enter, it is clear that young people are the most conventional composition of "netizens". Age is a key variable, which gives us good reasons to regard netizens as a kind of virtual peer group.

As we have discussed, as a primary group, the general peer group, in addition to similar age, also includes voluntary entry, emotional communication, equal interaction, and distinct subculture. In contrast, the virtuality of the Internet makes netizens more prominently display the above characteristics of peer groups. First, in the anonymous state, members are more free to enter, and the restriction of the network area no longer exists.[10] This breaks the physical space and occupational proximity of the average peer group, and even biological age is no longer necessary for membership. As long as you are interested in the topic of a certain section or Forum, you can participate in it, and you don't need to worry about group pressure when you quit the communication space (Wang & Liu, 2006). Second, in anonymity, people's emotional communication is more natural and convenient, especially when the discussion involves politics, sex, or personal privacy, because there is no face-to-face pressure and mutual restriction. In this regard, IRC (Internet Relay Chat) is better than BBS and Forum. Although it is generally not as long-winded as BBS, it has the characteristics of real-time interaction, which, if coupled with microphone and camera, guarantees the free and full communication of emotions and generates much network love and friendship. Third, in anonymity, there is no pressure or "threat" due to age or social differences, so even the weaker party in the real world is free to organize the topic (or to use Goffman's language, to construct the "conversation starter" as the basis of interaction) or not reply after reading the post. The network and even the mobile phone and other peer-to-peer communication technologies are characterized by "decentralization" (Zhou, 2011a). On the one hand, this effectively deconstructs the "narrator's discourse" of propaganda usually used by the dominant party;[11] on the other hand, it also endows the communication of netizens with unprecedented interactivity. Fourth, also in anonymity, peer groups like netizens have more distinct subcultural characteristics. Not only do they deliberately seek to maintain a degree of independence from mainstream culture, but it is easy to form some subculture atmosphere or network environment completely different from the mainstream culture through the Internet. In such an atmosphere or environment, there are no more hierarchical systems and top-down communication channels, and their own subcultural values and network rules are formed. The network buzzwords we discussed in Chapter 4 of the first volume of this book are the prominent representation of this youth subculture.

If the emergence of Internet technology, especially the promotion of web2.0 technology and the arrival of the network society, is embedded into the social structure at the macro-level and changes it to some extent, and creates a new way of life or of surviving at the micro-level, then this process will naturally have a profound impact on the daily life and spiritual growth of human beings, especially the younger generation, and make the molding process of the latter begin to shift from the traditional single real socialization model to the modern multi-socialization model, including the virtual one (Yao & Zhang, 2004). In this sense, although the Internet and the resulting peer group are virtual, what we call "growing up in cyber culture" is a real psychological consequence. Here, we can at least discuss the influence of network culture on the spiritual world of the younger generation in terms of the following aspects.

First of all, through online interaction, virtual peer groups meet the psychological needs of individuals, especially adolescents, for self-formation and belonging in the socialization process. On the other hand, it enriches the social communication among individuals, and provides them with a participation path to cultivate their communication ability, understand the rules of interaction, and adapt to the social environment. From this point of view, we can be sure that the network virtual peer group is of positive significance to the growth of the younger generation's spiritual world.

From the perspective of social psychology, the mature self is the basis of personality formation, which then forms the necessary psychological dynamic system for people to adapt to society. However, the self grows through interaction with others, that is, through social interaction. Because as a social person, you can only exist in other people's minds or imagination, as we have discussed before with Cooley's "looking-glass" concept, "a social self of this sort might be called the reflected or looking-glass self: 'Each to each a looking-glass'" (Cooley, 1992: 184). Furthermore, if daily interactions provide people with opportunities to reflect on each other, then interactions on the Internet can provide people with channels to "watch" each other. This is because anonymity allows a person's online "presence" (Goffman, 1959) to often be closer to reality, and the two people interacting with each other have a more accurate view of each other.

SAB is a young man who has benefited a lot from the Internet. This boy we mentioned in Chapter 1. He was studying economics at Shanghai University of Finance and Economics, was addicted to online games, and could not extricate himself before his sophomore year. For this reason, his mother SAM even consulted with her best friend in college, Shu Chang, a professor who later studied psychology. As the saying goes, "Whoever started the trouble should end it". It was the Internet that SAB was later able to use to mend his ways—he fell in love online in his junior year! At first, his own parents, SAF and SAM, thought his relationship was unreliable, while his girlfriend's parents were terrified that their child would be cheated by a bad guy. After a semester of dating, SAB and his girlfriend made an appointment to meet each other in the summer vacation. First SAB flew to Lanzhou, where his girlfriend was attending college; her mother was very nervous during their two days of dating there. Two days later, SAB went with his girlfriend back to her hometown in Lvliang, Shanxi province, where her parents finally felt relieved. Interestingly, SAB had to give up online gaming because he was too busy dating his girlfriend online in his spare time; the Internet gave them a whole new way of dating:

> And that's when I realized that the Internet was actually quite positive. For example, MM and I watch movies together through QQ video on the Internet, record songs and discuss learning together—I can teach her Japanese, while I have always been interested in ancient Chinese and ancient phonology, and MM happens to be studying literature, so she can also teach me. ... We communicated on the Internet for half a year. After we met in the summer vacation, we found that the other person was the one we were familiar with on the Internet. There was no difference at all, so we hit it off. In addition, because I am in a good mood now, not only has my academic performance improved, increasing from 1.92 GPA (1.8 is the pass line, 4.0 is full marks) to 3.2 GPA.
>
> But I also fell in love with fitness, and have gradually become more confident and physically better. Now I am a graduate student in the United States, and MM has been recommended to the school of literature of Wuhan University, so I think this love is really OK!
>
> (SAB, 2014)

In terms of social interaction or social participation, the Internet is also an effective path. Although most of the text on the Internet seems random to some adults, in fact, the important issues related to publicity have always attracted the attention of netizens. Taking 2010 as an example, the top ten issues of concern to network opinion leaders with regard to young people as the main body were as follows: the Qian Yunhui case in Yueqing; the campus car accident; the case of the Fenghuang girl who jumped from a building after being molested by the police; the shipping collision in the Diaoyu Islands; frequent campus kills; the "bloody" demolition incident in Yihuang; the Tang Jun "diplomagate"; the Jing'an fire in Shanghai; the sweatshop for mentally handicapped people in Xinjiang; and the attack on Fang Zhouzi (Yu, 2011: 9). In China, the Internet is often a powerful tool for citizens to fight corruption, as officials are increasingly corrupt and the mass media such as television and newspapers lack active and effective supervision. Numerous corrupt officials have been dismissed in recent years by "human flesh searches" on the Internet, among which the most famous are Zhou Jiugeng, who smoked "Nine-Five Supreme" cigarettes, and Yang Dacai, or "Brother Watch". The former was subjected to a human flesh search by netizens in late 2008 for making inappropriate comments to the media, such as "no lowering of housing prices". He was found, as a section chief of housing administration, to smoke daily Nine-Five Supreme cigarettes, which cost as much as 150 CNY per pack. The latter was disliked by netizens for smiling at the scene of the "Yan'an traffic accident" in the summer of 2012, and a following online human flesh search revealed that this Shanxi provincial security chief had worn 11 watches on different occasions, the most expensive of which was worth 400,000 CNY. Zhou Jiugeng and Yang Dacai were both punished by the relevant departments shortly after they were searched on the Internet, and "Nine-Five Supreme" cigarette and "Brother Watch" became popular Internet phrases of the year.

Secondly, through network interaction, online virtual peer groups can smoothly realize the "transition" or "bond crossing" from family to school, from school to society, or from one social environment to another. In this process of transition or bond crossing, online virtual peer groups can serve as intermediaries or bridges for families, schools, and societies—what the American sociologist Patricia Phelan calls "multiworlds". In other words, the emergence of the Internet and the formation of virtual communities online provides the possibility for the younger generation to exercise their identities or play roles and transform their environment, which also lays a foundation for them to enter society smoothly in the future.

When Phelan began his experiments in the fall of 1989, titled "The multiple worlds of students and their displacement", most studies of youth socialization were separate ones about the social impact of family, school, and peer groups on student growth. Through a study of 54 high school students at four schools, Phelan et al. argued that students are minors living in a multiworld. This multiworld consists primarily of families, schools, and peer groups, and each world contains the values, beliefs, expectations, actions, and emotional reactions familiar to those in the circle (Phelan & Yu, 1993: 53), which constitute the so-called social setting in which children grow up. In the process of socialization, children who adapt well can easily jump from one environment to another, a phenomenon known as "social transition". What's remarkable about Phelan is that she shows that children are at risk when their environment shifts, and may be faced with conflicting worlds, or worlds with closed borders, and thus become loners who fail in their attempt to cross borders. To avoid this outcome, what is required is not just understanding other people's cultures, but that students must acquire the skills and strategies to work closely with different groups of people, not just themselves, in a conflictual society (Phelan & Yu, 1993: 85).

As far as Phelan's research is concerned in understanding the growth of Chinese youth, in the last three decades, with the quickening pace of life, the miniaturization of families, the rigidity of school systems, and the solidification of classes, as well as the hardening of the walls or barriers between families, schools, peer groups, and even classes, the younger generation is indeed increasingly likely to be the losers who cross the line. In Internet chatrooms, you can express your warmth and concerns; on BBS, you can learn about the dynamics of the school and society and express your opinions; and on Forum, the electronic public domain, you are able to communicate and discuss public topics that appear in society or are of general concern to the public. Secondly, in the network society, "crossing the boundary" in different environments, such as home, school, and society, only requires tapping on the keyboard. This kind of "intervention" provides a convenience for the younger generation who have not really entered society sufficiently to be familiar with its rules and public expectations. Although this kind of intervention is usually far away from the real world due to the lack of adult participation, it still provides a simulated path for the younger generation to be exposed to reality earlier.

Thirdly, online virtual peer groups can further form various non-governmental organizations and communities spontaneously formed by "netizens", especially young netizens, through online interaction. Considering that "the virtual 'society' is certainly not satisfied with the virtual interaction on the Internet, but must be transformed into actual social action" (Chen, 1998), we can even say that virtual peer groups can promote the development of civil society in real life and ultimately contribute to the formation of democratic politics and civil society in China.

The relationship between the Internet and civil society and even the construction of political democracy in China has always been a hot topic. Given the lack of democracy in China, the low level of freedom of the media, and the poor tolerance of citizens to the views of others,[12] since its advent, especially in China, many people hope that the Internet can contribute to the construction of civil society and political democratization by promoting the formation of the public sphere. In 2004, Mary Meeker, a researcher at Morgan Stanley, pointed out in the "China Internet report" that large numbers of Internet users gathered in BBS, chat rooms, and Forum, indicating that the Internet opens the way for increased interactivity in a Chinese culture that is not known for self-expression and interaction (Meeker, 2004: 17). In 2005, in this "new world", Zhou Yongming discussed the delicate relationship between folk political writers and the government in China's cyberspace through his field study of Beijing:

> On the one hand, folk writers express their new citizenship by deeply accepting and interpreting information and accepting different political views. On the other hand, the state also uses new resources such as private capital to serve its control purposes as much as possible.
>
> (Zhou, 2005)

Apparently, for the young netizens with a more democratic consciousness, the significance of the Internet, as an article in *Beijing News* reported in 2006, "lies in freedom, which may be one of their few channels of expression" (Hu, 2008: 303). This expression channel fully demonstrated its power in the Xiamen XP event in 2007. Esarey and Xiao Qiang discussed this event and proposed that "bloggers in China have succeeded at spreading the word about government malfeasance, misleading media reports, and political dissent" and "controlling the information available to Chinese citizens will become more difficult as new communication technology, such as blogging, empowers people to broadcast their views to an unprecedented degree" (Esarey & Xiao, 2008: 759, 772). Further, through the analysis of the two famous Forums "Strengthening the Nation Forum" and "Huaxia Educated Youth", the question was raised as to "how the Internet and civil society in China interact in a mutually plastic way". In China, "this co-change process also means that the development of civil society will promote the democratic application of the Internet, and the promotion of the Internet will also shape the civil society" (Yang, 2003).

The "tree preservation movement" in Nanjing in March 2011 is an excellent example of the connection between the Internet and the development of civil society. It is well known that Sun Yat-sen's body was moved from Biyun Temple in Beijing to Zhongshan Mausoleum in Nanjing in May 1929. In 1928, in honor of Sun Yat-sen's "Feng'an ceremony", Liu Jiwen, then the first mayor of Nanjing, selected 1,500 *wutongs* (sycamores), presented by the Ministry of Works of the French Concession in Shanghai, as roadside trees, and planted them along the tens of kilometers of road from Xiaguan Pier to Zhongshan Mausoleum where the coffin passed. Later, after the founding of the Communist Party of China (CPC) in 1949, *wutongs* were planted on both sides of the roads in Nanjing, tens of thousands of which shaded the sky and became the best symbol of the natural ecology of the ancient city.

The problem occurred in the "development" era after 1978, which was "centered on economic construction". Back in the mid-1990s, Wang Wulong, then mayor of Nanjing and a graduate of Nanjing Forestry University majoring in forestry and the chemical industry, cut down thousands of *wutongs* along Zhongshan North Road, Zhongshan Road, and Zhongshan East Road, thus gaining the title of "mayor of tree cutting". In 2000, as roads in Nanjing were widened and subways were built, the *wutongs* were felled again. By 2005, as many as 20,000 trees had been felled in a decade (Ju, 2011). In 2011, when Nanjing subway lines three and ten were ready for construction, the authorities expected to move 1,100 street trees, more than 200 of which were *wutongs*, some more than 60 years old. On March 9, more than 40 *wutongs* on Taiping North Road were "laid down" to make way for Daxinggong Station of subway line three. And the good news this time is that the Internet changed the fate of the *wutongs*, which were decimated in the 1990s: Huang Jian-xiang, a media man, Meng Fei, a host, and Lu Chuan, a director, each with thousands of fans on their blogs, all wrote about the felling of the *wutongs*, and within a week or so, tens of thousands of people had joined, with 16,909 comments. "Nanjing Greenstone", a local environmental NGO in Nanjing, launched the "smile campaign" on their blog, participants of which tied green ribbons to trees along the road and held up signs that read "Please use your smile to keep the trees in Nanjing". On March 19, thousands of young citizens holding hands online gathered in front of the Nanjing library square near the Grand Palace. Meanwhile, a poem titled "The winter is too long in this spring" was repeated:

What disappears at the fingertips
Is more than just
Feeling

What vanishes in the mind
Is not all
Memory

What's lost in the heart
Is not mere
Conscience

What's missing in the world
Is not simply
Affection

It's a tree, a path that records the rise and fall of a nation.

By coincidence, 2011 marks the 100th anniversary of the 1911 revolution. The unique political position of Nanjing in modern Chinese history finally determined that this tree preservation movement aroused the attention of the Kuomintang people and media across the strait. Faced with the dual pressure of Internet crowds and Taiwan compatriots, on March 15, the Nanjing municipal government responded positively for the first time by optimizing the plan to protect the big trees. On March 18, tree removal work was halted on subway line three, and soon after a "green assessment commission" was established with the participation of ordinary citizens to draw up a new tree removal plan. An environmental storm on both sides of the Taiwan straits finally subsided:

> Under the new plan, Line Three will claim 318 trees, mostly wutongs, but it will spare more than two-thirds of trees that were to be moved. The city promised to give each uprooted tree a number and track its health wherever it is replanted. And henceforth, Mr. He said, every construction plan that affects ordinary citizens will first be reviewed by a green assessment commission.
>
> Moreover, the government will get citizens involved before, not after, it digs up trees, he said. All in hopes of preserving a separate, arboreal peace.
>
> (Shiho Fukada, 2011)

For more than a year after the Nanjing tree preservation movement, on various occasions, I kept meeting friends who had tied green ribbons on *wutongs* or gathered in front of the library. Most of them worked in schools, media, companies, social groups, institutions, and youth and higher education; a strong sense of participation was a common characteristic of this group. The other common feature of them was that they were all senior "netizens". They spent their spare time or even work time on the Internet, immersed in the democratic and equal atmosphere created by the culture. They were sad that the towering trees of the same age as the republic or even older were felled; they were even more intolerant of such decisions being made by a handful of GDP-oriented urban construction officials. If in the 1990s, faced with rows of fallen trees, citizens had no choice but to ridicule officials like "Wang Wulong", then today, with the ubiquity of the Internet, a self-organizing, low-cost, responsive, and interventionist tree conservation campaign had indeed stopped the hand of indiscriminate cutting. Although the March 19 tree protection movement was quickly dispersed, and the "green review" work was, to a large extent, just a "show of democracy", I remember that over the course of a week, many underage children followed their young mothers to the movement, and their little faces flushed with the chill of spring and passion—let me believe that once the door of democracy is opened, generations will flock to it.

The salon: building a society-shared governance via communication and interaction

Although in this age the Internet is of great significance in the construction of civil society, and even been called "the largest special zone in transitional China" (Xiong, 2010: 282), it is clear that in a country of great change and transformation, such special zones are not limited to the Internet. In terms of our theme of the peer group here, the Habermas-style public sphere, in which young people participate and thus acquire knowledge, dialogue, and practical ability, also includes "salon". Although the word "salon" here is not the same as that which came into the French from the Italian in the 17th and 18th centuries, in that the latter was a social place derived from the luxurious sitting room of an aristocratic family, I refer to the public domain where a group of young people mainly participate in discussions around a certain public topic, which, after all, inherits the tradition of kindred spirits and free conversation. This is the reason why Habermas regarded the early salon as an extension of the private sphere of the citizen family (Habermas, 1962: 54). From this point of view, the communication and interaction in the salon or public sphere is obviously conducive to promoting the enlightenment and construction of civil society or the co-governance society.

In China, the earliest salons were introduced by intellectuals studying abroad in the 1930s, one of the most famous was the "Star Six Party" hosted by Lin Huiyin at 3–1 Zongbu Hutong, Beijing. Besides Liang Sicheng and Lin Huiyin, there were also a large number of cultural elites such as Xu Zhimo, Jin Yuelin, Zhang Xiruo, Hu Shi, and Shen Congwen, as well as Mr. and Mrs. Fairbank, who later became "China experts". It is said that an equally famous salon at the same time was the "Poetry Reading Meeting" hosted by Zhu Guangqian at No. 3 Cihuidian, Di'an Gate in Beijing.

For more than half a century, war and political repression squeezed the more or less romantic salons out of Chinese daily life. Except for the "underground art salon" of Li Li and Xu Haoyuan during the Cultural Revolution that we mentioned at the beginning of this chapter, this embryonic public sphere was completely erased not only from the structure of Chinese society but also from the memory of the people. This naturally leads to the fact that when the reform and opening-up started, the only remaining idealism under political pressure turned the 1980s into a new peak of "salon culture". So much so that many years later, Li Tuo, a trendsetter of the salon in the 1980s, would say with regret,

> One of the characteristics of the 1980s was that everyone had passion. What passion? Not just any passion, but a passion to carry on. Everyone had such an ambition. ... There were also parties and dinners, but the real attraction was the discussion of so many issues in politics, philosophy, and literature.
>
> (Zha, 2006: 252–256)

However, the "bookstore salon" or "book bar" that appeared after the mid-2000s was the first salon with the nature of a modern public sphere or civil society, because only from then on did dialogue begin to be a distinct feature of the bookstore salon. In January 2006, the "One-way Street" bookstore set up by Xu Zhiyuan and others became a banner of the bookstore salon. From the start, One-way Street positioned itself not only as a bookstore, but also as a "public space". It declared with unprecedented candor: "'One-way Street' is dedicated to providing a public space for intellectual, ideological and cultural life." In fact, the public space of One-way Street is not composed of the bookstore, but by the salons held regularly by it on weekends. Since the speech of the poet Xi Chuan on March 5, 2006, more than ten years ago, One-way Street bookstore has held more than 1,000 salons, invited more than 1,200 speakers, and the audience has reached 150,000 people. Mo Yan, Chen Danqing, Bai Xianyong, Yan Geling, Tian Qinxin, Jia Zhangke, Lai Shengchuan, Chai Jing, Liang Wendao, Zhang Yueran, Shi Hang, Luo Yijun, Li Yinhe, Feng Tang, Yu Xiuhua, Ji Di, Fan Ye, Kato Yoshikazu, Zhang Ming, Liu Yu, Ye Fu and others have hosted the One-way Street salon, and the topics are multifarious: from art to life, from tradition to postmodernism, from the Qing dynasty to the Republic of China, from public life to the private sector, from life to faith.

Of course, with topics ranging from political reform to free speech to personal life, One-way Street salon topics are not always suave, and often contain ground-breaking boldness, which no wonder causes excessive attention from the "authorities concerned". Zhang Jiping, a reporter from *Asia Weekly* in Hong Kong, once listened to a "speech" given by Xiong Peiyun, a young scholar, and Kato Yoshikazu, a Japanese student: "How can individuals transform society?" The scheduled lecture time was less than half an hour, but more than 200 participants spent two hours discussing with each other, which fully reflects the public space nature of One-way Street:

> When Xiong Peiyun said that more important than facing the society is facing the heart, immediately a woman in the audience stood up and retorted. She said, in a mournful tone, that it was cowardice, and that how you could do nothing about the injustice of society. Xiong Peiyun also said that the transformation of the world can only start from the transformation of their own: "There are no enemies in the heart, only those whom you want to help." Another male listener stood up in support of Xiong Peiyun. And then they moved on. More people were telling their personal stories and worrying about social realities. Some mentioned petitioning, others talked about political reform, and still others said they were "transformed" from childhood to adulthood.
>
> Every weekend, seven or eight salons focused on civic issues are held in different parts of the city at the same time, every one of which is attended by about a hundred people. There are at least seven or eight cafes where documentaries are screened and discussed at the same time. In addition to social issues, salons also involve reading clubs, horoscopes, spirituality, science and

technology, and office politics – holding more life-oriented public salons has become the most fashionable choice for cafes.

(Zhang, 2010)

If you want to keep going, Beijing's Sanwei Book Store, Chuan Zhixing, UCCA, Yulan Book Store, Shanghai's Read and Digest, Waitan Forum, Guangzhou's Concave Bar, New Media Women's Salon, Chengdu's Cottage Reading Club, and Nanjing's Pioneer Forum all have become local popular folk salon landmarks. The most important feature of these folk salons is that in addition to the people involved in free discussion, the theme directly concerns society. The participants are also mostly young college students or white-collar workers fresh out of college, who have not only a strong sense of social participation, but also considerable communication skills. This determines that, although speakers are often eloquent "public intellectuals" such as Chen Danqing, Mo Yan, He Weifang, Zhang Ming, Liang Wendao, Zhu Tianwen, Ye Fu, Yu Jianrong, Zhang Yihe, and Qian Wenzhong, the active communication and interaction of salon participants endow it with the nature of a public space. This makes the salon no longer one of pure "enlightenment", nor one of simple "preaching", but a construction in the modern sense—mutual construction.

In discussing the various new structures of modern European cities, Habermas repeatedly emphasized the special role of cafes and salons in the formation of civil society. These new institutions, while different, had the same social function in Britain and France, where coffee houses flourished between 1680 and 1780, and the salon between the regency period and the French Revolution. Everywhere, they were centers of literary criticism first, political criticism second. In the course of criticism, an educated middle class, somewhere between aristocratic society and civic intellectuals, began to form (Habermas, 1962: 37).

The extent to which China's cafes and salons will contribute to the growth of the middle class and further promote the formation of civil society or community society is not yet known, but in these spaces open to the public, general issues or so-called public topics related to human civilization or dignity are subject to discussion or even controversy, which will undoubtedly promote people's consideration of these issues, and also form a common sense of style and responsibility in such discussions. Obviously, as a result of this discussion or controversy, public opinion will not only affect or restrict individuals in their social lives, but also exert some influence or restriction on the executive side of public power. For example, while all agree that the state is too powerful in China, squeezing social space and muzzling public opinion, one can see that, in 2003, it was the extensive media coverage of the "Sun Zhigang case" and the great discussion about the "detention and repatriation system" it triggered that led to the abolition of the system, which had been in place for more than half a century, in three months.[13] In 2012, another university student, Ren Jianyu, also attracted wide attention online and in the media.[14] Under the continuous fermentation of public opinion, Guangming Net stated bluntly,

Ren Jianyu case makes people feel the necessity of abolishing the reeducation through labor system again. It is safe to say that as long as the system of reeducation through labor violates basic legal principles, the so-called "mishandled" re-education through labor decisions like Ren Jianyu's case will not disappear.

(Guangming.com Commentator, 2012)

It was against this background that the Third Plenary Session of the 18th CPC Central Committee made the decision to "abolish the system of re-education through labor" (CPC Central Committee, 2013: 53) in order to conform to public sentiment. Aware of this, you can understand why Habermas said: Sometimes, the public sphere is the field of public opinion, which directly confronts the public authority (Habermas, 1962: 2). Similarly, we can naturally regard the public sphere as a bridge or transition between civil society and the state.

The reason why we pay so much attention to the construction of the public sphere is that the corresponding society or civil society in China has not been developed and grown for a long time. Historically, "civilian government" has been a classic Chinese expression of state–society relations. As a result, "the 'folk' people in China hardly believe that it is possible to establish a benign inter-active relationship between the society and the state" (Gan, 1998: 34). In reality, China after 1949 is a totalitarian or highly centralized country. Therefore, for a long time, "the state's strong control over society" has been the main narrative line of the western Chinese research circle about China in the Mao Zedong era (Zhou, 2010). However, since the reform and opening-up in 1978, the withdrawal or "delegation" of state power from many areas of grass-roots society, and the reforms in various economic and political fields, including the contract responsibility system, villagers' self-governance, fostering private enterprise, fostering communities, and non-governmental organizations (NGOs), provided society with unprecedented vitality. People began to look forward to fostering a civil society or co-governance society in China as soon as was possible.

What we call a civil society can also be called a society in a narrow sense, referring to the civil sphere corresponding to the state or its agents. It is made up of citizens and the various civic organizations and communities that citizens spontaneously form, so it needs a social "self-organizing" environment and the ability of citizens to self-organize. Such societies can be called "co-governance societies", which generally includes the following basic characteristics. First, individual standards, that is to say, citizens have the ability to act independently above the modern social system. Second, the spirit of autonomy, which is associated with the individual standard. Citizens have a strong sense of responsibility for their words, deeds, and social affairs, and can exercise their rights according to law and manage themselves through various social organizations. Third, the concept of public welfare, including the charity, volunteer, and mutual aid spirit. Fourth, corporatism, that is, citizens actively participate in social life and social affairs through various associations. Fifth, the principle of the legal system, where civil society is built on the basis of the legal system, and all kinds of social relations (including the relations between citizens, citizens and societies, and societies and governments) are strictly contractual. Finally, the private domain and public domain. Civil society includes the "private domain" established on the basis of the market economy and social differentiation, and the "public domain" where citizens can influence national policies through the exchange and expression of opinions (Huang, 2002).

Here, we have spent a lot of time discussing whether the salon or cafe is such a public domain. From the above analysis of the facts, it can be seen that a small salon or cafe not only creates a public sphere where opinions can be exchanged and expressed, but in fact also cultivates a lot of modern civic awareness and capacity for action through active interaction between the participants, especially the young participants who are the majority, such as the individual standard, the spirit of autonomy, the concept of public welfare, corporatism, and the principle of law mentioned above. Although there is no shortage of eloquent speakers in salons and cafes, as we have pointed out, because these public areas have procedures that limit the speaker's control of the interactive process (i.e., no more than half an hour), empowering all listeners to participate, so the roles of speaker and audience are relative and changeable. With this in mind, given that the participants are basically what we now call the post-70s, post-80s, or post-90s generation, we can think of these public spheres as a very special kind of communal public space for peer groups, where the beginnings of a community society are taking shape in China. Further, new integrations and alliances are quietly taking place between this kind of real space and virtual space, such as the Internet. What happens in a small salon or cafe, like "Co-China" in Hong Kong, radiates through the Internet and has an even more incredible impact. It makes it possible that the cultivation of a modern co-ruling society may progress in China at an unexpected speed.

Whether it is online posts or salon gatherings, all this happens in the form of peer group interaction that the older generation never experienced. With all this, we have come to understand to some extent how today's younger generation has acquired the ability to nurture their parents and even their grandparents. But that is clearly not the whole answer. In fact, so far, although we have discussed the subtlety of the Internet, we have not fully explained the influence and power of the whole mass media, including but not limited to the Internet. We will see how the rapid development of the media in mainland China from 1978 to 2020 and the resulting wave of information and knowledge ultimately has subverted the intergenerational relationship of the entire society and made the younger generation the undisputed trendsetter or bellwether of a country that has embraced tradition for centuries.

Notes

1 It must be admitted that in the early Red Guard rebellion, the strong consciousness of "factionalism" disintegrated the complete intergenerational consciousness or group consciousness of the younger generation. At that time, the Red Guards belonging to different factions fought fiercely for Mao Zedong and Mao Zedong's thought, something which they all fought to the death to defend. But the experience of going to the countryside after 1968 changed all that.

2 In fact, the most famous "educated youth novel" is Zhang Yang's *The Second Hand-shake*, because it describes the fate of returning intellectuals, which we do not discuss here. Also, interestingly, in the 1970s no one would have thought that Baiyangdian, where "dragons" and "tigers" lurk, would become the cradle of "underground poetry". In addition to the above several "educated youth" poets, Bei Dao, Jiang He, and Gan Tiesheng, who were also famous "underground poets", visited Baiyangdian successively (Yang, 1993: 108). Considering that these people were, in fact, the nucleus of the unofficial literary publication *Today* that emerged during the Beijing spring, we do have reason to believe that these underground or semi-underground gatherings or encounters set the stage for the new literature that emerged in 1978 as a result of changes in the political environment (Bonnin, 2004: 334).

3 "The song of the educated youth in Nanjing", also known as "The song of the educated youth in China", was written by Ren Yi of the educated youth in Nanjing. Today's young people don't understand how such a simple nostalgic song could have led to the writer being nearly sentenced to death (later sentenced to ten years in prison) during the Mao era. More than 40 years later, my friend X, who was on the scene of the sentencing meeting, still gasps at the horror of that era.

4 Erickson's own early life history provides a realistic proof of the relationship between identity and early life, and facilitates the psychoanalyst's creative research on identity or identity crisis. Erickson grew up with a sense of not belonging to his family, which was exacerbated by the fact that his mother and stepfather were Jewish, but he was tall, blue-eyed, and blond, of Scandinavian origin. At school he was called a Jew, but at his stepfather's ancestral temple he was called a heretic.

5 According to the view of Edward P. Thompson, class consciousness is a class and its members' consciousness of their own economic, political status, and social belonging; but class consciousness is not necessarily a direct reflection of the objective economic state, it is also a way of cultural formation. Specifically, a class is created when a group of people, drawing conclusions from a common experience (whether derived from their predecessors or from their own experience), feel and clearly state that they have common interests and that their interests are different from (and often opposed to) those of others (Thompson, 2001, Vol. I: 2).

6 "Substitution", in which adult children take over their parents' jobs, was often made at the expense of younger parents having to retire early. The policy of substitution was applied before 1966 to families who were in difficulties due to the early death of their parents. In 1978, at the beginning of the reform and opening-up, it began to be widely adopted in cities when a large number of educated youth and "decentralized families" returned to the cities, making career arrangements more difficult.

7 As for the history of the Western, mainly European universities, I should like to thank Professor Walter Ruegg, former President of the University of Frankfurt, Germany, and chairman of the Permanent Conference of European University presidents, for the generous gift of his edited *History of European Universities*. In November 2008, when I went to the University of Hamburg, Germany, for an international conference on "1968: German Universities: Historical Context, Events and Implications", knowing that I, a sociologist from China, would be attending the conference, Professor Ruegg, then 90 years old, handed me the first two volumes of the published *History of European Universities* in Chinese which he had carried all the way from his home in Switzerland, and showed great interest in my lectures on the Red Guard movement of 1966–1968. Although in the first volume of the *History of European Universities*, Professor Ruegg questioned whether the University of Bologna was founded in 1088, here I am going to use the Bologna authorities' version of the date. In fact, as a prominent sociologist, Professor Ruegg has also realized that the University of Bologna, the mother of European universities, has an unparalleled political and symbolic function (Ruegg, 2007, Vol. I: 5).

8 According to the data of the sixth census conducted in 2010, compared with the 2000 census, the number of people with college education increased from 3,611 to 8,930, the number of people with high school education increased from 11,146 to 14,032, the number of people with junior middle school education increased from 33,961 to 38,788, and the number of people with primary school education decreased from 35,701 to 26,779 (Ma, 2011). This suggests that in just ten years, as the number of years of education has increased, young Chinese have been entering the work force much later.

9 The reason for the decline of school tradition or influence lies not only in the decline of the supremacy of teachers in the electronic age due to the diversity of information sources, but also in the decline of the frequency of teacher–student interaction. In the past four decades, with the rapid growth of higher education in China, the ratio of teachers to students has been increasing. In the 1990s, when Professor Pei Xiansheng, a journalism professor, saw nearly a thousand students in my social psychology class, he once lamented that in the late 1940s, "when I was in college, only three students were enrolled in my major that year". Obviously, the results of teacher–student interaction of 1 to 3, 1 to 100, and 1 to 1,000 are not the same.

10 In the past, according to Negroponte, proximity was the basis of everything from friendship and cooperation to games and neighborhood. Today's children are completely unconstrained by geography. Digital technology can become a natural motivator to draw people into a more harmonious world (Negroponte, 1995: 271).

11 The cable broadcasting in Mao Zedong's time is a typical example of this kind of strong "narrator's discourse". People who know about cable broadcasting know that there was no switch available for personal control in the terminal of each house. Not only what you listened to was determined by the "superiors", but when you listened to it was also determined by them. Except for a few intellectuals who were relatively independent of the control of the village, the local farmers dared not take the risk of cutting off the cable broadcasting (Zhou, 1998a: 218).

12 In 1990, Li Anyou and Shi Tianjian conducted a nationwide survey of political behaviors and attitudes in China, and the results showed that respondents' perceptions of the influence of the government, the role of the system, and their tolerance of dissidents were all lower. However, "low awareness of the influence of the government and the role of the system, as well as less tolerant attitudes, may become roadblocks to democratization" (Guo, 2003: 110).

13 In March 2003, Sun Zhigang, a college student who had just found a job in Guangzhou, was taken into a shelter as a "social drifter" by the authorities, where he was beaten to death on May 20. "The death of Sun Zhigang" triggered extensive discussion and doubt on the detention and repatriation system once it was reported by the media. On May 14, three law doctors, Yu Jiang, Teng Biao, and Xu Zhiyong, submitted a proposal to the standing committee of the National People's Congress (NPC) on examining the measures for the detention and repatriation of urban vagabonds and beggars, arguing that the restrictions on citizens' personal freedom contained in the measures contradict the Chinese constitution and relevant laws and should be changed or revoked. On May 23, 2003, five famous jurists, He Weifang, Sheng Hong, Shen Kuikui, Xiao Han, and He Haibo, jointly submitted a letter to the standing committee of the NPC on behalf of Chinese citizens, requesting the launch of a special investigation procedure concerning Sun Zhigang's case and the implementation of the detention and repatriation system. On June 20 of the same year, Premier Wen Jiabao of the state council of the People's Republic of China signed the decree of the state council, promulgating the "Measures for Relief and Management of Vagrants and Beggars Who Have No Means to Live in the City". The promulgation of the measures marked the abolition of the "Measures for Reception and Repatriation of Vagrants and Beggars in the City".

14 Ren Jianyu, a college student village official in Chongqing, was sentenced to two years of reeducation through labor in 2011 for copying, forwarding, and commenting on "more than 100 negative messages" on Tencent Microblog and QQ Spaces. A year later, against the backdrop of the fall of Bo Xilai, the commission reversed its decision and Ren Jianyu was freed. One of the surprising details in Ren's case was that a T-shirt printed with the slogan "Give me liberty or give me death" that his girlfriend bought online for him became one of the most important pieces of evidence that the defendant, Chongqing Reeducation Through Labor Commission, argued that Ren was guilty. Recalling how Scottish–American Patrick Henry's famous saying "Give me liberty or give me death" inspired many people with great ideals to follow one another during the years when the Chinese people fought for freedom and liberation, it is really a shock to learn that after 30 years of reform and opening-up, some people in Chongqing under Bo Xilai were even convicted of this crime, which fully illustrates the essence of Bo's political line, and how significant it is for the 18th National Congress of the Communist Party of China (CPC) to list such values as freedom, democracy, and equality as the core values of socialism.

3 The media

More about survival than information

I have thought all day long, but found that it is not as fruitful as a moment of learning; I have stood on tiptoe to look far, but found that it is better to climb to the top to see more. A man who reaches a height and waves does not lengthen his arms, but is seen at a distance; if a man calls along with the wind, even if his voice is not louder than before, the listener can hear clearly. Those who use chariots and horses can travel thousands of miles without walking fast; those who use boats can cross rivers, not necessarily being able to swim. So the nature of the gentleman is no different from that of the average man, except that the gentleman is good at using external things.

Xuncius, 2011

Computing is not about computers any more. It is about living.

Nicholas Negroponte

The significance of the media

Following our discussion of peer groups, the analysis of the influence of mass media on the cultural feedback ability of the younger generation reminds us of David Riesman, the sociologist who became famous throughout the United States in the 1950s, mentioned at the beginning of Chapter 2 of this book. In his later classic, *The Lonely Crowd: A Study of the Changing American Character*, Riesman vividly compared the influence of peer groups and mass media on the changing American character:

The peer-group stands midway between the individual and the messages which flow from the mass media. The mass media are the wholesalers; the peer-groups, the retailers of the communications industry. But the flow is not all one way. Not only do the peers decide, to a large extent, which tastes, skills, and words, appearing for the first time within their circle, shall be given approval, but they also select some for wider publicity through contiguous groups and eventually back to the mass media for still wider distribution.

(Riesman et al., 2001: 84)

Riesman's thinking is clear. Firstly, peer groups and mass media interact with each other, which cannot be achieved by a single factor. Secondly, if the peer group as a "retailer" has the function of "acceptance" and "selection", then the mass media as a "wholesaler" has the function of "spreading" and "promotion" which the peer group cannot compare with.

The spreading and promotion ability of mass media determines its powerful shaping and influence on social life. Back in 1916, before the advent of radio, television, and the Internet, the mass media that would later transform the world, John Dewey, an educator at the University of Chicago, wrote with confidence that society exists not only through communication, but also, we can boldly say, in communication (Dewey, 1916: 5). Although there is no evidence that Harold Innis, who later became famous in communications, took Dewey's course when he was a student in Chicago, he did inherit Dewey's ideas, and together with Marshall McLuhan preached the influence of the media on society all his life. Innis and McLuhan creatively put the history of the mass media at the center of the whole history of civilization. Both of them regard it not only as a technological appendage of society, but also as a crucial determinant of social structure (Carey, 1967). This view of what Everett M. Rogers called "technological determinism" was later widely criticized: that a technology was often embedded in a social structure, which affected its invention, development, and diffusion, as well as its affect on society. In other words, technology was influenced by society, not the other way around. But Rogers may be more fair here in fact. This social embedding of technology does not condemn the fact that technology may be a force for social change, though it is not the only force (Rogers, 1994: 510).

If technology, especially communication technology or the media as discussed here, is not regarded as the only driving force of social change, we can really understand social change from the side of media development, and thus further understand the significance of the media to human social progress. Table 3.1 is a global communication development timeline based on various research works and institutional reports on the history of human communication. It roughly describes the great media events and their processes that have had an important impact on human communication during the 5,000 years of human civilization. In order to simplify the description of the progress of human media, in *Understanding Media: The Extensions of Man*, Marshall McLuhan, through the change of media and the extension of the human senses, divided the forward history of human society into three stages: tribalization, non-tribalization, and retribalization. In the primitive days of wandering and hunting, when man perceived the world as a whole and intuitively, he could neither analyze nor concentrate; he was a whole man, or a tribesman. Next, because of the division of labor and the invention of writing, especially the Pinyin, man learned to analyze, and at the same time made himself a fragmented and incomplete non-tribesman. Mechanical printing and the whole industrial civilization pushed non-tribalization to the extreme. Further, with the advent of the electronic age, the way people perceived the world was no longer just visual, literal, and linear.

Table 3.1 Global media development timeline

Events Related to Media Development

In 100, began the development of papermaking in China and its spread in Asia and the
Arab world up until AD 600
In 170 the Arabs introduced Chinese papermaking to the West
In 1000 came the invention and use of clay type printing in China
In 1400 came the development of metal type printing in Asia
In 1456, the German Gutenberg perfected metal movable-type printing and printed the
Bible by hand
In 1600 the world's first "newspapers" appeared in Germany, France, and Belgium
In 1702, the *Daily News* of London became the first daily newspaper
Mass media began in 1833 with the publication of the *New York Sun*, the first penny
newspaper
In 1837, the telegraph was first demonstrated
In 1839, Daguerre invented photography
In 1876, Alexander Graham Bell spoke on the telephone for the first time
In 1879, Edison invented the electric lamp
In 1884, Eastman perfected the film
In 1894, moving pictures were produced, and people saw movies for the first time
In 1895, Marconi broadcast a radio message
In 1920, the first regular radio station was established in Pittsburgh, USA
In 1927, the first feature-length film with a soundtrack, the *Jazz Singer*, was released
In 1933, the Radio Corporation of America (RCA) first experimented with television
In 1937, the first digital computer was created with telephone parts
In 1941, the first commercial television station broadcast programs
In 1946, the first large computer was developed at the University of Pennsylvania
In 1949, television networks appeared in the United States
In 1956, tape recorders came out
In 1957, the Soviet Union launched the world's first communications satellite
In 1958, China Central Television (CCTV) began to broadcast officially
In 1961, the first cable television connection was made between San Diego and Los
Angeles
In 1969, on the basis of ARPANET of the Pentagon Advanced Research Institute, the first
Internet network was established
In 1970, video cassette recorders (VCRs) were introduced
In 1973, Motorola made the first call on a small mobile phone
In 1975, American engineer Henry Roberts built the first personal computer, the Altair,
which became the basis for the Apple I. The first commercially successful personal
computer Apple II came out; at the same time, home theater (HBO) began distributing
programs via satellite to cable systems
In 1982, CDs went on sale
In 1987, mobile phones began to be used in China, with 3,200 people becoming early
adopters
In 1990, the Internet began to present various types of data with a simple and friendly user
interface
In 1994, the first network television (that is, television programs broadcast via the Internet)
appeared, and the "Education and scientific research demonstration network" in Zhong-
guancun, Beijing, China was officially connected to the Internet
In 1997, DVDs came out
In 1998, digital televisions came out
In 1999, mp3s made music downloads possible, while computer viruses were rampant
In 2000, Napster made music downloads easier

(*Continued*)

Table 3.1 (Cont.)

Events Related to Media Development
In 2001, satellite-based digital audio broadcasting services began to increase
In 2006, the number of landlines in mainland China peaked at 368 million and has since fallen
In 2008, mobile phones were used by 4 billion people worldwide, accounting for 61% of the world's population. Meanwhile, 23 of the world's 6.7 billion people had Internet access
In 2009, the total number of Internet users in mainland China reached 384 million, and the penetration rate reached 28.9%, exceeding the world average for the first time
In 2010, the iPhone3 and 4, developed by Apple, and the iPod, a tablet computer, were introduced. The number of mobile phone users in China reached 805 million, while the number of landlines dropped to 305 million
In December 2013, the Chinese mainland had 632 million Internet users, with a penetration rate of 46.9%

Sources: Crowley and Heyer (1991), USAID (2008), Croteau and Hoynes (2009), ITU (2009), State Council Information Office (2010), China Internet Network Information Center (2010, 2015:15)

Thus, "after three thousand years of specialist explosion and of increasing specialism and alienation in the technological extensions of our bodies, our world has become compressional by dramatic reversal". That is to say, it became a "global village" and achieved a higher level of retribalization (Rogers, 1994: 22).

Despite criticism of McLuhan's theory, the concept of "global village" has spread and become one of the world's most fashionable buzzwords. In 1999, Paul Levinson further separated the concept of a global village into three parts, dividing the world after the emergence of electronic media into children's villages, voyeurs' villages, and earth villages according to the different social participation abilities provided to the public by media in different times. In historical order, in the small pre-agrarian villages, people had almost equal access to information, and every villager could hear the peddler's voice at the entrance to the village. The advent of the written word and printing expanded the scope of communication, but changed the way humans communicate in two ways. On the one hand, printing destroyed the synchronicity of human communication. All people did not read books or newspapers at the same time. On the other hand, printing also destroyed the interactivity of human communication, so villagers could no longer directly ask peddlers questions. With the advent of electronic media, synchronization was restored, but neither radio nor television has been able to restore the instant feedback and interaction between the shopping "villagers" and the "peddler". Broadcasting was the voice of paternalism, and the public, like children in a family, could only listen and not speak; Levinson realized the similarities between Stalin, Hitler, Churchill, and Roosevelt: They had successfully used the power of broadcasting to "instill".[1] Television turned the audience from children into peepers: People saw more intuitive and reliable pictures and became more rational,[2] although they still did not have the right to make their voices heard. Interactivity was restored with the advent of the Internet. At this point, millions of people began to actively talk online, and individual citizens were no longer what Lippmann calls "deaf bystanders in the back"; instead, they have access to most of the information about most things and are free to react to that information. Thus, the Internet transformed (McLuhan's) global village from a metaphor to a near-reality (Levinson, 2001: 103, 97).

From Table 3.1 and the description of McLuhan and Levinson, we can roughly outline the great progress of the media revolution in human history. The first media revolution was the emergence of language, which made it possible for human beings to communicate and think, and thus provided tools for human beings to interact face to face, further enabling them to form the primitive clan society on the basis of blood relationship. The second media revolution was the emergence of the written word. As we have said in the previous chapter, the emergence of written language makes up for the inconvenience of communication caused by body language and oral language, "thus separating the spoken from the speaker, and making possible conceptual discourse" (Castells, 2010a: 355). More importantly, writing created a new communication order and established new social relations. On the one hand, writing enables human communication to break through the limitations of regions and expand the scope of human communication; on the other hand, because of the meaning of privacy provided by writing, it promotes the privatization of social communication and enables individuals to establish their own social networks centered on their own production and life. The third media revolution was the invention and promotion of printing. "The message of the print and of typography is primarily that of repeatability. With typography, the principle of movable type introduced the means of mechanizing any handicraft by the process of segmenting and fragmenting an integral action" (McLuhan, 1994: 204). The fourth media revolution was the emergence of electronic media. From the end of the 19th century to the first half of the 20th century, the emergence and popularization of mass media represented by telegraph, film, radio, and television throughout the world made a historic breakthrough in the audio-visual culture of mankind. "The explosion of communication brought about the transformation of social communication from closed to open, from dependence to autonomy, and from monism to diversity, thus bringing about a more complete revolution in social relations" (Meng, 2010). In fact, the climax of this revolution was the Internet revolution based on the computer technology popularized after the 1980s. It has completely changed the means of human communication and once again highlighted the significance of media to human beings.

There is a great deal of discussion about the significance of media to human beings, which can be summarized in two aspects: psychological cognition and social structure. In terms of human psychology or cognition, the significance of media is most importantly reflected in two aspects. First, in a deep sense, the medium is not just the means or carrier of information transmission, but, as McLuhan said, the medium is the message itself (McLuhan, 1994: 39). That is to say, different media not only take other media as the content of their communication (for example, text is the content of printing, while printing is the content of telegraph), but also determine the means and clarity of the human perception of information due to its nature; they also determine or shape the cognitive structure of the human perception of information. When people listen to music, it is easy to understand, because the melody they hear is both the style and the content of music. The same is true of other media, which makes our understanding of certain media at least to a certain extent determined by their nature. Second, on the surface, different media extend and expand the range of human perception and cognition in different ways, so McLuhan would say that "all media are extensions of our own bodies and senses" (McLuhan, 1994: 116). For example, a telegraph or radio is an extension of our ears, a film or television is an extension of our eyes, and an electronic computer or network is an extension of our central nervous system.[3] Such extensions not only makes the distance between people and things or information shorter and shorter, but also makes the distance between people shorter and shorter, and we know that this is exactly the premise of the global village.

In this sense, the history of media is actually the history of narrowing the distance between human beings. Since the telegraph was invented by Morse in 1844 and the telephone was invented by Bell in 1876 we see humans getting closer

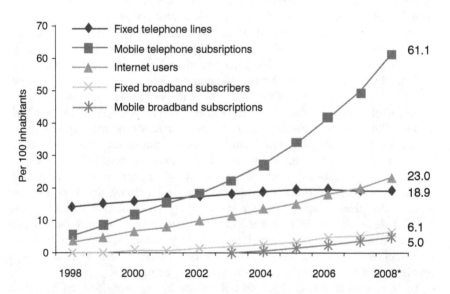

Figure 3.1 Development of global information communication technologies, 1998–2008
ITU (2009: 3)

and closer to each other, but it was the Internet (based on computer technology) we mentioned in Chapter 5 of the first volume of this book and the first call of the small mobile phone made by Motorola in 1973 that made the distance disappear. Since then, new information technologies have swept the world at lightning speed (Castells, 2010b: 38). Especially in the last decade of the 20th century, information and communication technology (ICT), which was based on mobile phones and the Internet, was developed rapidly. Figure 3.1 shows the statistics according to the "Measurement information society", the 2009 report of the International Telecommunication Union (ITU). By the end of 2008, the number of people using mobile phones had reached 4 billion, accounting for 61% of the world's population (after 132 years of development, the total number of fixed telephone households is only 130 million). At the same time, nearly a quarter (23%) of the world's 6.7 billion people have access to the Internet, and in developed countries the figure is even higher (ITU, 2009: 71). In fact, China, a country with a telephone penetration rate of only 0.45% (2.13 million) at the beginning of the reform and opening-up, is the best epitome of the development of new information technology "at lightning speed". By June 2012, the number of fixed telephones in China had reached 285 million and the number of mobile telephones exceeded 1 billion (CNNIC, 2012). Furthermore, by the end of June 2014, the number of Internet users had reached 632 million, among which the number of mobile Internet users reached 527 million, surpassing traditional PC Internet users for the first time (CNNIC, 2015:12) (Figure 3.1).

Compared with the influence of media on human psychological cognition, its influence on human society is more significant. We can discuss this effect from both macroscopic and microscopic dimensions. From a macro-perspective, because the media is a bridge to building social relations, and even a driving force for the transformation of social relations, it is quite natural that every media revolution introduces a new scale and changes social relations. To be specific, the emergence of language is adapted to the consanguinity society, while the emergence of writing is accompanied by the breaking up of the *gens* united by consanguinity. Further, although the invention and promotion of printing had only a mild influence in eastern society, it also promoted the differentiation of industries and classes, and the development of "business relationships" centered on trade, industry, chamber of commerce, and other elements. However, in the West, it has brought tremendous changes, breaking the domination of blood and geographical relations over personal relationship networks (Meng, 2010), and promoted the transformation of the human community from the "*Gemeinschaft*" or "custom society" mentioned by sociologists Tonnies and Fei Xiaotong to "*Gesellschaft*" or "legal-rational society" (Fei, 1998: 9; Tonnies, 1988). During the American Civil War, and later during the reform movement, the dominant form of print—newspapers—played an unprecedented progressive role (Zhou, 2006). Finally, electronic media, especially the network information technology popularized after the 1980s, has brought the whole world into an interactive network. At this point, the traditional concept of space and time is broken, and anyone with "individual needs" and a "shared code of conduct" can connect via the Internet. This initiative has allowed Robin Dunbar's "Rule of 150" to be expanded as never before, using the social psychologist Stanley Milgram's "Six degrees of separation" theory: Anyone can theoretically connect with any other person in the world through a chain of six people (Ximen et al., 2009: 6–7).[4] Most importantly, in cyberspace, we also form the fourth kind of human relationship after blood relationship, geographical relationship, and karma relationship—virtual social relationship.

On the micro-level, the most prominent influence of media on human society is that it is a powerful tool to shape human modernity. Back in 1958, American social psychologist Daniel Lerner, in his book *The Passing of Traditional Society*, regards the relationship between the individual and the media as one of the basic elements of the theoretical framework that divides traditional people, transitional people, and modern people. More than a decade later, American social psychologists Alex Inkeles and David H. Smith, following Lerner's basic train of thought, in a study of personal modernity in the six developing countries of Argentina, Chile, India, Israel, Nigeria, and Bangladesh, proposed a similar hypothesis regarding the relationship between the media and human modernity: A modern man should have more frequent access to the mass media, newspapers, radio, films, and television (if any). They are quite strongly convinced that, in evaluating different sources of information, more modern people will have greater confidence in the newer mass media and less modern people will rely more on more traditional sources (Inkeles & Smith, 1975: 37).

Inkeles and Smith carefully designed the mass media scale, and divided people's contact level with the media into seven levels. The lowest level 1 does not read the newspaper or listen to the radio, and the highest level 7 does both. The results show that there is a close relationship between the increase of mass media contact and the increase of the score of the comprehensive modernity scale: In each of the six countries, for every level of advancement in the mass media, there is almost a roughly proportional increase in personal modernity. This common trend is also reflected in the strong zero-order correlation coefficient between comprehensive modernity and mass media. For the whole sample, its average correlation coefficient is 0.45 (Inkeles & Smith, 1975: 218).

In fact, before Lerner and Inkeles, Yan Yangchu, a "folk educator" in China, realized that the media had a great influence on cultivating people's modernity or "opening up people's wisdom"; he started from Ding county in Hebei province and began to promote the rural construction movement to the whole country and even the world.[5] Especially in the ten years from 1926 to 1936, Yan Yangchu led hundreds of elite intellectuals to launch a vigorous campaign of civilian education and rural construction in Ding county. In the ten years of the "Ding county experiment", in order to improve the intelligence, productivity, strength, and solidarity of farmers and create a generation of "new people" (Song, 2012), the Chinese Association for the Promotion of Education for the Common People led by Yan Yangchu carried out a large number of pioneering communication practices, among which the most effective ones included the use of newspapers, radio, and drama. They taught peasants how to read newspapers and use them as their mouthpieces, established radio broadcasts covering several counties in the vicinity of Ding county to broadcast radio programs in local dialects and to teach farmers news, knowledge, and livelihood techniques, and even cultivated civilized behavior and public emotion adapted to the new life by organizing farmers to rehearse and watch the new plays with farmers in the leading roles. So many years later it is still recognized that "the mass media in the Ding county experiment is just such a liberating force, exerting its functions of spreading new knowledge, cultural entertainment and social coordination: It is not only a convenient tool to help farmers learn to read, but also an effective means to mobilize farmers, improve the social atmosphere, and promote rural modernization in Ding county, and also to create a favorable public opinion environment for the national rural construction movement" (Cao, 2005).

Both Inkeles's research and Yan Yangchu's experiment demonstrate the social significance of media from different perspectives. As American communicator Wilbur Schramm said, the media are a liberating force, because they can break down barriers of distance and isolation and transport people from traditional society to the "great society" (Schramm, 1990: 134). Then we will see how the revolutionary development of mass media, including newspapers, radio, television, and the Internet, has gradually brought the younger generation from traditional China into the great society of contemporary China over the past four decades.

The impetus for social opening-up

The influence of media, especially the modern mass media, on the whole society is not limited to re-establishing people's social relations, nor is it limited to giving modern values and social behaviors to the masses immersed in tradition. Fundamentally, it will directly promote the openness of a society. In fact, it is only when a society moves from a closed society to an open one that it is possible to absorb the dynamic elements of foreign culture or publicize the local culture, break the previously solid social relations, change the behavior patterns that people have taken for granted, and finally regenerate a society with new vitality.

In modern times, when Chinese society with deeply rooted traditions underwent unprecedented changes under the "impact of the West", as we put it in the words of the American historian Cohen in Chapter 2 of the first volume of this book, then society became all-directional and open to the world (Cohen, 1989: 145). This all-round opening inevitably leads to a flood of new economic, political, social, cultural, educational, and gender concepts from the West. Both the "eastward advance" of these new concepts and their popularity in Chinese society are closely related to the popularity and promotion of mass media such as magazines, newspapers, books, dramas (civilized dramas), and broadcasting. The mass media has played an important role in the opening up of Chinese society and its transition to modernity.

Shiwu Newspaper, founded by the reformists Huang Zunxian, Wang Kang-nian, and Liang Qichao after the Sino-Japanese war in 1896, is an example of how mass media plays an important role in promoting the opening-up of modern Chinese society. This political journal, written by Liang Qichao, aimed at the preservation of reform laws and setting up columns such as argumenta-tions, oracles, recent events outside Beijing, and translations of overseas news-papers, serialized Liang Qichao's "Reform of laws and regulations", which lashed out against the conformism of feudal diehard groups, and generated great repercussions in Chinese society at the end of the Qing dynasty. Although *Shiwu Newspaper* lasted only two years and published only 69 issues in total, it not only promoted the reform movement politically, but also gave birth to the openness of the whole society and cultural changes. For example, it opposed the social reality and traditional value orientation, which subtly changed the values of officials and gentry. Scholars no longer regarded officiating as the only way out, and people no longer regarded associations as a political taboo. For another example, *Shiwu Newspaper* promoted great changes in the cultural market. From then on, self-run newspapers and publishing organizations of Chinese people broke the monopoly of outsiders on the dissemination of new learning. At the same time, the publication of works and translations on new learning led by *Shiwu Newspaper* formed a cultural market with the newspaper office as the core and from which it radiated to the whole country. For example, the modern values and nationalism advocated by *Shiwu Newspaper* also led to the large-scale improvement of traditional customs, the most prominent of which were the prohibition of foot binding and the promotion of female educa-tion. The Shanghai "Foot-binding-prohibition association", located in the *Shiwu Newspaper* office, once collected donations and printed 20,000 copies of "Female learning songs" and 3,000 copies of "The simple story of literacy instead of foot binding", which were distributed widely among its members, creating the social public opinion of female learning and foot unbinding, and the registered members of the "Foot-binding-prohibition association" in Shang-hai alone reached 300,000 (Lv, 1994).

In addition to *Shiwu Newspaper*, the emergence of many newspapers, publi-cations, and broadcasts in the turbulent period of the late Qing dynasty and the early Republic of China all contributed to the opening of Chinese society's pol-itics and ethos. At that time, Beijing, Nanjing, Guangzhou, Wuhan, Hangzhou, and Shanghai, a metropolis in particular, often led the way. It was closely related to the developed industry and commerce and the rapid population move-ment there, but it was fundamentally driven by the increasingly developed com-munication media of modern times. Take the illustrated newspaper *Good Friend*, which was opened by Wu Liande in Shanghai in 1926 as an example. This "large, image-based, popular and cheap publication" (Li, 2002: 2) not only focused on current affairs, opened people's wisdom, and carried forward culture, but also led the trend, advocated fashion, and influenced the general mood, becoming the most important and influential pictorial newspaper in China at that time. Every issue of *Good Friend* featured a portrait on the cover. Among the 172 issues of the magazine, only 11 were male,[6] and the other 169 were all female, including Hu Die, Ruan Lingyu, Bai Yang, and Lu Xiaoman, most of whom were movie or sports stars, and a few were ladies. What is interesting is that this practice not only boldly broke through the Chinese tradition of women not leaving their homes, but also developed the public space of middle and upper-class women and influenced the colorful urban culture in Shanghai consumer society (Wu, 2009). For example, in the early days of *Good Friend*, the women not only wore traditional clothes, but also showed cuteness and affectation, but in the later days, the clothes and expressions of the cover figures became more and more "obviously signifying modernity" (Li, 2005: 80).[7] These portraits "recommended a modern lifestyle to young women in Shanghai, instilled a new value concept, and stirred up a series of fashion trends" (Meng, 2005: 179), which affected the social opening of this metropolitan city.

If the reform at the beginning of the last century, though violent, was confined to the south-east coastal cities and limited in scope, then the reform and opening-up that began after 1978 was not only more vigorous, but also broader in scope. What it formed was "a change not seen in 5,000 years". In this "change", ideological confrontation or thought liberation was hanging by a thread yet also thrilling, but each time it was promoted by the media to further emancipate the minds of the whole people. Ma Licheng and Ling Zhijun, political writers at the *People's Daily*, summed up the 30 years of ideological confrontation into four big debates: (a) "Two whatevers" or reform and opening-up? (b) Planned economy or market economy? (c) Is the private economy a curse or a vitalizer? (d) Are there mistakes in China's reforms? (Ma, 2008; Ma & Ling, 1998). For the sake of space, we will take the first two arguments discussed in Chapter 3 of the first volume of this book as examples. The first debate, in the years after Mao Zedong's death, focused on "two whatevers",[8] the essence of which was that we could not turn over the case of "cultural revolution" or change any political decisions made in the Mao Zedong era. On May 11, 1978, Hu Fuming published "Practice is the only criterion for testing truth" in the *Guangming Daily*. Then, mainstream media, including the *Guangming Daily*, the *People's Daily*, the *PLA Daily*, and the *Xinhua News Agency*, initiated and organized a discussion on "Practice is the only criterion for testing truth". During the theoretical debate that lasted for half a year, more than 650 articles were published in various newspapers and magazines, and their influence went far beyond press and theoretical circles and involved all fields of the country, thus forming the climax of the first ideological liberation movement in contemporary China (Yin, 2007). More than a decade later, the "June fourth turbulence" of 1989 and the upheaval of 1990 in eastern Europe led those on the left to argue again that reform and opening-up would inevitably lead China to "peaceful evolution" towards capitalism. They also questioned whether China's reform was capitalist or socialist. In 1991, Huangfu Ping published four signed articles in the *Jiefang Daily*. The articles not only proposed "break[ing] through the shackles of any kind of rigid way of thinking", and "chang[ing] the whole situation through reform", but also explicitly emphasized that "we cannot simply equate the development of a social commodity economy and the socialist market with capitalism, and assume that market regulation is capitalism" (Ma & Ling, 1998: 172). These articles not only further expanded people's awareness of reform and opening-up, but in fact caused the debate that contributed to Deng Xiaoping's "southern tour speech" a year later (Ma, 2008: 154–157). At the age of 88, Deng Xiaoping once again endorsed reform and opening-up with his own actions.

If every progress in the field of ideology is thrilling, then every opening in the field of daily life is more like a "quiet revolution". Since the beginning of the reform and opening-up, with the opening of the country and the gradual development of the West wind, the songs, dances, paintings, novels, films, and works of art that we used to think of as exclusively bourgeois, a vast variety of refreshing ideas in philosophy and the social sciences, as well as the entire material lifestyle including food, catering, clothing, electronics, and cosmetics, all poured into mainland China, becoming the object of desire of ordinary people, especially the younger generation. In the process of the introduction of these material and non-material civilizations, the increasingly prosperous and diversified mass media themselves played an important role. Although people have different opinions on this role, it is an accepted fact that the mass media has triggered unprecedented openness in Chinese society.

Henry Bergson and Karl Popper believed that an open society should guarantee individual freedom and allow criticism from the masses; George Soros went further and said that in addition to having a democratic and efficient government, and regarding the promotion of freedom, democracy, the rule of law, human rights, social justice, and social responsibility as a universal concept, its most important foundation should be the recognition that any society is an imperfect society ready for improvement (Soros, 2002: 1, 140, 139). Although these expressions of "open society" have multiple political and social implications, in the context of the intergenerational relations we are discussing, it at least shows us that in a society that can be called "open", no individual has any reason to reject new experience or oppose any attempt at social change, because this is the basic premise for improving social or individual imperfections. As the two social psychologists Inkeles and Smith, whom we have repeatedly quoted in this book, say, a modern person should be able to embrace the process of social change that is taking place around him, and more freely accept the changed opportunities that others are now enjoying. In a sense, he is not too stubborn and is not too anxious about others acting in new or unconventional ways (Inkeles & Smith, 1975: 26).

The reason why the mass media can lead to the opening of a society and lead people to accept new things and social changes is that it can bring different values and attitude towards life, show different people's ways of life, publicly display the different or even radically contradictory views of the same thing or event, show the imperfection of the society in which we live and the possibilities of transformation, encourage people to explore and debate the value and relevance of each possibility, and eventually make people accept or at least tolerate other values and lifestyles. In our study, through interviews with dozens of families, it was found that the convenience of access to the mass media makes the younger generation more open in values and lifestyle than their parents:

> I think children know more and are more receptive because of social development. For example, the development of mass media, such as newspapers, television, movies and the Internet, has led to a flood of information and reports, making them completely different from when we were young. When we were little, we couldn't afford even newspapers, let alone TV. If you said you had newspapers in the home, for example the *Beijing Daily* or the *Reference News*, others must guess you were from a cadre family. The only insights we had as children came from wandering from one alley to another around home; at most, we were led by our grandparents to travel from east Beijing to west Beijing. How could we travel the world as children do today? Those children from well-off families can even go to a summer school abroad during the summer vacation, so, of course, they know more things than we do, and they are not as conservative as we are. You see, I sell health care products, but a lot of my information comes from my son BOB. He knows where to look for information, and happens to be an English major, so he not only helps me find Chinese materials, but sometimes also helps me translate English materials. He has also sent a lot of emails for me to get orders, and said that he will help me to build a sales website, which can sell through the Internet. If only.
>
> (BOM, 2004)

In fact, the openness of a society is not only reflected in the fact that the younger generation is abler to accept new values and behavior patterns than their parents, but also in the fact that the older generation is able to tolerate the values and behavior patterns pursued by the younger generation even if they do not agree with them. Tolerance of the ideas and behaviors that one does not agree with or is unwilling to adopt is also a sign of the openness of a society, which, to a certain extent, also comes from the influence and promotion of the media. Obviously, a society with developed mass media will provide diversified channels for the expression and communication of different ideas and behaviors, and thus increase the understanding and tolerance of social members to various ideas and behaviors. Over the past four decades of reform and opening-up, Chinese people, including the elders, have gradually accepted the following principle: I may disagree with you, but I will defend to the death your right to say so. In this sense, the tolerance of the older generation in the face of a new set of values, life attitudes, or behaviors is sometimes an equal or even greater progress than the bold acceptance of the younger generation. In the interview in Guangzhou, a sociologist over 50 whom I know very well expressed basically the same view:

I think the media can bring a lot of things to our society that were not there before, and the biggest change it will make is that the tolerance of the society will increase. In theory, only when the society is more tolerant can it accept new things. I think this is probably the biggest change that has occurred as a result of the proliferation of media and information.

A young person may not change the old person's behavior easily, but the old person will become more tolerant, which is probably called "diversity". More precisely, here by "diversity" I mean that I or the older generation can accept greater changes in society. This change may be the biggest change since the reform and opening-up, but it is not about who has changed whom or who has transformed whom. In other words, the fact that the elderly become more tolerant itself is a kind of social progress.

(Interview with Cai, 2003)

Cai He is right. From the perspective of intergenerational relations, one of the signs of whether a society is open or not is that different generations no longer complain or even hate each other, but tolerate each other. In general, of course, because much of the power or wealth of a society is in the hands of the older generation, it is often the older generation that makes a complaint or shows hostility, and the younger generation that receives it. Thus, when the elders of a society are able or willing to tolerate the bold words or actions of the young, even though they themselves would not accept such words and deeds, such words and deeds also have the possibility of gradually expanding or spreading in society, which will surely lay the foundation for its progress.

At the beginning of the last century, the Dutch–American writer Willem van Loon wrote his later famous book *Tolerance* (Van Loon, 1985: 13). In van Loon's works, the intolerance of modern society often stems from three aspects. First, out of laziness. People are unwilling to change their own concepts and lifestyles just because of habits, and therefore all people with new ideas become enemies of humanity. Next, out of ignorance. Because of ignorance, a person builds in his soul a fortress of granite, proclaiming himself infallible. Last, out of selfishness. Selfishness is often a sign of jealousy (Van Loon, 1985: 140–143). If we can seriously consider the function of the mass media, we can understand why it can promote tolerance of a society to a certain extent. Obviously, the mass media can break the habits or conventions of a society by spreading novel knowledge or other living habits, and can also make the ignorant become relatively wise through comparison. As for jealousy, although it is difficult to resolve by relying solely on the mass media, and it is also believed that there is no such thing as a society without jealousy,[9] reasonable and effective communications can help people to appropriately suppress and channel envy by publicizing facts, suppressing differences, and building trust (Schoeck, 1988: 312). In any case, in a society where there is reasonable, just, and effective communication, people will have a sense of forgiveness and tolerance for others.

Advertisements: to promote commodities or living styles?

If the modern mass media establish a huge empire of symbols by sending speech, text, and especially image symbols to the rest of human society, then the advertisements we are going to discuss are called the "emperor" of this empire. Tao Dongfeng noticed that the living environment of human beings is being advertised on an unprecedented scale (Tao, 2006); in other words, in today's society, advertising is an integral part of the rich world of experience in which we live. In the 1960s, American advertising scientists Raymond Bauer and Stephen Greyser proved through research that, on average, Americans encountered more than 300 advertisements a day (Bauer et al., 1968: 173–176). In the 1970s, this figure rose to 560 in Stuart Barrett's survey (Britt, 1972); in Schulz's study in the 1980s, however, this figure rose to more than 1,500 (Schultz, 1987: 124). Although we have not seen relevant data on China yet, no one can doubt that, since 1979, when the advertising business was re-granted a "birth permit" in China,[10] along with the economic development and reform and opening-up of Chinese society, advertising has become omnipresent and unavoidable (Zhou, 1994: 7). In 1979, after China reintroduced commercial advertising, the annual turnover of advertising in mainland China was only 10 million RMB. But 40 years later, in 2019, the figure climbed to 867.4 billion CNY, the growth rate of which is far higher than that of the GDP in the same period, when China became the world's leading advertising power after the United States.

The reason why we say that advertising is the "emperor" in the symbol empire established by mass communication is not only because advertising is the most effective facility and technology to influence human behavior (Di et al., 1991: 216), but also because, in essence, the whole modern mass communication system is supported by advertising. As early as the beginning of the 20th century, when the modern advertising industry was just starting, the advertising revenue of American newspapers accounted for 64% of its total revenue (Wang & Su, 2006). In 2005, when China's TV population reached 1.254 billion and became the largest TV country in the world (Chen & Yu, 2005), the advertising turnover of CCTV alone exceeded 8.6 billion CNY, accounting for nearly 70% of the total revenue of 12.4 billion CNY (Huang & Chen, 2006).[11] So we can say, on the one hand, there would be no modern advertising without mass media.

> In many countries, advertising is the most important source of income for the media through which it is conducted. In addition to newspapers, magazines, and broadcast media, advertising media include direct mail, billboards and posters, transit advertising, the Internet, and promotional items such as matchbooks or calendars. Advertisers attempt to choose media that are favored by the advertisers' target audience.
>
> (*Encyclopedia Britannica*, 1985, Vol. III: 524)

On the other hand, there would not have been such a developed mass communication system without modern advertising. Advertising, relying on its increasing income, provides a realistic possibility for the expansion and diversification of the mass media.

Just as the influence of the mass media cannot be ignored, the influence of advertising as its core content is also of great significance. Even since advertising has essentially been a professional technique for producing persuasive messages (Di et al., 1991: 7), its influence is often greater than that of the general mass media because more intelligence and money are invested over the same time period. For this reason, the famous American historian David Porter admitted that the social influence of modern advertising can rival that of churches and schools with a long tradition (Ogilvy, 1991: Preface); Mark Poster, another historian, even saw advertising not as an economic event, but as a sociological event that told or participated in the ongoing game of forces in the social field (Poster, 2000: 67). The reason why Poster regarded advertising as a social and political event is based on the two basic characteristics of modern society. For one, television is becoming more and more popular, and watching it is one of the most time-consuming social activities after work and sleep.[12] For another, almost all social groups watch advertisements on TV, especially children, the elderly, and housewives (Poster, 2000: 70, 67). In fact, no sociologist or even an advertising scientist would be so naive as to think that advertising's influence on the public is limited to shopping. The reason why people sigh that "the air we breathe is composed of oxygen, nitrogen and advertisements" (Huang, 1998: 348) is that advertisements have been comprehensively embedded into human daily life and become one of the most important social and cultural factors shaping people's beliefs, values, and lifestyles.

If the impact of advertising on people's daily lives is an indisputable fact, it is true that, as Poster said, its impact on different statistical groups is not the same. For the younger generation we are talking about here, the reason why they are more concerned about advertising and more receptive to its influence than the older generation is, on the one hand, because children have a keen interest in new and different stimuli, have no instinctive repulsion, and are often open to anything foreign. And, as we have discussed in the previous chapter, peer groups have a distinct tendency to imitate, and almost all smarter businesses know that "teena and her teenmates come in bunches, like bananas ... sell one, and the chances are you'll sell them all" (Savage, 2007: 452). On the other hand, since the end of World War II, the whole of modern industry and commerce, which mainly focuses on fashion manufacturing, has been coveting teenagers for a long time. They realized the stimulating effect of this age group on the post-war market and successfully transformed the teenager from a restless group to a consumer group through overwhelming commodity advertisements. The power of consumption and advertising that promotes consumer awareness on the younger generation has a clear universal significance. In 1945, it was not the war that ultimately was won for the United States, but the culture of consumption that we talked about in the last chapter in the youth magazine

Seventeen. Through this culture and the flood of fashion products, including clothing, Coca-Cola, jeans, baseball, soda, ice cream, and crackers, it began to sweep through the vacuum of post-Nazi Europe (Savage, 2007: 445). Nearly half a century later, in the early 1990s, what really dispelled the excessive political resentment of the younger generation, and thus completely eased the intergenerational antagonism that had become increasingly tense because of the "June fourth political turmoil", perhaps is not tighter ideological education, or even more open economic policies, but what Deborah Davis-Friedmann calls the "revolution" in Chinese consumption, especially among the younger generation, brought about by openness and economic development.

Two examples can be used to discuss the case of China. Firstly, as mentioned above, the annual sales of the advertising industry in China has increased from 10 million CNY to 867.4 billion CNY over the past 40 years, with an average annual growth rate of 54.2%. This growth rate is much higher than the amazing GDP growth rate over the same period, and the average annual growth rate is as high as 78% in the three years (from 1991 to 1994) after Deng Xiaoping's "southern tour speech" in 1992. Secondly, when talking about China's consumer revolution, Davis observed that, starting in 1992, at least in Shanghai, children or teenagers as an independent consumer group were directly targeted by advertisers. As a result, "China's headlong plunge into 'market socialism' immersed an entire generation of 'singletons' into an increasingly commodified environment deeply engaged with the products and advertising of global capitalism" (Davis, 2000: 54). And, interestingly, international foods such as pizza, donuts, bagels, and sushi, along with greater mobility and the spread of mobile phones, computers, and the Internet, which began in the 1990s, instead of bringing about ideological troubles, promoted the growth of a real national culture and the understanding of foreign cultures, which greatly strengthens people's identification with the whole country (Vogel, 2012: 652).

The younger generation's preference for advertising is borne out by local research. A study of household consumption in urban China found that children are the least resistant members of the family to advertising. They use it more as a playmate in their daily lives. In particular, advertising provides them with cutting-edge fashion culture, the most fashionable public topics, so children are more likely to use advertising as information for entertainment, and are also more likely than their parents to believe in its truth. Their shopping desire is also more likely to be stimulated by advertising (Chen, 2005).

Almost at the same time as this research, when we interviewed in Beijing in 2004, several middle school students in Beijing 31 Middle School talked about the influence of advertising, and they all said at the same time that there was an extremely popular post on the Internet:

(On the first day, the principal caught the student climbing the wall.)
Principal: Why don't you go in and out of the gate?
Student: Metersbonwe, no ordinary way.
Principal: How did you get over such a high wall?

Student: (Points to his pants) Li Ning, anything is possible.
Principal: How does it feel to climb over the wall?
Student: (Points to his shoes) Xstep, an unusual feeling.

(The next day, the student entered the school through the gate, and the principal saw him again.)
Principal: Why not over the wall?
Student: Anta, I choose, so I like it.

(On the third day, the student was dressed like a social hoodlum.)
Principal: Don't you know there's a school rule against wearing hoodlum clothes?
Student: You are what you wear, Semir.

(On the fourth day, students wore a vest to school.)
Principal: You can't wear a vest to school. Be civilized.
Student: Man, just be simple, Edenbo.
Principal: I'll give you a major demerit recording.
Student: Why?
Principal: M-zone, I am the master of my site.

As the title of this section suggests, modern advertising sells not just goods or services, but a whole way of life. Considering that at the time of reform and opening-up in 1978, in China, a country with a population of more than 1 billion, commercial advertising was basically zero, as mentioned above, so in a way, the 40-year history of China's reform and opening-up is the rapid growth of modern advertising from nothing. Over the course of more than four decades, guided by advertisements, children chose transformers, Rubik's cube, SuperBot, Poli seaweed, Bugles, and *Pleasant Goat and Big Big Wolf*; young people chose jeans, sneakers, lovers' suits, beepers, hand-held computers, and iPhones or iPads; women chose fashion trends, gold and silver accessories, beauty products, spas, Louis Vuitton, or Prada handbags; men chose Shanshan suits, Goldlion ties, Lacoste jackets and Hermes belts, Porsche SUVs, Rolex or Vacheron watches; and the old people chose oral liquid, medicine, a pension mode, and a health care mode. As for choosing a color TV, refrigerator, recorder, video recorder, VCD or DVD, washing machine, air conditioner, home computer, and private car according to the advertisement, it is something that almost every family has experienced. In fact, in the consumption experience of Chinese, as Daniel Bell described Americans in the 1970s, "advertising begins to play a subtler role in changing habits than merely stimulating wants" (Bell, 1996: 69). In other words, while advertising becomes an incubator of our desires, it also becomes deeply embedded in our daily life and as a part of our lifestyle. And the younger generation's natural affinity for advertising also often makes our way of life present a "bamboo" type renewal and replacement from the young age group to the old age group.

The significance and function of advertising to the progress of human society need not be said, but people of insight often reveal the other side of advertising. As we have already pointed out in Chapter 1 when we talked about consumerism, because advertising, on the one hand, satisfies people's needs, and on the other hand, as Galbraith said, "creates" people's needs endlessly (Galbraith, 1958), modern advertising is essentially the twin brother of consumerism, which bears the responsibility for our society slipping into the mire of consumerism step by step. Thus, the historian Arnold Toynbee even asserted that the fate of Western civilization will depend on the outcome of our struggle against what Madison Avenue stands for (Zhou, 1994: 21).

Compared with Toynbee, sociologists evaluate the negative meaning of advertisements in more detail. In *The Lonely Crowd*, which we quote over and over again, David Riesman explains vividly how modern businesses rely on psychologists, market surveyors, and statisticians for market analysis and consumer research, and on this basis "systematically" sell their products to consumers through the mass media, including advertising. In Riesman's eyes, the terrible thing about advertising is not that it exaggerates the goods themselves, but that it has a great power to shape people's lifestyles:

> Just as it is impossible to separate the messages of advertising in the media from the "messages" carried by the goods themselves, displayed in the stores, the streets, and the home. We still believe that the long-run impact of the media on the style of perception, the understanding (or, more often, the misunderstanding) of life, the sense of what it means to be an American boy or girl, man or woman, or old folk, is immense—more important than the often overestimated power of the media to push one marginally differentiated product or candidate over another.
>
> (Riesman et al., 2001: lxiv)

Twenty-five years later, Daniel Bell further analyzed that the dependence of the modern market economy on advertising or the mass media, while emphasizing consumption and cultivating hedonism, also formed a fierce conflict with the old values of hard work, thrift, and moderation advocated by Protestants, and constituted an irreconcilable cultural contradiction of capitalism (Bell, 1996). So far, consumerism has shaken the use of goods and become an illusory symbol of their holders' social class or so-called "status". Due to the prevalence of consumerism, our age is the first age in which both food expenditure and "reputation" expenditure is called "consumption" and thus falls into the trap of goods and their apparent affluence (Baudrillard, 1998: 163, 165).

Do not assume that criticism of advertising and consumerism is directed only at the Western hemisphere. In fact, because of its openness to the world and the globalization that comes with it, China has become a link, even the most important link, in the production and consumption chain of global capitalism.[13] The culture of consumerism that began in the West has flooded into this once impoverished country with Coca-Cola, McDonald's, Barbie dolls, French perfume, Italian fashion, Japanese electronics, and German cars. While changing the living standards of the people in this country, it also completely reconstructs the values and lifestyles of Chinese people, including consumption, through advertising. Almost overnight, the life idols of Chinese people changed from productive idols like Lei Feng, Wang Jinxi, Chen Yonggui, Chen Jingrun, and Lu Wenting to consumption idols composed of sports stars, performing stars, and entertainment stars (Tao, 2006). The extravagance and waste, fuelled by the unique "Chinese characteristic" of "consumption by public funds", have eroded the foundation of this ancient civilization.

In Chapter 1, when discussing globalization and the wave of consumerism, we have already shown from the perspective of generational differences that while the older generation is generally a stickler for traditional consumer ethics, and the younger generation are advocates and spokesmen for consumerism, China's current so-called middle class, or "successful people", aged 45 to 60, have generally gone from extreme scarcity to extreme abundance, so their consumption may be more conspicuous than that of the younger generation (Veblen, 1967: 75). It is based on distrust of this generation that I would prefer to believe that younger generations raised in real affluence are likely to take a hard look at the meaning of consumption. In other words, while affluence does not necessarily form a detached attitude towards material life, it is a necessary prerequisite for such a detached attitude. From the Russian Decembrists and their wives to the American hippies who led the "global rebellion" 150 years later, the reason why the two radically different groups of people are willing to give up their wealth, status, and fame is more or less related to the indifference they developed due to the wealthy life of their early years. In the interviews, we also repeatedly meet the "rich second generation" with ideals. They not only take the family business earned by their parents calmly, but also show disdain for their parents' face-saving and vainglorious extravagant behavior. If the overall atmosphere of this country can develop in such a manner, our 42-year GDP growth or wealth accumulation may one day breed true "spiritual aristocrats". In that sense, today the modern building of advertising which is tilted against human ideals by its aggressive promotion of consumerist values may possibly be righted in the hands of a younger generation. And the younger generation, who have grown up under the bombardment of advertising since childhood, may also become the first generation to truly understand the professional teachings of advertising master David Ogilvy.[14]

Digitized "natives" and "immigrants"

Despite the complexity of our discussions, all of them have been guided by basic theoretical principles—"generation" is both a biological fact and a social fact, and it is always the great historical events that divide the two generations in the social sense. Now, when discussing the impact of different types of mass media on human groups, including different generations, such theories are somewhat challenged. The development of the mass media itself can also be an effective tool to divide different generations. Of course, if we regard the leap-forward development of the media as a major historical event or even a historical period, we can easily turn such challenges into powerful theoretical assistance.

In 2001, just as humanity was entering the new century, American author, educator, and game designer Mike Prensky proposed that, over the past 20 years, the rapid development of electronic media, especially the Internet, has divided two radically different generations: digital natives and digital immigrants. The former were born and grew up together with network technology over recent decades. They regard modern science and technology represented by the network as an inevitable part of their living environment. For them, using a computer or other electronic device is as natural as breathing air. Thus, you can call them the net generation or the digital generation, but the label Prensky finds most useful is the "digital natives". Today, our students are native speakers of digital languages such as computers, video games, and the Internet. The latter, in terms of age alone, would be adults over 40 or 50. The new digital environment that emerged in the 1990s was like a new continent to them. Accordingly, "as Digital Immigrants learn—like all immigrants, some better than others—to adapt to their environment, they always retain, to some degree, their 'accent', that is, their foot in the past" (Prensky, 2001). In 2008, when Hu Yong, a budding communicator, read Mike Prensky's short but surprisingly imaginative essay, obviously, while accepting the two wonderful concepts of digital natives and digital immigrants, he was also shocked by Prensky's description of the young Americans or the so-called "digital natives":

> Currently, before graduating from college, the average American teenagers spend nearly 10,000 hours playing video games, send and receive 200,000 emails and chat messages, spend 10,000 hours talking, playing games and downloading data on mobile phones, watch TV for more than 20,000 hours (fast-switching MTV is their favorite), view about half a million TV commercials—at the same time, they read only about 5,000 hours.
>
> (Hu, 2008: 367)

As two living generations in today's world, digital natives and digital immigrants are radically different not only in the way they receive information and the time they spend on it, but also in the way they operate. In his essay, Prensky enumerates the "accents" of the digital immigrants: They often print their mails out to read or save,[15] while those who ask secretaries to do it for them are even more "provincial"; they also often pull people into their offices to look at an interesting website, rather than sending it out to others. By contrast, digital natives are accustomed to receiving information very quickly, preferring to multitask, preferring diagrams over text, and preferring random access (as in hypertext). They are excited when they go online, like instant affirmation and frequent rewards, and prefer games to "serious" work (Prensky, 2001).

Do not assume that the difference in electronics or digital usage between generations is only happening in Prensky's world tech powerhouse, the United States, the phenomenon of giants and dwarfs in the electronic world that we described in Chapter 5 of the first volume of this book has become a global intergenerational landscape. This distinction between giant and midget has nothing to do with physical height, or even with spiritual nobility and inferiority; it is only related to age. Take what we call the digital generation here. Although China's comments on the generation that grow up with globalization and the Internet after the 1990s vary, almost all pre-80s think that they are really not our species, and the main factor that causes this "new species" to appear is the emergence of the Internet and the information age that follows it in leaps and bounds.

> In this age, proficiency coexists with non-proficiency. They were born in the Internet age with a mouse in their mouth. The degree of their proficiency in computer control makes parents and other "newbies" unable to supervise, so "Green Dam" (an Internet filtering software) is indeed a helpless choice. Now an 11-year-old primary school student in Beijing has to do his homework in PPT format, while his father doesn't even know what the PPT template is.
>
> (Xiao, 2010: 191)

Also based on globalization, what happened in China, a big developing country, is just as common in other developing countries today. Sometimes, in the absence of strong state control, the picture of change created by the development of the Internet in the developing world is even more startling than in China:

> When Aung San Suu Kyi was first released, she took a knee-jerk step back from supporters holding up their cell phones to take pictures of her. She had never used a cell phone, and when she was asked to talk to her youngest son, Kim, in Bangkok, she wasn't sure the gadget would actually connect people. She didn't even know where to speak. The world had changed so much that while there was no Twitter or Facebook, and mobile phones were not popular enough, let alone developed into an omnipotent mobile terminal, when she was placed under house arrest for the third time in 2003, now, the Internet and its generation have changed the world, and perhaps Myanmar too. On many occasions, she said that one of the happiest things in this year was to see more young people participating in movements.
>
> (Yang, 2012)

While China today does not have the same space as Myanmar to engage in radical social movements, the Internet is creating a space for younger generations that their parents never had. We found in the interview that many children, or the younger generation, not only learn information and things that their parents did not know through the Internet, but also form their unique hobbies and lifestyles through the Internet. During the interview in Nanjing, I met NNB who was 19 years old. The boy, who graduated from Nanjing Foreign Language School last year and enrolled in his freshman year at the University of Rochester, hoped to major in biomedical engineering, but his hobby was bodybuilding. NMB, one of NNB's high school classmates, said that NNB used to be a good basketball player, especially a very good shot, but he was not as well-known for this as he was later for bodybuilding.

> After all, there are a lot of good basketball players in our school, but it was different when he became a bodybuilder. He was the undisputed "alpha male" of our grade. Now whenever students talk about NNB, they say, "Oh, that guy. He's strong."
>
> (NMB, 2013)

NNB's mother, who studied computer science and later worked in technical management, could not explain why her son was interested in bodybuilding. Actually, NNB's first idea for bodybuilding probably came from his deskmate, whose love of physical fitness stimulated NNB to a certain extent by reading in front of him magazines like *Health and Beauty* and *Bodybuilder*. But his motivation for later bodybuilding came from the Internet, or the microblog of professional bodybuilders.

> NNB expanded his network by practicing fitness. Although he was young, he was often in contact with various members of society, far from his age. For example, in his first vacation after studying abroad, when he just came back from abroad for a few days, there were engineers and general managers who invited him to dinner now and then. I asked him why the general manager wanted to have dinner with him, and he replied he was a buddy he had met in the gym back home. But it's probably the Internet that has helped him the most with his fitness. Through the Internet, he not only establishes regular contact with a large group of bodybuilding enthusiasts, and frequently exchanges experience and knowledge about bodybuilding with them, but also turns directly to professional athletes for advice. One day, when he was still in middle school, he said to me excitedly, "Mom, that man talked to me!" I said, "Who talked to you?" He replied, "Ronnie Coleman. Don't you remember? The strongest man in the history of bodybuilding!" I took a closer look, and it was. NNB emailed Ronnie on his twitter address, and the African-American, who had been crowned "Mr. Olympia" for seven consecutive years, replied, giving him his home address. NNB would talk to Coleman about fitness and ask him about his physical or strength statistics, such as how thick the arms are, how many pounds to squat, and how many pounds to lift the legs. One time NNB asked Coleman in a skeptical tone, "They say you can lift 1080 pounds in

a squat. You might not be able to lift it, right?" As a result, Coleman gave an ambiguous answer, which I can't remember was "should be" or "may be", probably "should be". You see how much help the Internet has given him.

(NNM, 2013)

NNB's friendship with Ronnie Coleman reminds me of Negroponte's friendship with another high school student, Michael Schrage, who also made personal connections with Internet gurus like Negroponte through the Internet. And as Schrage's father said, he met all kinds of people online, and most surprising of all, "all sorts of people, Nobel Prize winners and senior executives, seemed to have time for Michael's questions. The reason is that it is so easy to reply" (Negroponte, 1995: 202–203). But do not assume that the Internet is simply a way for young people to meet celebrities, get fit, or, more broadly, indulge a wide variety of personal interests. In fact, the Internet and the resulting digital way of life, as Negroponte said, make computing no longer just about computing, but something that determines our survival (Negroponte, 1995: 15). For example, the nature of the job market will change dramatically as we use fewer atoms and more bits; as businesses become more global and the Internet grows, there will be fully digital offices; the mass media will be redefined as a system for sending and receiving personal information and entertainment, and "as we interconnect ourselves, many of the values of a nation- state will give way to those of both larger and smaller electronic communities" (Negroponte, 1995: 7).

In fact, like Prensky, Negroponte sees the biggest change in the online world as the "upending" of two generations. Convinced that each generation of humanity will be more digital than the last, the founder of the new media lab has no doubt that "the control bits of that digital future are more than ever before in the hands of the young" (Negroponte, 1995: 231). As a citation, Rainie Lee, in "Digital 'natives' invade the workplace", brilliantly describes the gap between the two generations facing the digital world through a 22-year-old college student: "I'm the one living in the digital world. Playing with more equipment, for my father, is work, and for me, is life" (Lee, 2006). As a result, advocates of digital society, such as Negroponte and Prensky, naturally agree that human society is facing huge discontinuity as never before—a gap between generations. The brains and ways of thinking of the young or digital natives are very different from ours or those of the digital immigrants. The human dilemma is related to this: Our generation of digital immigrants who speak outdated languages are educating digital natives who have mastered new languages!

Prensky came up with all sorts of ideas for how humans could get out of this dilemma. While these ideas may not actually solve the problem, at least two of Prensky's assumptions are valuable. For one, we must acknowledge that the brains of the young and digital natives have changed, and that we do not know much about their new world, so we should humbly use their help to learn about and integrate into this new world. We must strive to learn to communicate with them in their language and manner, which means faster learning, less rigidity in behavior, more synchronic and parallel learning, and the ability to randomly shift to other events. What's more, after this huge break, human learning has split in two: the traditional contents, including reading, writing, arithmetic, logical thinking, understanding of past works and thoughts; and future contents, which are mostly about digitization and technology, including software, hardware, robotics, nanotechnology, and genetics, as well as the new ethics, politics, sociology, and linguistics that come with them (Prensky, 2001). Obviously, if we want to continue to be educators, we need to find ways to use digital natives' languages to teach these traditional and future contents.

Like the title of Chapter 4, Volume 3 of Negroponte's book, *Digital Life*, the best way to combine educational contents and methods in the Internet age, as Prensky suggests, is to "learn from games". From MIT Professor Nicholas Negroponte to online game designer Prensky, they have repeatedly argued that we can embed skill learning in games. Thus, just as Prensky believes that educational games are not whimsy, but reason rather than illusion (Prensky, 2001), Negroponte also believes that

> most adults fail to see how children learn with electronic games. The common assumption is that these mesmerizing toys turn kids into twitchy addicts and have even fewer redeeming features than the boob tube. But there is no question that many electronic games teach kids strategies and demand planning skills that they will use later in life.
>
> (Negroponte, 1995: 204)

And, of course, if you think about it differently, not all things brought by the network society or information technology are beautiful things; there are also hidden dangers. Among them, the increasingly popular mass media and network information technology make it possible for the virtual environment to replace the natural environment of people, especially children, so that children may lose their innocence (Li, 2001). Children and teenagers spend a lot of time on TV, computers, or video games, as a result, their reading time is greatly reduced and their thinking becomes flat (Odland, 2004), and they gradually lose their interest in real social life to become "otaku" and even "otaku babies". Because human interactions are increasingly conducted through virtual worlds or cyberspace, this leads to "people being online all the time. In the cyberspace, spreading new technologies can bring tens of thousands of friends or fans, but human beings are lonelier than ever" (Cao & Zhuang, 2013). Further, because of the advance of Internet technology, young children rush into the virtual world or cyberspace in advance. Intelligent electronic devices such as iPads or iPhones have aroused great interest among children, and technological alienation transforms the young population of the global village into the "play labor" of the online society— people who play games on the Internet. They provide a kind of free labor for information manufacturers like Apple or Microsoft, and become an indispensable link in the global expansion chain of capitalism in the information age (Kucklich, 2005; Qiu, 2009).

In recent years, more and more Chinese scholars pay attention to the hidden dangers brought by the network society or information technology. In 2012, Cao Jin, a communications scientist, studied nearly 100 middle-class families in Yangpu district, where Fudan University is located, and found that developing countries like China are vulnerable to technology myths, making it easier for middle-class parents to consider computer skills as an important aspect of their children's abilities. Thus, with the popularization of multimedia terminals represented by tablet computers and smart phones in Chinese society, children's leisure time is increasingly occupied by various new media devices. However, when training information skills, improving media literacy, and assisting children in learning become the most common reasons for children to be exposed to a large number of new media, they will not just get entertainment and computer skills, but also become "qualified" consumers and young "play labors" in the information society, and they have used their supposedly colorful childhood to provide multinationals with the most tamed and fun-loving market available (Cao & Zhuang, 2013).

Information is power

As I write this subheading, I naturally think of a quote from science historian Michael Saylor about the information revolution. In his recent book *The Mobile Wave: How Mobile Intelligence Will Change Everything*, the CEO of MicroStrategy, a company with a dual interest in human history and information technology, wrote:

> The Agricultural Revolution took thousands of years to transform vast tracts of land, populated by nomads, into cities, towns and villages around the world. The Industrial Revolution imposed its massive socio-economic changes over a period of a few hundred years. By simple extrapolation, we might expect that the Information Revolution will require tens of years to achieve pervasive changes in our lives and businesses.
>
> (Saylor, 2013: 229)

Saylor's confidence in the information revolution came from his insight into human history and the nature of information itself. In terms of human history, the information revolution can be regarded as a significant historical progress of human society comparable with the agricultural revolution and industrial revolution. The information revolution can be traced back to the appearance of cuneiform script in 4,000 BC, but its large-scale impact on human society begins with the invention of Gutenberg printing in the 15th century, which was inspired by the Chinese movable type printing. The advent of the telegraph and telephone in the 19th century extended the coverage and immediacy of the information revolution, and the emergence and popularization of mass media such as radio and television from 1920 to 1950 further enhanced the coverage and immediacy of information.

In terms of information itself, it is its particularity that gives the information revolution unprecedented power. Saylor realizes that first, although information is the "core energy" of the revolution, it is not the same as physical energy sources like fuel or electricity; in fact, all human actions create new information, so it is constantly increasing. Second, unlike oil or electricity, every drop of information has a different energy value. For example, "The house is on fire" has much more energy than "The temperature is 68 degrees Fahrenheit". Furthermore, for different consumers of information, even the same "drop" of information can produce completely different energy values. The dollar's exchange rate against the euro, for example, has a completely different energy value for currency traders and taxi drivers. Third, the energy sources of oil or electricity are a superposition, with ten drops of oil or ten kilowatt-hours of electricity containing ten times as much energy as a drop of oil or a kilowatt-hour of electricity, but the information energy content is exponentially distributed. In other words, a collection of information droplets may contain much more energy than the sum of the individual droplets. For example, the total production of wheat in a given year is valuable information, and information on the total yield of wheat over ten years, plus the rainfall data and fertilization conditions during the same period, makes 30 times the amount of information, but it may contain 100 times the information energy. Obviously, the trend and related effects it presents will lead to more decisions (Saylor, 2013: 255).

It is because information is so powerful, and there is so much information in modern society,[16] that faced with an information explosion, almost all theorists will emphasize the technical capabilities related to information acquisition. Manuel Castells, for one, believes that

> the information technology revolution induced the emergence of informationalism, as the material foundation of a new society. Under informationalism, the generation of wealth, the exercise of power, and the creation of cultural codes came to depend on the technological capacity of societies and individuals, with information technology as the core of this capacity.
>
> (Castells, 2010b: 372)

In today's information society, almost all service industries, especially those high-end services where technology is king, are, after all, professions dealing with information. Aviation scheduling, for example, uses flight, airport, and weather data to determine aircraft movements and landings; investment bankers make decisions on corporate financing, mergers and acquisitions, sales and trading of financial products such as stocks and bonds, as well as asset management and venture capital business based on trading information in the financial markets; insurance companies use risk information to evaluate policies; doctors use physical information (e.g., electrocardiograms, imaging data, blood biochemical indicators) to develop treatment plans; teachers choose the appropriate content from the vast amount of relevant information to instruct students of different ages; even supermarket clerks deal with customers' transaction information every day; and bus drivers have to use traffic information to choose a smooth route.

Thanks to the development of computers, the Internet, and all kinds of software, we are now able to gather information at a speed we have never seen before. For developed countries with high computer penetration rates, as mentioned above, collecting information and processing data through electronic computers is of great convenience. In developing countries including China, mobile phones, which are increasingly developed to personal handheld computers and mobile terminals through 3G or 4G technology, provide ordinary white-collar workers and even grassroots people with convenient access to daily information. For example, the use of mobile phones enables: Tanzanian fishermen to easily collect weather information, enhance cooperation in fishing, deal with emergencies, and negotiate prices for seafood (Myhr & Nordstrom, 2006); migrant workers in India, Mozambique, and Tanzania to respond to emergencies, maintain family relationships, and save on living expenses (Souter et al., 2005); small businessmen in Rwanda to better broaden their business vision, adjust their working place and procedures (Donner, 2005: 39); and migrant workers in the Pearl River Delta in China to obtain employment information sent by friends, former workers, and employers, thus improving their employability (Ngan & Ma, 2008). The mobile phone survey we mentioned in Chapter 5 of the first volume of this book also found that for low and middle income groups, mobile phones are not communication tools in the general sense, but more of a means of livelihood. For example, even those "bangbangs" who live at the bottom of society in Chongqing and work as porters for others are also now using mobile phones for business. For a bangbang without a mobile phone, he can only rely on another bangbang who does have a mobile phone to get daily job opportunities (Zhu, 2011).

While everyone, from airline dispatchers and venture capital managers to Tanzanian fishermen and Chongqing bangbangs, has benefited from the information revolution, the undisputed reality is that the millions of people caught up in the maelstrom of the information revolution differ greatly in how they get information and the quantity and quality of that information. If we call this huge difference in access to information the "digital divide", we can find that in the popularization process of almost all information communication technology (ICTs), there is an insurmountable divide between different users in various fields such as mobile phones, computers, and the Internet and broadband. Some people think that this difference can be regarded as the technology divide, which is caused by the technical differences between developed countries and developing countries, and between the middle class and grassroots people in developing countries in the application of ICTs (*The Economist*, 2005). Some other people think that this difference is an economic divide, that is to say, the digital divide essentially reflects the imbalance of economic development. The International Telecommunication Report, for one, confirms that there is an association between the level of development of ICTs and income, and that this is becoming more and more apparent over time (ITU, 2009: 271). We admit that the technology divide, the economic divide, and even the social divide caused by the stratification of the information society (Xue & Liu, 2010) reveal the profound significance of the digital divide regarding different aspects, but the problem is that none of the existing concepts can explain why there is a stark digital divide in countries and regions with the same economic and social development conditions, or in social groups at the same level of education, occupation, class, and income, or between parents and children, and between the older generation and the younger generation, within the same family. Although some, such as the International Telecommunication Union (ITU), recognize that demographic characteristics, including age, sex, race, income, and urban and rural area, are all linked to the digital divide (ITU, 2009: 45), no one refers to the digital divide just as an "intergenerational divide" as we do (Zhou, 2011a).

When we say that the digital divide is an intergenerational divide, we do not mean something that is merely subjective imagination. According to the statistical report on the development of the Internet in China, by the end of June 2019, 65.1% of China's 854 million Internet users were under the age of 40, while the number of Internet users over 40 was declining rapidly. The 20–29 age group was 24.6%, 40–49 age group was 17.3%, the over-50 age group was 13.6% (CNNIC, 2019), so it is true that the number of ICT users is declining with age. In the last ten years, the elder's disadvantage in the use of electronic computers has become increasingly obvious with the popularization of computer networks, as well as the structural complexity of computer hardware and the functional complexity of software. Home computers are far faster than they used to be in terms of information processing speed and hard disk capacity, especially with all kinds of operating and editing software. You can use a computer to process words, translate between languages, edit and typeset, make graphics and tables, process digital or quantitative or even qualitative data, and make Power-Point documents; you can also use it to download text or photos, make photo folders, watch movies and TV, find maps or weather forecasts; you can even use it to send emails, participate in discussions on bulletin boards (BBS) and Forum, write blogs or microblogs, and share your radio or TV programs by sending audio or video files. Clearly, the more computer and network technologies are developed, the more disadvantaged parents become. Just operating the computer and surfing the Internet is not easy for many less-educated parents, because it requires operational ability, professional knowledge, and even a good foundation of English (although there are more and more Chinese materials on the Internet, many materials and information on the Internet are still in English), which makes most parents feel powerless. Therefore, it is indisputable that since children have the advantages of computer operation and language use, combined with their great energy and wide range of interests, they basically monopolize the "discourse power" of the Internet and its information. It is further conceivable that this intergenerational divide in information access cannot but have an immeasurable impact on the values, attitudes, perspectives, participation abilities, and even survival opportunities of the two generations.

In fact, the differences between parents and children are not only reflected in the skills of information acquisition, but also in the content of information acquisition. Although in theory parents can also watch TV, listen to the radio, or surf the Internet and tweet, in real life, they tend to be distracted by work and family affairs, have a single interest, and have a poor ability to obtain information, so the amount and quality of knowledge and information they obtain from television, the Internet, or other mass media are not as good as those of their children. In our interviews, many parents said that after a hard day at work and housework, they would naturally choose something relaxing to watch: football games (father), romantic dramas or soap operas (mother), but for their curious children, the conflict in Bosnia and Herzegovina, the US–Iraq war, the feminist movement, the Indonesian riots, green food, Microsoft technology, viral mutations, the NBA, and the financial crisis all arouse their keen interest. If young children, as Guo Yuhua's research shows, often only get knowledge about food and toys from TV (Guo, 1998), the teens and twenties we are studying are learning much more from television, newspapers, and other media. But this is only the first step, and the content that children get on the Internet is incredibly rich. For trendy parents, the main way to get online is through so-called "portals" like Sohu, Sina, and Netease, where they learn the simple information technology of browsing the news, and the information they get is mostly the news on the home page of these websites. However, for children, they can get almost any information they want through the Internet. They can use the Internet to find MTV clips of singers they are interested in, search or download movies of videos, search for homework materials, and solicit votes for Yao Ming to enter the NBA all-star game, which is often not accessible to their parents. In this way, children become very comfortable with the vast amount of information on the Internet.

Like the Tanzanian fisherman or the Chongqing bangbang, SCB from Shanghai is also a beneficiary of the spread of information technology, but the young "rich second generation" uses information far more technologically than the average migrant worker. SCB got average grades in middle school, and the Shanghai Petrochemical Junior College he later attended was far from a prestigious university, but his major—computing—satisfied him. After graduation, it was difficult to find a job, so SCF, who was engaged in a sales agency of the wine industry, asked his son to assist him in the company. At the beginning, SCB had no interest in "selling wine", but had to do it because of his father's urging. Just at this time, online shopping began to catch on in China. Led by a number of shopping websites, such as Taobao, Tmall, Dangdang, JD, and Suning, online sales had surged. For example, in 2014, the annual sales of Taobao alone reached 1.8 trillion CNY, and the one-day sales of singles' day (November 11) exceeded 60 billion CNY. So SCB, with his quick mind and professional skills, quickly proposed to his father SCF to act as the agent of Zhejiang "Tower" yellow wine and set up a flagship store on yhd.com to sell it. SCF accepted his son's advice and left him in charge. After just over a year, the yellow rice wine sold by SCF and SCB on yhd.com, known as the "online supermarket", entered the top three online sellers and increased the overall sales volume of SCF's Tianyuan Wine Industry by 40%. Now SCB was considering setting up a Tianyuan flagship store on Yes My Wine, China's largest B2C Wine sales platform, to help his father expand his online reach beyond yellow wine into other wine.

Further, the impact of computer and Internet technology on our lives, and especially on intergenerational relationships, has been fueled in the last decade by what Saylor calls the "tipping point" of the information revolution—mobile technology—fueled by the proliferation of mobile phones and iPads. As we all know, in the process of the information revolution, the emergence of business computer information processing technology in the 1960s is a key step. If the use of the steam engine contributed to the emergence of the Industrial Revolution, then computer information processing technology is the "steam engine" of the information revolution. But just as the discovery of electricity was the tipping point of the Industrial Revolution, the next step, the advent of mobile computing, is more important. It is mobility that makes all previous applications more valuable because it has the following advantages: eternity (24 hours, 7 days a week), instant access (wireless network), convenience (various applications), and accessibility (lower cost) (Saylor, 2013: 254).

If the media and information revolution driven by Internet technology brings about a revolution in the content and way of information acquisition, then by combining with mobile computing technology, the information revolution truly brings about an all-round change in the way of human life. Communication master McLuhan once said that any new media is an evolutionary process, because it opens the door to new areas of perception and activity. The medium is not only information, but also all human cultures (McLuhan, 1994: 422). In this sense, the media and information revolution we are talking about is not only the product of social change, but also social change itself. Accordingly, the differences between parents and children in the content, ability, and way of obtaining information are in fact part of the transformation of human life style. Thirty years ago, or even twenty years ago, parents who controlled the use of home phones by their teenage children (it was almost a routine sight of urban Chinese families three decades ago that parents sat by the telephone in the living room after dinner to control their children's so-called "bad interactions") were almost the only "social presence" or partner these only children had outside school. But after 2000, the spread of the Internet, especially mobile web technologies like the iPhone or iPad, allowed children to break out of their parents' control, Through QQ, Renren, blog, and especially WeChat, which developed rapidly, they were able to keep close communication with their partners from the moment they step into their house until they go to bed. This time–space extension of peer group communication not only replaces the traditional top-down communication between parents and children, but also forms a new communication and lifestyle for children.

As a matter of fact, with the development of mass media, computers, and the Internet, children are not only likely to be separated from their parents, but also from their teachers, classrooms, and textbooks, and gain knowledge and information often unheard of by parents, teachers, and other adults. This has become the most important way for them to acquire the "feedback" ability or "discourse power" in their interaction with parents, teachers, and even the whole adult world. In this book, we have presented a multi-dimensional picture of how children or younger generations gain discourse power through their excellent ability to acquire information in their interactions with parents or older generations. Further, if with the future development of mobile computing technology, actions like reading the morning paper, queuing to conduct banking business, checking in and out at the hotel, shopping in the mall, learning in the library, using the copier in the office, and waiting for others to clean up the paper copier all become what Saylor calls "old habits" that would be eliminated by automation, then the younger generation, who have a natural affinity for mobile software operating on mobile technology, may form a more distinct life guidance or "action hegemony" in the face of the older generation struggling in the mobile world. In this sense, in the future of mobile technology, younger generations will write more detailed historical footnotes to the belief that "information is power".

Notes

1 In the world of communication, an example of the power of radio is President Roosevelt's "fireside talk" during World War II. At that time, more than half of the 100 million Americans heard "fireside talk" on the radio, and he received an average of 4,000 letters from listeners every day (Zhan & Yang, 1991: 171–174). Hitler's path to power in Germany also benefited from total control of broadcasting, and simplification and repetition were the secret to the "success" of Nazi propaganda minister Joseph Goebbels. But it is cable broadcasting, as we have already discussed for China under Mao Zedong, that most controls ordinary people. Clearly, cable radio controls not only the audience's choice of media content, but also the freedom to listen and not listen.

2 There are two examples of the argument that television promotes rationality. For one, McLuhan said that if television had existed before Hitler, there would have been no such figure (McLuhan, 1994: 368). For another, in the 1960 U.S. presidential election, the debate between Kennedy and Nixon was televised live, and Kennedy won. Kennedy's victory was a bit lucky because most radio listeners thought Nixon would win and a few television viewers thought Kennedy would win. In that debate, more people watched TV than listened to the radio, so Kennedy won not only because he spoke beautiful words, but because he looked beautiful (Levinson, 2001: 99, 98).

3 Of course, I've always believed that every extension is an overuse of a sensory organ that eventually becomes a detriment to that organ. For example, the use of radios, tape recorders, and especially earphones causes damage to the ears, and the use of television, especially computers, causes damage to the eyes (I have also suffered from dry eye syndrome as a result of 20 years of writing on a computer). The

most comprehensive statement, therefore, should be that every medium is an extension of, and a detriment to, some sense organ.

4 In 1967, Milgram found through experiments that the average person can make contact with anyone they don't know through an average of less than six people, which is called "Six degrees of separation". Anthropologist Robin Dunbar suggested that the stable social network defined by human intelligence was 148 people, rounded to 150, and is known as the "Rule of 150" or "Dunbar's number". If these two laws are true, the number of people theoretically accessible through a network of six people is 150 to the sixth power, or 11,396,250 million. That's more than all the people in human history put together. Thus, network theorists assert that it is theoretically possible to connect with anyone in the world through six people.

5 After 1949, the political environment did not allow Yan Yangchu to continue to promote the rural construction movement anymore. After he was forced to leave, he expanded the original slogan of the Chinese People's Education Promotion Association from "eliminating illiteracy and be new citizens" at the beginning of its establishment to "eliminating worldwide illiteracy and be new citizens of the world". From the 1950s to the 1980s, civilian education organizations were set up in Thailand, the Philippines, India, Ghana, Colombia, Guatemala, Cuba, and other countries to continue to carry out the theory and experience summarized in the "Ding county experiment". In 1967, the International Institute of Rural Reconstruction (IIRR) was established in the Philippines. In 1943, Yan Yangchu, along with Einstein and Dewey, won the honor of "Ten Great Men with the Most Revolutionary Contributions in the Modern World" issued by the Copernicus Quadricentennial National Committee. He was honored as the "father of the world's civilian education" (Song, 2003: 3).

6 Most of the main characters in the 11 issues of male photos are related to the Anti-Japanese War after 1937, including Chiang Kaishek, Feng Yuxiang, Zhang Fakui, Bai Chongxi, Li Zongren, Zhu De, and "the new soldiers of China".

7 For example, the cover of the 69th issue was an image of a young and fit woman holding a tennis racket and wearing sportswear; the 77th issue showed the swimmer Yang Xiuqiong, who was called "mermaid" at that time, wearing simple and lightweight sportswear and full of strength and beauty; the cover of the 86th issue was Ms. Hu Die who was trying out riding a horse on the outskirts in spring; on the cover of issue 118 was a picture of a bodybuilding lady; the cover of issue 139, the "new era Chinese women" issue, was a picture of a woman in military uniform, holding a steel gun, and being gentle and containing masculinity; and the cover of the 148th issue was a picture of a new woman bending a bow and shooting arrows.

8 The exact words of the "two whatevers" are "Whatever decisions Chairman Mao makes, we firmly support them; whatever instructions Chairman Mao gives, we resolutely carry them out." The "two whatevers" was first proposed by Hua Guofeng and proposed by the editorial of "two newspapers and one magazine"— the *People's Daily*, the *People's Liberation Army Daily*, and the *Red Flag* magazine—on February 7, 1977.

9 On the contrary, it has been noted that a moderate amount of jealousy can often promote social competition and progress. For example, the anthropologist Homer Garner Barnett has long observed through his study of primitive peoples that the envious man is often deprived of resources and therefore has much less to lose in any new attempt, which often makes him an adventurer in social life or an agent of innovation (Barnett, 1953: 401–406).

10 The spring of 1979 was the first spring after China's social reform and opening-up. On January 25 of this year, Shanghai TV set up the advertising business section, and on January 28, the first commercial advertisement in the history of Chinese TV was born: the one-and-a-half-minute "Ginseng Tonic Wine" advertisement (Huang & Chen, 2006). Then, on March 9, a live international women's basketball match on Shanghai TV was interrupted by a TV advertisement for "happy coke". This ordinary

advertisement caught people in Shanghai, who had always thought they were well-informed, by surprise. It caused Shanghai viewers, who had gathered to watch because of the low TV penetration rate, to exclaim "Wrong broadcast! Wrong!", so much so that the next day the Shanghai newspaper had to print a message explaining that what was broadcast during the match was not a live broadcast of the match, but one of the first TV advertisements just shot by Shanghai TV. Then, on March 15, CCTV also broadcast the first foreign commercial advertisement—that of Citizen Watch in Japan, which was "famous all over the world" (Zhou, 1994: 2).

11 In 2011, CCTV's annual advertising revenue had reached 22.8 billion RMB, followed by Shanghai Oriental TV (7 billion RMB), Hunan TV (6 billion RMB), and Jiangsu TV (4.3 billion RMB) (The Member Department of China Advertising Association, 2012). In terms of individual columns, the top three programs in 2012 were CCTV's "News Broadcast" (4 billion RMB in advertising revenue), CCTV's "Focus Interviews" (3 billion RMB in advertising revenue), and "If You Are the One" (2 billion RMB in advertising revenue).

12 In the 1980s, in a developed society like the United States, the average person spent 20,000 hours watching TV from birth to the end of high school, but they accumulated no more than 14,000 hours of formal education in the classroom (Cutlip & Center, 1988: 351). Considering that the average viewing time over 18 years was 20,000 hours, and that the average daily viewing time was only three hours, it can be speculated that the average Chinese today watches as much TV as Americans did in the 1980s.

13 If you consider that China, a country with the second largest GDP in the world and the 87th largest per capita GDP in the world, ranked first in luxury consumption in 2012, you get an idea of the extent to which people, especially the affluent, worship "consumption" in China. A country that barely had enough to eat four decades ago has become a country where a materialist or consumerist ideology prevails.

14 In 1962, while David Ogilvy was making a name for himself as an international advertising scientist, his sister, Lady Hendy, advised him that advertising should be scrapped. Ogilvy calmly and presciently told his sister that advertising should not be abolished, but it must be reformed (Ogilvy, 1991: 149). So far, though advertising is getting better at technology, the transformation of its sense of social responsibility gets further and further away.

15 It's the same with me. Although I have been writing on a computer for more than 20 years, I always print out a page after finishing it. Over the years, I have also asked students to finish their assignments, print them out, put the text in my college mailbox, and repeat over and over again: "I do not accept electronic assignments."

16 In 2011, Walmart alone handled more than a million customer transactions an hour. Large companies like eBay, Bank of America, and Dell each manage a huge amount of data in petabytes (1,000 terabytes, or 10 raised to the power 15), while the global data volume has reached the level of zettabytes (10 trillion gigabytes, or 10 raised to the power 21). In fact, social networks have contributed a lot to the growth of data volume. In 2011, Facebook hosted more than 50 billion photos, equivalent to seven photos per person worldwide, and people shared 30 billion pieces of content every month. In 2006, Twitter appeared in the United States, and only six years later, it grew to 155 million tweets a day (Saylor, 2013: 256). On August 28, 2009, Sina microblog was launched in China. In July of the following year, the total number of microblogs generated by Sina alone exceeded 90 million, which means the average number of microblogs generated every day was more than 3 million, and the average number generated every second was nearly 40 (Sina.com, 2010). The number of users of WeChat created in October 2010 had reached 1.1 billion by June 2019, and the number of WeChat messages generated every day was countless.

4 What has been ushered in by cultural reverse?

Instead of rebelling directly against parental authority in favor of a contrary ethic, the modernizing Chinese sought to establish warmer and more sympathetic relationships with their parents. The ethic they championed was so innocent that, if understood by their parents, it could only make the latter proud. The significance of this pattern of revolt is that Chinese youth generally have steadfastly denied, under great provocation, any hostile feelings toward their parents in spite. Their need to speak of the goodness of parents has been an almost absolute imperative, which in turn reflects the intensity and completeness with which they have learned to repress their emotions of hostility and aggression.

Lucian Pye 1992

The modern dilemma concerning filial duty

Our fast-changing times, with their rapid economic development, changing social structures, increasing access to information, and the growing power of peer groups, have turned traditional intergenerational relationships on their head from 1978 to 2020. When the phenomenon of cultural reverse discussed in this book becomes a common way to reconstruct the intergenerational relations of Chinese society, it will also have an unprecedented impact on the long tradition and changing reality of this ancient nation.

The first to suffer from this turbulent tide of history is the concept of filial piety, which we discussed in detail in Chapter 2 of the first volume of this book, and the tradition of filial piety developed on this basis—because it is the concept of filial piety centered on "obedience" and "no violation" that lays down the most basic code of conduct for the traditional parent–child relationship in China (Zhou, 2008a). As we have explained, this code of conduct gives rural Chinese parents the right to educate their children, and further forms the basis of their daily authority, by forcing the younger generation to gradually accept it in daily life through the indoctrination of etiquette and custom, and then to become a part of traditional Chinese culture. Although "filial piety" is broad in content, its basic meaning is nothing more than "serving parents", "respecting parents", and "obeying parents"; in short, children must "try their best to obey and meet their parents' requirements and wishes" (Yang, 2008).

Children's filial duty is based on two motives. One is reward. Parents have worked so hard to raise their children, and have suffered so much for this, that the latter have to reward the former beyond adulthood. The other motive is justification. Children are filial to their parents, not only because they are loved by them, but also because they are "parents" and we are "children", which is what people call "justification". We do what corresponds to "justification". Xu Fuguan calls filial piety based on the above two motives "filial piety out of love" and "filial piety out of respect" (Xu, 1975), which are two different levels of filial piety. The former is based on emotional factors, which involve the mutual affection between parents and children, while the latter is based on rational factors, which involve the rational obedience of children to parents due to their different roles.

As the core of Confucian morality and Chinese tradition, filial piety has suffered from the tide of changes of modern times. It has experienced three major impacts in the past hundred years. The first onslaught began after 1840 and peaked around the May Fourth Movement of 1919. At this time, all sectors of society, led by the intelligentsia, began to challenge the rationality of filial piety, in addition a variety of "non-filial" trends of thought prevailed in the world. The reason why the filial piety advocated in China for thousands of years began to encounter a crisis and fall into its modern predicament is not only because people at that time "felt deeply the irrationality of filial piety from the perspective of children" because of the changes of the times (Ni, 2004), but also because Western influence was gradually spreading into China. The result of the Opium Wars allowed the Western colonists to drive straight into China with their powerful ships and cannons. In a series of humiliating treaties, the Chinese civilization, which had endured for thousands of years, was severely challenged, and the cultural superiority of its subjects was completely lost. Failure and humiliation began to cause people to question the national tradition and culture, including filial piety, and then to voice it negatively.

What can be understood is that the result of the Opium Wars first made the Chinese realize that what was backward with their civilization was the science and technology on which the strong ships and cannons were built. Therefore, Wei Yuan, who advocated "adopting the skills of the western countries to control them", clearly defined the strength of the West in terms of warships, firearms, and military training (Wei Yuan, 1998: 26). In 1861, Feng Guifen, who was the first to clearly express the idea of "Chinese knowledge as fundamental, and western knowledge as application", proposed a way to save the nation from its crisis by "taking Chinese traditional ethics as the basics, supplemented by the art of prosperity of various countries" (Feng, 1994: 84). Under the guidance of this thought, the Westernization school, which tried to "strengthen the nation" and "seek wealth" in the face of national crisis and collapse, naturally believed that "China's civil and military systems are far more advanced than those of the west, except for firearms" (Wen et al., 2002: 398). Thus, in almost the whole of the 19th century, even when the crisis came, the mainstream of Chinese thought was to stick to tradition. While introducing Western knowledge, the school advocating "Chinese knowledge as fundamental, and western knowledge as application" always kept it within a range acceptable to Chinese society, so as to maintain the ethics behind the system. At that time, "all those who talk about current affairs and teach western knowledge accept or agree with this proposition, and even the early reformists are the majority of those who advocate it" (Chen, 1982), so that for the time "the whole country has taken it for granted" (Liang, 1998: 97).

As we have already mentioned in Chapter 2 of the first volume of this book, the Westernization movement soon after, especially the Sino-Japanese War of 1894–1895, declared the end of "Chinese knowledge as fundamental, and western knowledge as application", and prompted the reformers represented by Kang Youwei to advocate the fundamental reform of China's system. However, the moral code and its core filial piety, based on Confucianism, were finally pushed to the forefront of the tide of reform. For example, by attacking the "three cardinal guides", Tan Sitong attacked the key point of traditional filial piety and advocated the equality between father and son. As the saying goes, "The son is the son of heaven, and the father is also the son of heaven. The status of the father is not earned by himself, but derived from generations. Therefore, father and son should be equal by nature" (Tan, 1981: 348). Although the reform that lasted from the Reform Movement of 1898 to the May Fourth New Culture Movement was often accompanied by the trend of restoration, it is just this "failure of the new, and restoration of the old" (Chen, 1959) that finally led to the emotional radicalization of the elites of the new culture movement. Therefore, Chen Duxiu advocated that "if we are determined to reform, everything should adopt the new methods of the western countries, and there is no need to make trouble with the myths about the essence of Chinese culture and national conditions" (Chen, 1984: 270). Qian Xuantong also believed that "in order to keep China alive and make the Chinese nation a civilized nation in the 20th century, the fundamental solution must be to abolish Confucianism and Taoism, especially the traditional Chinese language that records Confucian doctrine and Taoist demonology" (Qian, 1918). In such a radical atmosphere, Chen Duxiu, Li Dazhao, Hu Shi, Qian Xuantong, Lu Xun, and Zhou Zuoren, the giants of the new cultural movement, criticized the traditional concept of filial piety under the banner of "down with Confucius". Even Mao Zedong, who had read the *New Youth* and worshipped Chen Duxiu, did not hesitate to regard traditional Chinese thought and morality as "hypocrisy", and believed that only with "magnanimous people" could the reform be carried out fundamentally. In the eyes of the rebellious young Mao Zedong, Confucius was a symbol of the great power of the ideological circle, so that "there are many reasons for our opposition to Confucius, and we cannot help but oppose it simply because it monopolized China, prevented our intellectual circle from being free, and made us slaves to idols for two thousand years in repression" (Mao, 1995: 368).

But within a decade, the first shock of traditional filial piety began to wear off. Not only did the conservative Beiyang government advocate "respecting

Confucius and restoring ancient ways", but even the revolutionary Sun Yat-sen advocated "taking democracy from Europe and America as an example, while still integrating the old culture from thousands of years ago" (Sun, 1981: 560). In 1928, the national government of Nanjing decided to offer Confucius a sacrificial ceremony, requiring that "the day of Confucius' birth should be set as a national memorial day, and the words and deeds of Confucius should be narrated to show admiration" (The Ministry of the Interior, 1928). At the same time, in the name of Sun Yat-sen and the Three People's Principles, the national government elevated "carrying forward the inherent virtues of the Chinese nation" to "the highest guiding principle of the revolution", and "made loyalty, filial piety, benevolence, faith, righteousness and peace the guiding principles of the people", which should be "popularized" for all people to "follow proper customs" through such forms as "incorporating them into primary and middle school textbooks", "engraving them on steles", "hanging them on plaques", and "publicity speeches delivered anytime and anywhere" (The Ministry of Administration, 1994). In 1934, Chiang Kai-shek launched the New Life Movement with "the core of restoring traditional Chinese morality and advocating ethics, righteousness, integrity and shame". Although the aim of the movement was to "achieve the modernization of the Chinese people" (Chiang, 1946: 99), its foundation was still the traditional national morality. Chiang Kai-shek not only made "filial piety and observance of marital fidelity" the essence of the New Life Movement, but also regarded "filial piety for parents, respect for the elders, love for the country and defense of the nation" as an important content of school education and the basic requirements of life (He Riqu, 2013: 207). Three years later, because of the outbreak of the war of resistance against Japanese aggression, nationalist sentiments were running high, and the national government even tried to use traditional culture to unite the people. "Loyalty and filial piety" was regarded as "the foundation of the Republic of China" in the "Program for the founding of the People's Republic of China" adopted in 1938, which called upon "all the compatriots to show their utmost loyalty and filial piety to the state and the nation at this time of national crisis" (Supreme Council for National Defense, 1939), thus once again extending the object of filial piety to the country and nation.

If in the field of political life, the rulers, under internal and external pressures, had repeatedly invoked the traditional culture with loyalty and filial piety at its core as a means of rallying the people and inspiring the nation, in the realm of everyday life, although at this time, under the influence of the new ideological trend spread by the May Fourth Movement, the public, especially the urban youth, had shown a distinct modern tendency regarding the aspects of values as described in Chapter 2 of the first volume of this book, most people did not completely abandon the traditional concept of filial piety—they usually did not have a real conflict with their parents. When in conflict with their elders, the younger generation largely adopted the peaceful style of Lucian Pye, the American Sinologist whom we quoted at the outset. Further, as Pye continued to analyze in his book *The Spirit of Chinese Politics*, if generational conflicts were unavoidable:

> Another way in which the youth could make an oblique attack on parental authority was by following quite consciously a strategy of compliance while at the same time finding new areas for the expression of personality development beyond parental control. Parental authority could be accepted fully so long as this meant little more than adherence to the rituals of defer-ence within the home. Outside of the household the young Chinese felt free to seek a new world, and in doing so he told his parent little about what he discovered. This did not always entail a sharp conflict, for the individual could feel that he was complying with his old master even as he accepted new taskmasters. The young might turn to Western knowledge, something about which his father knew little, and believe, and make his father believe, that by becoming a dedicated physicist or modern scientist he was in fact bringing greater glory and honor to his family. By moving into a world completely removed the individual was able to escape from the tensions of parental control while claiming to be still respectful of traditional authority.
>
> (Pye, 1992: 113–114)

The second onslaught on China's traditional filial piety came after the victory of the Chinese revolution in 1949 and culminated in Mao Zedong's Cultural Revolution in 1966. The earth-shaking changes in Chinese society after 1949 and the establishment of a highly integrated social system made it possible to fully express the long-standing rebellious spirit of Mao Zedong as discussed in Chapter 2 of the first volume of this book. Traditional culture, including ances-tor worship and filial piety, once again bore the brunt of relentless criticism. In 1950, the Marriage Law of the People's Republic of China, the first law of the new China, emphasized the "freedom of marriage between men and women" and negated the "order of parents" by law. In 1956, Mao Zedong took the lead in criticizing traditional grand funerals and long bereavement, advocating cre-mation and the reform of funeral rites and customs (Mao, 1992).[1] At the same time, since the beginning of land reform and collectivization, ancestral halls, temples, genealogies, and public lands related to the traditional clan succession culture were confiscated or destroyed. Peasants who were mobilized smashed temples (Zhou, 1998a: 161), abolished genealogies of families and clans (He Riqu, 2013: 214–215), and destroyed and abandoned a large number of ances-tral halls (Zhu & Chen, 2009).

The impact of this devastating revolution on filial piety was, of course, far more dramatic than the comments of John King Fairbank and Edwin Reischauer, not just because of ideological radicalism, but because the sweeping social changes that took place after 1949 also hindered strict enforcement of the filial tradition in general. Anyone familiar with Chinese tradition knows that while filial piety is a virtue involving parent–child relationships, it is maintained partly on the condition that children inherit their parents' jobs or property—

children's filial piety to their parents can be the criterion for parents allocating to them their inheritance. This also shows that the intergenerational relationship in China is a reciprocal exchange relationship. As a result, older parents effectively control their adult children's filial piety and other behaviors until they die. However, after the revolution in 1949, the situation changed a lot, and the urban and rural elderly began to face different circumstances.

First the countryside. After the cooperation in 1953 and the people's commune in 1958, the collectivization movement that swept through rural China made land, livestock, and tools to be owned collectively by people's communes, which led to the middle-aged generation in rural areas basically losing their absolute power to restrict their children. This change accelerated the disintegration or collapse of traditional filial piety. American sociologist Deborah Davis-Friedmann noticed when she studied the intergenerational relationship of Chinese society that, before 1949, the sons of poor farm laborers, who had little family property, basically took over the decision-making power in family affairs when they reached their prime, but in the average family, because parents had property, they still had control over their adult children. However, collectivization eliminated the resources held by the parents before liberation, and by the end of the 1970s, this model, previously popular in the families of ordinary farm laborers and poor peasants, had become the mainstream model in the families of all economic classes in the countryside (Davis-Friedmann, 1991: 81). Similarly, Guo Yuhua's field studies in rural Hebei province also found that decades of revolution had led to a decline in the status of the elderly. Specifically,

> they have no assets, no property, no honor to pass on to the next generation, or that they have nothing to give in exchange for something in return, which means a change in the economic basis of the pay-reward intergenerational ethical relationship.

It further led to the crisis of filial piety in rural areas and even the difficulty of supporting the elderly (Guo, 2001).

Compared with the rural elderly, the urban elderly fared better. A 1994 study in Baoding, Hebei province, by Martin Whyte, an American sociologist, found that "most older urban Chinese are very satisfied with their lives and their relationships with their children". In answering the question of why filial piety had retained more power in modern cities than in more traditional rural areas, Whyte found that the survival of filial piety in urban China was linked to parents' higher economic and social status. It is precisely because the urban elderly enjoy higher pensions, more spacious housing, and medical treatment that today a considerable proportion of them can live apart from their adult children, and they can also be financially independent. At the same time, when they need support, support can come from both sons and married daughters (Whyte, 2003: 303–304). In fact, as we mentioned in Chapter 2, not only did the elderly no longer have to rely on the young, but they could even help the younger generation in terms of housing, living expenses, and career access. This unique mode of pay–reward alleviated the impact of radical ideological revolution on filial piety in this period to some extent. Except for the radical parent–child conflicts that occurred during the Cultural Revolution in 1966, the concept of filial piety among ordinary urban residents is still largely preserved by the children's material dependence on their parents. But outside the family, generational tensions and conflicts have never been higher. Because of the devastating "great rebellion" of the younger generation and the crazy trampling on the "dignity of teachers", the older generation has become more disappointed and vigilant towards the latter; the younger generation, abandoned by the "revolution" or "rebellion", and facing various obstacles in real society, also become more suspicious and resentful of the former than ever before.

The third shock to China's traditional filial piety began in 1978 with the reform and opening-up, and which peaked in the post-1992 market wave. To be frank, the reform and opening-up, to a certain extent, made up for the multiple fissures, including intergenerational conflicts, in Chinese society caused by the Cultural Revolution. The reopening of universities and the return of "old cadres", and the various changes that had taken place during this period, offered the best opportunity in life for both the young and the old. At this time, with the abandonment of the radical revolution, the country "revived the great Chinese civilization" and advocated "critically inheriting all the fine moral traditions in human history" (CPC Central Committee, 1986). As an echo, the academic circle also began to reiterate that filial piety is a "traditional virtue with Chinese characteristics", which "should not only be discussed, but also be discussed enthusiastically" (Yan, 1983). In this context, the metaphor of filial piety begins to imply hard work, responsibility, and selflessness. There is no inevitable conflict between being a filial son and a good communist (Davis-Friedmann, 1991: 69).

However, the rapid social changes triggered by the reform and opening-up does not provide a realistic basis for the revival of filial piety. On the contrary, more and more rapid social changes shake the realistic foundations of Chinese tradition in different aspects. For example, in terms of political concepts, while promoting the progress of Chinese society, changes also excessively raise the expectations of Chinese people, especially the younger generation, regarding the progress of their own country. In the first ten years, the rapid economic growth and inflation brought by price reform increased the dissatisfaction and anxiety of ordinary people while providing them with a better life. The opening of the market and the dual-track system of price made the first batch of "tide riders" of the market economy and the children of cadres engaged in "official corruption" to "get rich first" (Zhou, 2010), which increased the "sense of relative deprivation" of the public and even general cadres. Finally, due to the openness and the relatively free contact with Western society and Western ideological trends, the difference of views between the veteran cadres who fought for the revolution and the students who were accustomed to a comfortable life was further widened (Vogel, 2012: 566). First in late 1986, then in May–June 1989, the anxieties and grievances of the younger generation about a society that was already changing rapidly poured out violently through mass street rallies.

In fact, differences in political views are not the main reason for the intergenerational conflict and the decline of filial piety in Chinese society. Soon, as we have already seen in Chapter 3 of the first volume of this book, the gap between the younger generation and their not conservative elders was completely closed by Deng Xiaoping's policy of further reform and opening-up. However, as the political passion faded, the social transformation triggered by the transition from planned economy to market economy posed new challenges to traditional intergenerational relations. After 1992, with more and more young people going into business or going out to work, with the frequent "de-regionalization" of the population in urban and rural society, and with the promotion of the one-child policy and the change of family size and form, the traditional family structure and the foundation of intergenerational relationship in Chinese society were changed. This change finally eliminated the status and power of the older generation in the family, and traditional filial piety received a fatal blow.

With the causes of the eventual breakdown of traditional filial piety carefully sorted out, we may mention some of these factors. First, because young people are more attuned to the market, which in turn pays according to the market price of one's human capital or contribution to distributable outcomes. In both urban and rural areas of China after 1992, the income of young people began to exceed that of their parents, who generally had no economic accumulation during the Mao Zedong era. This made the domination or control of the older generation over the younger generation lose its economic or practical basis. For example, Yan Yunxiang's field research in Xiakuan village in Heilongjiang province found that villagers' "family property was mainly gathered during the reform period. During this period, the younger generation has proved that it is more adaptable to the market economy than the older generation" (Yan, 2006: 207), so most of the latter could but accept the fact that their children were in charge. They also gradually became resigned to their children's "disobedience". Second, social changes have brought about frequent population movements. The Sixth National Census conducted in 2010 confirmed that the floating population in Chinese society had reached 260 million, and the number of people who had mobile experience—including those previously from rural or inland areas who had settled down in cities or coastal areas—was even higher. We have argued that the greatest erosion of intergenerational relationships by de-regionalization flows in both geographical boundaries and old relationships is that they weaken parental control over offspring. Take the famous Zhejiang village in Beijing in the 1990s. Tens of thousands of young farmers from Yueqing Hongqiao, Wenzhou gathered in the Dahongmen area of Beijing. They made their own way by engaging in the production and trading of clothing, shoes, and hats, not only taking root in Beijing, but also breaking away from the traditional restrictions of Wenzhou rural communities, including elders' rights (Zhou, 1998a). Third, if market factors lead to the decline of the status of the elderly and mobility factors make young people "out of reach" for the elderly, then the one-child policy has led to changes in the family structure in China, and children have become more important than ever. After 1980, due to the promotion of the one-child policy and the change of Chinese people's parenting concepts, there are fewer and fewer traditional large-sized stem families or joint families and a large number of miniaturized nuclear families (the average population of Chinese families is only 3.1 people, according to the Sixth National Census), which changes the relative importance of parents and children in family life. Since most families have only one child, the "4–2–1" family structure tilts the focus of the family. This, as we have argued extensively in this book, has turned the lives of not only parents but also grandparents around their children. The needs of the child become the needs of the adult, the desires of the child become the desires of the adult, and the child becomes the ultimate master of a family's choices and decisions.

The reason I call the changes in Chinese society in the last 30 years or so the "real fatal blow" to the millennia-old tradition of filial piety is that the first two strikes were, in the strict sense, nothing more than a revolution in ideas or a subversion of ideas. They simply declared the irrationality of traditional filial piety in different ways. However, both the May Fourth Movement and the Cultural Revolution failed to overturn the social and economic basis on which the traditional intergenerational relationship and the tradition of filial piety were formed in terms of family structure and lifestyle, except for the appeal of ideas. In fact, as long as the Chinese live together, as long as the young are dependent on their elders, and as long as the elders have the economic or social power to hold the young in check, complaints, dissatisfaction, and even resistance are ultimately unable to change the subordinate status of the young; and even the abandoned filial piety will eventually return to life as the basic rules of intergenerational relations. We have seen that in the pre-1949 and post-1949 periods, once the younger generation that first revolted against the irrationality of adult society becomes the dominant one, they still unconsciously inherit the traditional intergenerational relationship principle that they had abandoned earlier, when they maintained or carried forward the original scorned filial piety in different ways. This is also the fundamental reason for the rise and fall of the revolutions around intergenerational relations and filial piety.

The technique of balance: giving directions without undermining parental authority

Although we have repeatedly stated that "obedience" and "no violation" are not only the core of the concept of filial piety, but also the most basic code of conduct to deal with the parent–child relationship in traditional China for thousands of years, we have also repeatedly stated that the content of "filial piety" is very broad, and it almost involves every aspect of the parent–child relationship and even the intergenerational relationship, including at least three aspects: serving parents, respecting parents, and obeying parents. In recent years, by analyzing the contents of 3,760 journal articles concerning "filial piety" from 1869 to

2009, He Riqu has operationalized the connotation of filial piety by dividing it into seven aspects: support, care-taking, respect, humble advice, love, consolation, and funeral sacrifice (He Riqu, 2013: 261). If carefully analyzed, it can be found that, although each of these seven aspects has its own independent meaning, support and care-taking basically belong to serving parents; respect, funeral sacrifice, love, and consolation belong to respecting parents; and humble advice belongs to obeying parents. More radically, so-called filial piety, according to Chinese folk belief, indicates that obedience is its core, or at least that it mainly includes the material "support" of parents and spiritual "obedience" to them. If material support is the reward for our parents' upbringing, and spiritual obedience is our nominal recognition of the father–son relationship, this division is then basically consistent with the views of Xu Fuguan and Yang Zhongfang cited at the beginning.

Here again, it is not pointless to discuss the meaning of filial piety. In Chapter 2 of the first volume of this book and the first section of this chapter, although we repeatedly use the concept of Taiwanese scholar Ye Guanghui, affirming that traditional filial piety has encountered a "modern dilemma" (Ye, 1995), and that it is declining in general, it should also be noted that, because of the broad nature of filial piety, its different connotations are not entirely uniform in their degree of challenge or decline. Whether it is studies in Taiwan, Hong Kong, or mainland China, scholars have found that modern Chinese people still have a higher acceptance level of "serving parents", followed by "respecting parents", while "obeying parents" is challenged the most (Ho, 1996; He et al., 2007: 27–28; Deng & Feng, 2003); in other words, in terms of the inheritance of the tradition of filial piety, people generally begin to feel that "service" is easy and "obedience" is difficult.[2]

In 2009, He Riqu conducted a questionnaire survey of 1,200 urban and rural residents in Qingdao, and found that there were significant differences in the recognition of the seven connotations of traditional filial piety among Qingdao citizens. In the five-point questionnaire survey, people's identification degrees are successively as follows: respect (mean 4.62), comfort (mean 4.61), love (4.59), support (mean 4.51), care (mean 4.45), funeral sacrifice (mean 3.78), and finally humble advice (mean 3.07). In response to the multiple choice question, "What do you think should be done to honor parents in the first place?", 72.1% of respondents select "respecting parents", followed by "taking care of parents in life" (65.4%), "caring for parents" (49.8%), "materially supporting parents" (41.7%), and "comforting parents" (39.8%), whereas only 14.9% select "obeying parents" and 0.5% select "holding a grand funeral for parents after their death". Obviously, this study also confirms that while "serving parents" and "respecting parents" are retained to a large extent, "obeying parents" is confronted with severe challenges. If He's study accurately reveals the reality of China's intergenerational relationship (our theme), the emergence of the phenomenon of cultural reverse and the continuous expansion of related fields also change China's traditional parent–child interaction mode, making "respect" and "disobedience" start to become a basic intergenerational "balance skill".

When discussing the social impact or consequences of the phenomenon of cultural reverse, we have pointed out that

> the "reverse" of the offspring to the parents usually does not affect the affection between the parents and the children, but it does change the original parent–child relationship mode, especially improves the status of the offspring in the family and their right to speak in family affairs.
>
> (Zhou, 2000a)

This statement actually includes two questions. For one, does the "reverse" of the offspring to the parents affect the relationship between parents and children? For another, does the "reverse" of the offspring change the status between parents and children?

On the first question concerning whether cultural reverse affects the relationship between parents and children, our interviews focused on whether parents are able to calmly accept their children's reverse and how their children behave when giving advice to their parents. Generally speaking, today's parents are more or less aware that their children are different from what they were like in their own childhood or youth due to the acceleration of social changes. In fact, it is a sign of social progress that the children or the younger generation are smarter or better-informed than themselves, so there is nothing to be ashamed of in accepting their reverse. For example, BNM, the woman we mentioned in Chapter 4 of the first volume of this book, who became the Party Branch Secretary of the brigade at the age of 22 in the Mao Zedong era, said with deep feeling:

> I did listen to my parents when I was young. I did whatever they asked me to do, and there was never any negotiation. Although I later became the Party Secretary of the brigade, to be honest, it was nothing but a king of children. I could be cocky on the outside, but not at home. Because my father was working away in the railroad army, everything in the family was decided by my mother. It's a completely different relationship than I have with my daughter now. Although the child is not the "decision maker" at home, I do put her in my heart and want to talk to her about everything. I think my daughter is very independent, so no matter what happens, after I discuss it with her father, I will discuss it with her again when she comes back, so that I can feel secure and decide what to do. For example, there is going to be a professional title examination for accountants in Beijing in May next year, and I hesitate whether I should take it as I have already obtained the accounting license. When I talked to my husband, he did not encourage me, insisting that an accounting license was enough for a person on the verge of retirement like me. However, when I talked to my daughter that evening, she was very supportive. She said maybe what I learned was not useful for my work, but it would be useful for the enrichment of my life, and I might be in need of it for

family finances even after retirement ... Therefore, I feel no pressure to learn from my daughter. On the contrary, I feel uneasy about many things without discussing with her. My experience tells me that when children's ideas are different from ours, especially when they can refute us, it is a sign that the children are mature and have their own ideas. Therefore, I always feel very gratified from the bottom of my heart that the next generation is better than the previous one.

(BNM, 2004)

Although in our interviews, most of the older generation said that they were able to accept the reverse from the younger generation, this "modesty" or "openness" is not without conditions. First of all, the children's attitude must be good; otherwise, even if what the children say is right, the parents, especially those who have a certain social status or social prestige, will find it difficult to accept their words emotionally, feeling that their own "face" is at stake. In 1998, among the seven families I interviewed in Nanjing, NBF was the political commissar of the aviation force stationed in the outskirts of Nanjing, and her daughter NBG was a third-year junior high school student. Having been in the army for years, NBF did not know as much about the new things in society and trendy things like computers and mobile phones as his shrewd-brained daughter, so it was a normal phenomenon that NBF received reverse from NBG in week-end family interactions. To this, NBF's feelings were mixed:

My daughter has really helped me a lot. I don't think this phenomenon is unreasonable, but it is difficult to accept it emotionally. In the army, the sub-ordinates must obey their superiors, but when back at home, sometimes I have to listen to my daughter and follow her orders, so it is really hard for me. Of course, if NBG's attitude is good, things will be made much easier.

(NBF, 1998)

Second, as NDM, who works in a long-distance bus station, said, "It is much more pleasant to accept 'advice' from one's own children than from other younger people" (NDM, 1998). This difference in the acceptance of reverse from younger generations can be explained by two possibilities. Personally, it is nothing shameful or embarrassing to accept that your children are better than you—you can even boast as to how great your children are,[3] but it is more or less humiliating to be dwarfed by other young people. Practically, if your children are better than you, maybe you will lose your face, but you will not suffer any real loss. However, if other young people, especially those who are more or less competitive with you in the workplace, are better than you, it can lead to real consequences, such as loss of position or interests. One of the interviewees in Beijing, BMF, a 47-year-old bank manager, had typical ideas:

I have no trouble communicating with my daughter, willing and relaxed to learn new things from her, and quick to forget those occasional unpleasant moments. After all, our child is part of us, an extension of us, so it's nothing bad for my child to be better than me; actually, we often expect him or her to be even better. But we don't think this way at work. When we have to learn new things with young people in the same position, we have no other choice but to surpass them; otherwise, we'll be replaced by them. This kind of competition is somewhat ruthless. Of course, if we can realize that it is a trend and a common phenomenon for young people to excel the old, we'll learn to relieve our own psychological pressure.

(BMF, 2005)

When parents or the older generation have some reservations about cultural reverse, children or the younger generation have a more positive view. Most of them not only affirm that cultural reverse has a positive impact on intergenerational communication and mutual understanding, but also realize that the ways and manners of giving advice to their parents are of critical importance. They should learn to find a balance between respecting their parents and advising them. In other words, non-compliance with parents' opinions should not affect their emotional or attitudinal respect or honoring of their parents. Take the NGF family we mentioned in Chapter 3 of the first volume of this book. NGF was a former air force pilot and later transferred to the bank as the chairman of the labor union. His son, NGB, who was a sophomore at the time, affirmed in our interview that cultural reverse

> would improve the relationship between parents and children. For example, I think both my father's temper and professional ability are much better than when he was just transferred to a local job. He is no longer so commanding as he used to be, but speaks in a consultative way. In fact, instead of damaging his image, this change makes us more aware of how he feels when we talk to each other, and enables him to get along well with his young colleagues in the unit. Now, all the young people in his unit say that he is a competent union president.
>
> (NGB, 1998)

There is a very simple reason why children, or the younger generation, learn to strike a balance between giving advice and retaining affection; after all, they are dealing with their parents or elders, who have made great efforts toward their growth, so no matter whether they can repay them or not, they should at least give them due respect, even if they don't know anything or their views are completely wrong. In our interviews with dozens of families, most of the children said that they told their parents what they did not know "to make progress with them" (NCG, 1998) rather than to disdain them. One girl even made the thought-provoking remark: "I don't think our respect and love for our parents is based on them knowing everything" (NDG, 1998).[4] In addition, the experience of interacting with parents makes children realize that whether or not their parents accept their advice often has nothing to do with "what you say", but a lot to do with "how you say it". Most of today's parents are able to be tolerant and receptive to children, especially their own, because they want to cultivate their children's ability of independent thinking through encouraging them to "challenge authorities" and to seize the opportunity to know more about current society so as to keep pace with social development. Of course, all this happens with the premise that children or the younger generation do not fundamentally challenge their elders' status and dignity.

At this point, we have come to the second question concerning whether the "back-feeding" of children to parents will change the status between them. It must be admitted that, while parents insist that accepting advice from their children does not jeopardize their status and dignity, results of our interviews reveal that cultural reverse quietly changes to a great extent the relative position between parents and children. That is, cultural reverse inevitably raises the voice and decision-making power of minor children in family life.

Many families now not only consult with their children when making decisions about daily purchases or collective actions, but often leave it entirely up to them. Parents now let their children make decisions ranging from what kind of drinks, foods, and clothes to buy, where to travel, what kind of transportation to take, and the specific transportation route, to the brand, size, model of TV, computer or car to buy, the style of house decoration and even the children's own major and profession. Even BNM is not alone in talking to children about how to make her career more fulfilling. Of course, we find that the improvement of the status of children was the most prominent in the BV and BW families in the Zhejiang village we discussed in Chapters 3 and 4 of the first volume of this book. Doing business in a new place made the parents of these two families face both language difficulties and the lack of social contacts, so they, both in their 40s, decided to hand the financial control of the family to their young children, with them playing second fiddle to their children. In such immigrant families, younger children learn from older children who get ahead, and then pass on knowledge or experience to elderly parents who stay at home. They make their own decisions, do their own things, deal with the outside world on their own, and their position in the family is often unmatched by that of urban children who do not have actual family financial or decision-making power.

NGG, who was studying for a master's degree in foreign literature at a university, was sensitive to this change in parentage and status within the family. She said,

> Of course it affects our positions in the family. For example, my brother and I are now having more say on major family decisions, the most obvious sign of which is that parents are giving fewer direct orders and more room for negotiation.
>
> (NGG, 1998)

Of course, it should be admitted that the rise of children or juniors in the parent–child relationship is not only due to their ability to back-feed their parents in all aspects of social life, but also to the changes in family structure caused by the one-child policy since the 1980s, which we have repeatedly discussed in this book. The popularity of the one-child family in China, especially in cities, not only makes the parent–child relationship significant in terms of the intergenerational tilt or the descending of the family orthocenter as mentioned in Chapter 1 of this book, but also increases the importance of the younger generation in this relationship. Moreover, the change of family structure increases the opportunities for parent–child interaction and shapes the mode of democratic participation and decision-making between parents and children (Lin, 2009: 2, 77). This mode of interaction improves the ability and insight of the offspring, and as we will soon see, also increases the likelihood that the parents will adapt to society.

Standing on the immature shoulders of the younger generation

If the phenomenon of cultural reverse merely increases children's status and voice in the family, then it is somewhat unfair to parents who are struggling to raise their children. In other words, if cultural reverse is merely an intergenerational subversive movement, which means the loss of the voice of parents or the older generation, then it is only a one-dimensional revolution: While children or younger generations have unprecedented opportunities to give directions, traditional educators, that is parents or the older generation, have apparently seen their status plummet. However, our interviews and research suggest that is not the case. This new mode of cultural inheritance not only endows children with confidence, knowledge, and power, but also broadens parents' horizons and improves their ability to cope with the increasingly unfamiliar world. In this sense, cultural reverse is ultimately conducive to the common growth of the two generations.

We interviewed dozens of families in five major cities—Beijing, Shanghai, Nanjing, Guangzhou, and Chongqing—over the course of a decade and generally confirmed that the cultural reverse from the children not only makes the parents understand a lot of unfamiliar knowledge and change their perspective, but also improves their social adaptability. Take BBB's family as an example. Although this is a family of intellectual parents—the father, BBF, a senior engineer, was one of the first 1977-grade undergraduates admitted to Tsinghua Chemical Engineering Department after the Cultural Revolution, and the mother BBM majored in English in university and then was engaged in management work in China Artists Association—they also benefit from the reverse from their son, BBB. Because BBB majored in automation in Tsinghua University, he naturally taught himself how to use computers and all kinds of electrical products. Whenever BBF and BBM argued over the use of a computer, BBM, who had previously trusted her husband's engineering background, said, "Come on, let's wait until BBB comes back. Or why don't we call BBB?" (BBM, 2005). BBF added, "That means I'm out" (BBF, 2005).

If you think that the advice from BBB is simply a way for parents to learn to use a computer or mobile phone, or just to learn how to use MP3 or Norton anti-virus software, then your view is too limited. In fact, the cultural reverse from BBB even reconstructs the knowledge structure of her parents, especially BBM, making her handier in her post than ever before:

> I was transferred to the membership department of our association before I retired. When I got there, I was stunned. The records of the association's tens of thousands of members over 50 years, from 1949 to 2000, were recorded on written cards—which, in other words, were a jumble of papers of varying sizes. Because members had to pay their dues every year and the association had to recruit new members, this pile of paper was very inconvenient to read. Managers before me simply avoided the problem because they either lacked the technical means or the knowledge and ability to amend it. But when I took over, it was different. Because I had more or less learned some computer knowledge from my son at home, I thought I could do it. What's more, I had BBB behind me as a technical backup who knew everything. I gathered my colleagues from the members' department, and at first no one was willing to do it. They all said they didn't know how. It didn't matter. For the problems they had, I would go home and ask BBB first, and then told my colleagues what to do at work. In this way, with the help of BBB, our association realized the computer management of member data for the first time, and our generation also caught up with the last bus to complete our historical duties.
>
> (BBM, 2005)

From the results of interviews with various families, it can be seen that the knowledge and information parents get from their children's guidance is indeed extensive and comprehensive. If there are no children, many parents say, they may neither have tried KFC and McDonald's, or know such catchwords as "new money", "fifty cent party", or "cyber manhunt", or stay up all night watching the World Cup or *If You Are the One*, or talk about stocks, play bowling, or wear jeans, or know of Pierre Cardin, Alain Delon, or Do Min Joon, or have any knowledge about the cloned sheep "Dolly", the Qinshan Nuclear Power Station, or the "Long March-2" carrier rocket, or care about the Gini coefficient, soil erosion, ecological balance, or PM2.5, or review Chinese history or poems that they failed to learn well in high school, or use Windows XP, the Internet, or WeChat, or understand the market economy, business regulations, or "generalized monetary quantity", or go shopping on Tmall or Dangdang. Indeed, today's parents learn not only from their children about new ways or habits of consumption, but also about the courage, knowledge, and ability it takes to live and take it easy in a rapidly changing society. We can really say that without children, the window of the new China and the new world would not be so open today to the eyes of parents.

As typical cases, many families we interviewed provide ample evidence for our point of view here. In the NG family we keep referring to, NGF, the former air force veteran who was widely regarded as "rigid", said that even the knowledge of leisure and entertainment he got from his children helped him in his work. For example, his children watched DVDs and knew which movies had artistic taste or were impressive, so he was inspired to raise funds in the company's union to set up a "DVD exchange center", and asked children to help recommend DVDs. It turned out to be well received by the staff. Also, after playing bowling with the children, the union organized a bowling competition for the staff, enriching their lives. So NGF admitted that it was the cultural reverse from NGG and NGB that made him a "competent union President" in the eyes of young people.

GGF, a senior engineer with management responsibilities in Guangzhou Iron and Steel Group, graduated from Wuhan University of Science and Technology and was only about 40 years old when we conducted the interview, but he also lamented that he had failed to catch up with the development of the times and often needed his 15-year-old daughter GGG to give him some cultural reverse. For example, when preparing for the annual work report, GGF thought that GGG could use PowerPoint and asked her to help. As a result, the PowerPoint produced was not only illustrated, but also included good animation, showing GGF's management practice and work performance in this year at a glance. Therefore, the report satisfied the leaders and convinced the workers, and GGF naturally won the "excellent" assessment of that year (GGF, 2003).

Like NGG, NGB, and GGG, SHG, a Shanghai girl majoring in psychology and mathematics in UCLA, was not only a good girl for her mother, but also a crutch for her grandmothers. Her paternal grandma lived in Shanghai, and her maternal grandma lived in Wuhan; one was a middle school teacher and the other a doctor before retirement, and both were nearly 80 years old then. Before going abroad, SHG went to Wuhan for vacations and taught her maternal grandma how to surf the Internet, send WeChat messages, chat with QQ, and play PC games. When she returned to Shanghai, she taught her paternal grandmother the same things, not only making it possible for the two families, which used to contact each other only a little, now to be connected by networks, as well as enriching their retirement lives. Whenever they had any problems with the Internet, they still sent WeChat or QQ massages to SHG across the Pacific Ocean for help. "The other day when I went to visit my mother-in-law," said SHM, SHG's mother,

> I found her busy working in front of her computer. When she saw me, she said to me immediately, "Come on! Here is your mom." I was curious, "How can my mom by here? Where is she?" As I approached her desk, I realized what was happening. They were playing the game "Open a restaurant" on the Internet, with my mother-in-law as the manager and my mom as the waitress. With the network technology taught by SHG, their lives are indeed more lively. In contrast, my father-in-law doesn't fit in well after he retires. He can do nothing but drink tea, read the newspaper and take a walk, so he seems quite lonely.
>
> (SHM, 2014)

NFF, a professor of sociology whom we mentioned earlier, felt a certain amount of anxiety from his "dependence" on his son, an anxiety that runs counter to the conventional wisdom in society. NFF believed that what we had to worry about was not the independence of children—many people are like the "Nine-*jin* old lady" in Lu Xun's literary work and worry that our children are "not as good as" ourselves—but the decline in parents' ability to live by relying on their children. NFF's analysis of various social problems often had unique perspectives and sharp views, and his views on current intergenerational relations were equally refreshing:

> Just think, if someday our children have to leave us for work, for business, or for a foreign country, we may not know how to listen to the stereo, how to choose a TV program, how to open a microwave oven, how to use the timing device of air conditioning, how to handle life insurance, and even how to see a doctor, not to mention sending and receiving E-mails, surfing the Internet, and driving to visit old friends.
>
> (NFF, 1998)

Although as far as he himself is concerned, NFF's anxiety may never come true—they have altogether three children (which is quite unusual for Chinese couples their age), among whom they rely most on NFB, who has grown from a junior student in 1998, the year of our interview, into a postdoctoral at Brown University in America and now a teacher in the Chemistry Department of Nanjing University. This ensures that NFF and his wife have somebody to rely on not only in family life, but also in the spiritual world. But for many other parents, the issues raised by NFF is indeed the Achilles heel of most Chinese families entering old age.

In fact, the only solution to NFF's anxiety is timely and thorough cultural reverse. This means that parents should update their knowledge, change their way of looking at the world, develop behavior patterns in conformity with modern society—in a word, enhance their ability at social adaptation and avoid becoming an "outman"[5] in this age of globalization and networking—with the help of their children before they leave home. We used to talk about standing on the shoulders of giants, but for almost all parents or the older generation today, the real secure and realistic choice is probably standing on the shoulders of their children or the younger generation.

For all parents who can see their weaknesses or deficiencies, and are willing to set foot on their children's young shoulders, they will not only broaden their vision and see enough of the scenery, but more importantly, they do not have to worry about "losing their footing"—their children will guarantee their parents' safety by looking over them with all their strength and loyalty. For all children, to carry their parents on their shoulders takes not only the courage not to be afraid of being "trampled" on or "thumped" by their parents and elders, but also a strong mind—a weak mind, after all, cannot bear their parents' increasingly heavy old concepts. It is in this sense that we have always thought that cultural reverse not only brings different spiritual wealth to the children and parents, two relatively independent generations, but also promotes the common growth of the two generations, bringing an unparalleled opportunity to facilitate good intergenerational communication and thereby reshape intergenerational relations in the Internet age.

The primary reason why cultural reverse can promote the common growth of two generations lies in the new two-way information communication mode, which bridges the gradual distance between generations created by rapid social changes, and thus facilitates the mutual understanding between two or several generations that are increasingly unfamiliar.

In the opening chapters of the first volume of this book, we repeatedly stated that the "generation", or "generation gap", which is the biological basis of cultural reverse, is a product of industrial society or modernity. It is the rapid change from traditional society to modern society that leads to the discontinuity between generations, which makes the contradiction and conflict between generations arise as an emergent social reality. Therefore, "generation gap" refers to

> the social phenomenon of difference, estrangement and conflict between different generations in terms of social ownership and choice of values and behavioral orientation due to the rapid changes of times and environmental conditions, the interruption of basic socialization processes or the trans-formation of patterns.
>
> (Zhou, 1994)

For the three generations living today, the first generation, from the post-1910s to the post-1930s, grew up with one political movement after another, the short supply of a planned economy, and a uniform life symbolized by the "blue uniform".[6] They have suffered from brutal politics, material deprivation, and a monotonous life, but they cannot imagine any possible alternative to such a life—they are comforted by today's abundance, and discomforted by its haste. The second generation, from the post-1940s to the post-1960s, who are now considered the backbone of society, have more critical consciousness than their parents and have a global perspective due to the reform and opening-up over the years, but they cannot shake off the traces of the old times, especially when they are in a hurry. Although the third generation, from the post-1970s to the post-1990s, that has just grown up now has the most global consciousness and knows all kinds of new devices in the Internet age, including computers, they are not only confused and complicated in regard to values, but also display bold and unusual behavior patterns and are heartless in daily life, which makes the previous two generations look at them with unrestrained contempt. Thankfully, cultural reverse promotes the mutual understanding between two or even three generations in an unprecedented reverse way that can also be regarded as the experience of modernity in addition to the traditional socialization path of father–son and son–grandson. If you are not paranoid, consider the "lethal" argument of NAF, the professor of aesthetics we mentioned in Chapter 1 of the first volume of this book—"My son says …", and consider Fan Jingyi, the old newspaper reporter mentioned in Chapter 1, who confesses to "go home and ask my grandson" whenever there is a problem. You must admit that this is a successful "counter-attack" of modernity in contemporary China!

The second reason why cultural reverse can promote the common growth of the two generations is the mutual understanding between them achieved through two-way information communication, so that the two or more generations living at the same time can truly realize the relativity of their own culture and the rationality of other cultures. The recognition of cultural diversity, including values, life attitudes, and behavior patterns, can promote the mutual tolerance between two or several generations that were originally contradictory or opposite.

If the rapid social changes in modern times lead to the generation break or generation gap, then one of the most important results may be that the intergenerational contradiction has become the most important form of conflict in human society, which is only inferior to the class contradiction. In modern China, the long-lasting traditional family culture ravages individuals to a suffocating extent. Once the growth of modernity (including modern democratic political thought, the school and factory system, the birth of freedom of the press and love) awakens the rebellion of the younger generation, the intensity of intergenerational conflicts is naturally unparalleled. For the older generation, the collapse of the old etiquette and system is for them like the death of their parents, so it is inevitable that some people will die for the sake of martyrdom. As for the younger generation, once they wake up, they will feel like Lu Xun:

> When I open up the history, I find that there was no date in it. On every page, the words "benevolence, justice and morality" are written askew. I can't sleep at all. I read it through the middle of the night, and there are two words written all over it: "eat people!"
>
> (Lu, 2005: 447, 455)

Therefore, for Lu Xun, the theme of social revolution was "save the children!" Furthermore, since the younger generation realizes that behind the suppression of their parents and families, there stands the feudal ethics and social system that has not collapsed for thousands of years, they must face a choice: they either return to the family to be filial, or become a fighter and declare war on society. Because of this, as Chen Yingfang said, the May Fourth generation developing "from resisting the family to reforming the society" is actually a continuous succession. This radicalism later even formed the social basis for the Communist Revolution to happen in full swing in China (Chen Yingfang, 2007: 83–157).[7]

Still, thanks to cultural reverse, we are living in a time of rapid change when two or more living generations are no longer competing or fighting with each other as their predecessors did. In other words, the emergence of a new way of intergenerational communication, cultural reverse, makes it possible to solve intergenerational conflicts in a post-revolutionary era or at least a non-violent revolutionary era. In my interview, because the older generation feels uncomfortable in the new social environment, they are surprised by the values, life attitudes, and behavior patterns of the younger generation. However, they gradually become tolerant and even receptive, so that cultural reverse becomes a powerful tool for them to adapt to the new era. For the younger generation, since the older one has increased their understanding and tolerance by receiving reverse, the homogeneity between generations is naturally enhanced, and mutual dissatisfaction or hostility disappears. The younger generation is discovering for the first time that the older one is neither recalcitrant nor defensive. Once they accept new things, they sometimes love new things more than themselves. NBM said that her mother used to hate her very much for wearing jeans and ballroom dancing, but when she retired, she became so addicted to disco that she refused to take off the old jeans that NBM did not wear (NBM, 1998). NMF, a professor of journalism and communication, also said that when he conducted telephone interviews with graduate students, he found that many elderly people learned shopping from their children and grandchildren. They went from opposing "Taobao" to later lingering in "Tmall" every day, buying a bunch of things that you cannot say are useful (NMF, 2013). Obviously, cultural reverse not only promotes the younger generation's understanding of the "eccentric" elders, but also enables the older generation to understand the children who have "grown more and more disagreeable", so that "learning from children" eventually becomes one of the important aspects of the older generation's lifelong learning to adapt to the changing society (Sun, 1998: 243).

Finally, the reason why cultural reverse can promote the common growth of the two generations is that it enables them to communicate, imitate, and learn from each other through the mutual tolerance of their multi-cultures, including intergenerational culture and intergenerational differences, and finally realize the harmony between them in the face of the ever-changing world.

From 1946 to 1947, when Fei Xiaotong wrote the *Fertility System* and *Rural China*, he saw that the older generation, who had "the power of education to compel the young" (Fei, 1998: 67), began to encounter the embarrassment of adapting to difficulties in the era of rapid changes. At the same time, the younger generation who has been exposed to new ideas and technologies feels that it "can't deny its hope and follow the predecessors in what they think is a dead end". Although the wise prophet of sociology realized that "the rise and fall of generations and the change of society have played this heart-wrenching game in the hearts of many people" (Fei, 1998: 210), the emotional balance of Fei Xiaotong, who was 37 years old when facing the turbulence of the changing times, obviously more inclined to the young people emotionally:

In the process of social change, people cannot be guided by experience. What can be relied on is the principle beyond the individual situation, but it is not necessarily the elder who can form and apply the principle. This ability has little to do with age. What matters is expertise, intelligence, and a bit of opportunity. When it comes to opportunities, the younger ones have more than the older ones. They are not afraid of change, curious and willing to experiment. In change, habits are obstacles to adaptation, and experience equals stubbornness and backwardness. Stubbornness and backwardness are not mere verbal sneers, but threats to survival chances.

(Fei, 1998: 68)

While Fei firmly believes that the older generation will not only be laughed at, but even reduced in their ability to survive, if they fail to adapt to the changes of the new era, he hopes to build some kind of more harmonious relationship between two or more generations. As early as the 1920s, Robert Park, a sociologist at the University of Chicago, was inspired by William Wheeler's work on ants (Wheeler, 1910: 339–424) to suggest that two types of beneficial social relationships can be established between people: (a) symbiosis, in which the secretions of aphids are good food for ants, and the aphids in turn are served by the ants (who take their aphids to suitable habitats), and they use each other, so that the relationship between these completely different insects can be regarded as a symbiosis (Park & Burgess, 1970: 87); (b) consensus, which is a relationship at a higher level than symbiosis that only exists in human society, and in which individuals are able to sacrifice their own interests for the benefit of other individuals. Park believed that mutual understanding and harmony were even more characteristic of human beings than cooperation or joint action (Park & Burgess, 1970: 84). Influenced by his teacher, Fei Xiaotong suggested that the most ideal intergenerational relationship should progress in this way: "The offspring is initially a physiological connection to the parents, then a symbiotic connection, and finally a harmonious connection" (Fei, 1998: 104).

As far as we are concerned, cultural reverse is not a physiological link between offspring and parents, but a cultural link between generations. This association at the symbiosis level is not controversial. Passing on the meaning and skills of new things in fast-changing times to parents seems to only increase parents' understanding of a changing society and their ability to adapt to it, though this understanding and adaptation, in turn, improves the children's own insight into society and reduces their own growth barriers caused by parental confusion and anger. Therefore, we always firmly believe that cultural reverse is the basic way for two or three generations to grow together.

So, does cultural reverse have the same positive implications in a uniquely human context of consensus? In terms of the way of inheritance from father to son in rural society, "the biggest difficulty for children is that they have no experience as parents ... The experience one does not have cannot be extended to others" (Fei, 1998: 104–105). In this way, the premise of consensus is the mutual empathy of both sides of the interaction. In traditional China, the way of intergenerational communication is one way, so no matter what kind of devotion parents make to their children, children will first feel one-way indoctrination and even repression. Therefore, the kind of "overall consensus relationship" Fei Xiaotong hoped to achieve is difficult in traditional intergenerational communication. And thanks to cultural reverse, for the first time, our children are likely to be "on duty" in advance—to start acting as educators—in the process of feeding their parents. The change from educatee to educator may make some children arrogant and perverse, but for most it may provide a positive reflexive experience; that is, to reflect on their own behavior from the perspective of parents and reconstruct healthy or "consensus" intergenerational relationships. In other words, the basic socialization path of traditional paternity, coupled with cultural reverse, provides a realistic possibility for the intergenerational relationship to change from one-way control or suppression to two-way interaction and communication. Almost all of the cases we interviewed—be it the NG family in Nanjing in Chapter 3 of the first volume of this book, the GE family in Guangzhou in Chapter 4 of the first volume of this book, the SE family in Shanghai, the BN family in Beijing, or the CO family in Chongqing in Chapter 5 of the first volume of this book—all proved that cultural reverse not only promotes the rapid growth of the younger generation, but also improves the social adaptability of the older generation. As a result, cultural reverse has become an unprecedented remolding experience of intergenerational relationship that almost all Chinese families have experienced since the reform and opening-up in 1978.

Chinese feeling: from "only here" to "only once"

So far, there is still a question worth discussing: Is the phenomenon of cultural reverse really a new way of cultural inheritance? Obviously, this is an unavoidable topic when discussing the social significance of the phenomenon of cultural reverse. In other words, what is the uniqueness of this phenomenon of intergenerational subversion in cultural inheritance if we examine it from the synchronic and diachronic perspectives?

This is one of the most common questions I have heard since I first proposed and studied the concept of cultural reverse. This question actually includes two aspects. First, from the synchronic perspective, is the phenomenon of cultural reverse really unique to China? Specifically, in this study, a variety of new food and information communication technologies (ICTs) have appeared in developed Western countries and emerging East Asian countries in recent decades. Is there no cultural reverse of offspring to parents or "subversion" of cultural inheritance in these countries? Second, from the diachronic perspective, is the phenomenon of cultural reverse really unique to China today? In Chinese history, especially in those important historical periods such as "dynasty change", is there no similar phenomenon that the younger generation backfeeds to the older generation?

Let's start with the first question. I still remember that in the discussions on this topic, since 1999, foreign scholars have asked me the same question.[8]

Apparently, they, like Nicholas Negroponte, the new media expert at the Massachusetts Institute of Technology we mentioned in Chapter 5 of the first volume of this book, saw that in front of various ICTs, the phenomenon that the parents are inferior to the children, or the elders are inferior to the young—that is, cultural reverse, as I call it—is a new phenomenon that has emerged globally with the promotion of ICTs. It does not seem to be unique to Chinese society.

I admit that parents all over the world are likely to experience inferior performance to their children or younger generations when it comes to new gadgets or the use of ICTs. However, the particularity of Chinese society lies in the fact that it is a country whose tradition is deeply rooted and which has been subjected to numerous internal and external troubles since modern times and failed to undergo a proper modern baptism. After 30 years of isolation, stagnation, and even the regression of the Cultural Revolution, such a country suddenly faced reform and opening-up. Faced with such a modern outside world and such a drastic social transformation, the sharp contrast makes the process of the older generation from "supreme" to "backward" almost instantaneous. In addition to the rapidity of change, the difference between two and even three generations of Chinese society caused by change is unparalleled, not to mention the generation of the post-1920s to the post-1930s who are still alive today, the generation of the post-1940s, especially the generation of the post-1950s and post-1960s, who experienced a series of waves such as "rebellion", joining the army, going to the countryside, returning to the city, being laid off, and seeking a career by themselves, though most people did not have the experience of modern higher education. However, those born after the Cultural Revolution or after the reform and opening-up, the so-called generation of the post-1970s to the post-1990s, have benefited from the rapid economic and social development in China over the past 42 years, enjoyed a good education and growth environment, and become the almost omniscient and omnipotent generation. Just look at this data: in 1977, when the college entrance examination was resumed after the Cultural Revolution, Chinese universities enrolled 278,000 students. Thirty years later, Chinese universities enrolled 5.67 million students in 2007. In just 30 years, enrollment has increased by a factor of 20, which means many families now face the embarrassment of having children who are "knowledgeable" and parents who are "know-nothings".[9] The differences between the lives of the children of the Great Depression and their children born after World War II in the 1930s are very similar to those between the Cultural Revolution generation and their children (Elder, 2002: 7), but it is clear that there is no such huge spiritual gap between the two generations in the United States as from "closed" to "open". The contrast between the material and spiritual lives of two or three living generations at the same time is so huge that it determines that, in China, the traditional parent–child relationship is subverted more thoroughly than in any other country, which is why it is called "only here".

Of course, here, the so-called "only here" is only a relative metaphor, so it is not necessary to make an absolute understanding of it. For example, in a speech

I gave at Ho Chi Minh National University in Vietnam in October 2011, a member of the audience told me that in Vietnam, which had been following China's example of reform and in some ways was even more advanced, there was a similar phenomenon of cultural reverse. I was not surprised. The country, which in many ways resembles China, despite its wars and more tortuous development path, had changed dramatically since the reform and opening-up beginning in 1986. For example, the Ho Chi Minh city I visited, the charming city formerly known as Saigon, with its endless bars and cafes and the French atmosphere, is more modern than Nanjing, my hometown. So I answered positively, "I believe you. Maybe the next country is North Korea?" Indeed, if North Korea can one day embark on the path of reform and opening-up, and also achieve a great leap forward in a few short decades, it will surely have the same cultural reverse phenomenon as China and Vietnam. This is why I firmly believe that China, which has taken the first step on the road of reform and opening-up or social transformation, has produced economic and social development achievements and undergone great changes in its people's spiritual world, which has a certain universal value for those developing countries with similar national conditions as China (Zhou, 2011b). In this sense, "only here" can also be understood as "only these few places".

Let's move on to the second question. Not long after I put forward the concept of cultural reverse in 1988, Lu Jie, an educator, asked me whether there was really no such phenomenon in history. First, as early as in the Tang dynasty, Han Yu said: "It is not necessary for a disciple to be inferior to his teacher, or for a teacher to be superior to his disciple" (*On Teaching* 2013). Second, during the period of the May Fourth Movement in 1919 and the great social transformation (such as after the victory of the revolution in 1949 and even the Cultural Revolution in 1966), the younger generation often dominated the times, while the older generation was often left behind as the "old fogy". Thus, the phenomenon of cultural reverse does not seem to be unique to China today.

I also admit that in any era, due to the fact that "people learn their way in different times and specialize in different subjects", and due to the difference in IQ and degree of effort, the phenomenon of disciples being stronger than teachers certainly exists, and it is also not uncommon for the father to be inferior to the son. I also admit that in those periods of great historical transformation, it is quite common for the younger generation to become the trendsetters of the times. However, the biggest difference between these two phenomena and what we call cultural reverse is: The former may exist as a specific case in a particular family or between particular teachers and students. The reason why parents are not as good as children or teachers is simply because some people "learn their way" early, while others learn late, the difference in profession, and the difference in IQ and diligence; or it may just exist in the realm of political or regime change, where acceptance of new political discourse or ideologies is often the result of a combination of social trends and personal circumstances, not entirely dependent on the single factor of age. On the contrary, the latter, what we call cultural reverse, is occurring on a large scale in the whole society of China today. On the one hand, it does not depend on the time of learning, or the similarities and differences in the field, and even has nothing to do with intelligence and diligence, but only with the great changes in the living environment between generations in the past decades. On the other hand, the phenomenon that the parents are inferior to the children or the elders are inferior to the juniors is neither limited to the "remembering" and understanding of certain kinds of knowledge, or the mastery and alienation of a particular profession, nor limited to class positions or political choices; on the contrary, it involves almost all areas of daily life, such as values, life attitudes, behavior patterns, and object civilization. In other words, this all-round gap between parents and children or between generations is another version of what the American sociologist Ogburn called "cultural lag" (Ogburn, 1950: 200). I think only by realizing this can we truly understand the unprecedented historical significance of cultural reverse.

In the history of the inheritance of human culture, cultural reverse has unique value, not only because it has never happened before, but also because it will not be repeated thereafter—it is "unprecedented and unique", which is called "only once". Obviously, the necessary condition for the phenomenon of cultural reverse is that the whole society has undergone drastic changes in a very short time, which has resulted in a huge gap between two or three generations living in the world at the same time. I remember when I visited Beijing, an ordinary fitter master BTF told me that none of the 40 or 50 workers in his workshop had gone to college, but now their children were all receiving college education (BTF, 2004). I acknowledge that society will continue on its journey of change, but after having seen many such cases that I am convinced that the great generational differences caused by the dramatic changes of the past few decades will not be repeated.

In recent years, while paying attention to a series of experiences accumulated in China's economic and social development and structural transformation, which is called the "Chinese experience" (Fan, 2005; Li, 2008; Wen, 2008),[10] I also propose to pay attention to the equally great changes in Chinese people's values and social mentality in these years—we call these changes the "Chinese feeling" (Zhou, 2009a, 2013, 2014a, 2014b). Just as the Chinese experience that people often talk about now, the "Chinese feeling"—that is, the micro-evolution of Chinese people's values and social mentality in the past few decades—discussed here should certainly become one of the themes that must be taken care of by the sociology of transition, or rather it is a kind of transformational social psychology, or what Fang Wen calls "transformational psychology" (Fang, 2008). The significance and influence of China's social transformation are not only reflected in the fact that it condenses many historical processes of human social changes, with implications of civilization transition (Sun, 2005), but that the generation or generations of people living in China in transition have undergone and condensed centuries of evolution in their short life cycle in a spiritual "duck-stuffing" manner, which is unprecedented for the spiritual or psychological reconstruction of these 1.3 billion people (Zhou, 2011b). All these have determined that the observation of the "Chinese feeling" and its sig-nificance has become an unavoidable historical mission of Chinese social psych-ology and even the whole of Chinese social science (Wang, 2012).

Compared with the Chinese experience, the Chinese feeling is a brand new concept, which does not mean that we should replace the previous Chinese experience or other similar concepts, such as the Chinese road, the Chinese model, and the Chinese miracle. The novelty of the concept of the Chinese feel-ing on the one hand refers to that like the Chinese experience, it is also the result of the rapid changes or social transformation of Chinese society over the past few decades, so previous social scientists did not and could not pay atten-tion to such a social phenomenon. On the other hand, it means that although Chinese feeling, like Chinese experience, is the result of social change or trans-formation, the former has not yet attracted enough attention compared with the latter. Few people realize that while the macro-economic and social structure of Chinese society is changing, the micro-values and social mentality of its people are also changing unprecedently. The Chinese experience and the Chinese feel-ing, as an integral part of this unprecedented social transformation that began in 1978, have endowed our unique era with complete historical significance and cultural value. If we simply sum up the Chinese experience and ignore the Chinese feeling, it is impossible to find out what role the spirit of the Chinese, as the main body of modernization, has played in this process involving 1.3 billion people; what changes have happened to their desires and personal-ities while they are changing China; how their social mentality of happiness and sorrow ebbs and flows with the changes of society; and what kind of embarrassment and loss they are facing in their spiritual world (Zhou, 2011b, 2013, 2014).

In a series of papers published in recent years, I have repeatedly stated the basic connotation of the Chinese feeling. First, different from the Chinese experience, the Chinese path, the Chinese model, or the Chinese miracle, the Chinese feeling is not the structural or institutional macro-changes of Chinese society in the past few decades, but the micro-changes of Chinese people's values and social mentality in the context of macro-changes. Second, the Chin-ese feeling includes both positive psychological experience and negative psy-chological experience. The former includes openness, mobility, competition, aggressiveness, peace, and tolerance, while the latter includes materialistic desire, money worship, impetuosity, indifference, lack of integrity, hatred, and flaunting of wealth (Zhou et al., 2014).[11] The marginalization of personality or polarization of social mentality are just the most important characteristics of Chinese feeling, which indicates that it itself is a spiritual landscape of change to a certain extent. Third, although the Chinese feeling is a kind of personality and social psychological evolution that may occur in any society that changes from tradition to modernity, due to China's specific population size, differences in economic and social structure before and after the transformation, a traditional culture with a long history, the promotion of globalization, and the speed of change, it has some characteristics that general spiritual evolution does not have. These characteristics make social psychologists' research into the evolution of the human spiritual world have new significance. Finally, while the Chinese feeling is unique, it is not without some universal significance; that is to say, this "feeling" may be useful for other ethnic groups or countries, especially the developing countries in upheaval, and some may even be copied to some extent. As Shi Zhiyu said, the results of Chinese research can be connected with "the universal law of human behavior" (Shi, 2006).

If indeed the Chinese experience and the Chinese feeling can be regarded as two sides of the great change or social transformation that this ancient country is undergoing, and the understanding of change is inextricably linked with social science itself, which pays attention to the path and causes of change, then the study of the Chinese experience and Chinese feeling can not only promote the healthy development of Chinese social science, but also fundamentally provide a God-given opportunity to realize the sinicization of social science. It is precisely in terms of the unique significance that the transformation of Chinese society may have for human society that the dual care for the structure (Chinese experience) and significance (Chinese feeling) of the transformation not only provides an unprecedented opportunity to forge Chinese social science, but also may prevent the transformation from becoming a mere wealth growth or GDP accumulation. This will help lift the spiritual significance of this change on a global scale.

If we look back over the 100-year history of social psychology, we can find at least two studies that have some historic value in explaining human behavior, especially social behavior, because they reveal the special significance of people's spiritual evolution, making the transformation discussed by the authors and the changes of people born of transformation go beyond the simple significance of economic growth.

The first study was *The Protestant Ethic and the Spirits of Capitalism*, written in 1904–1905 by Max Weber, a German sociologist. Clearly, in Weber's view, the spirit of capitalism is a kind of spiritual power, or a kind of social mentality that emerged in the European and American world after the Protestant Reformation, which paved the way for the emergence of modern capitalism or the transformation of European and American societies.

Before the emergence of the capitalist spirit, the so-called traditionalism dominated people's life attitudes and behaviors, in which labor is just a means of making a living, which makes people not try to change the existing way of life as long as they can meet their habitual needs. However, the religious reform triggered the collapse of traditionalism. In addition to the change of people's religious beliefs, it also promoted the change of their values and social psychology towards modernity, including the following. First is the change of career concept, that is, from the original concept of fate to the concept of calling. In Weber's words, "the only way of living acceptably to God was not to surpass worldly morality in monastic asceticism, but solely through the fulfilment of the obligations imposed upon the individual by his position in the world" (Weber, 2005: 40). Thus, secular behaviors have religious significance, and the struggle to earn money has a certain sanctity. The second is a change in the concept of money. If earning money and other worldly things are an unquestioned duty, attitudes to money also limit the spirit of capitalism in another way: The individual who is diligent in earning money must at the same time possess the ability to abstain, to be thrifty, to invest the money saved as new capital; only by realizing that money can beget money, that is to say, by realizing the self-reproduction of money, can an individual truly possess the concept of money in modern capitalism. The third is a change in the concept of time. Since our earthly life can add to the glory of God, there is no reason for us to slack off every moment. Thus Weber not only highly respected Franklin's moral maxim that "time is money", but also deeply believed that "waste of time is thus the first and in principle the deadliest of sins" (Weber, 2005: 104). Clearly, this view of time not only facilitated the precision of the measurement of time (including the invention of mechanical clocks, a hallmark of modernity), but later became the most important attitude in the entire capitalist management system.

It is precisely this that brings about a shift in the patterns of human social behavior, which, in Weber's words, leads to the emergence of instrumental or formal rational behavior. At this time, people's behavior is no longer only based on tradition and emotion, or even the meaning and value of behavior. Instrumental rational behavior, which emphasizes efficiency and predictability, starts to become the main mode of human social behaviors.

The second study, *From Traditional to Modern Man: Personal Change in Six Developing Countries*, was published in 1974 by U.S. sociologists Alex Inkeles and David Smith. The study, which was originally conducted in 1962–1964, looked at 6,000 farmers, industrial workers, and people in more traditional occupations in cities and towns in six countries: Argentina, Chile, India, Israel, Nigeria, and Bangladesh. The two sociologists wanted to show through this large-scale empirical study that people are not born with modernity, but that it is their particular experiences that drive the shift to modern success.

Since man is the product of the social environment, then a man with modernity is the product of modern society. From this point of view, Inkeles and Smith first identified some of the increasingly salient factors typical of the six developing countries that could be called modern: the factory system, mass media, urban life, and modern education. Although the actual research process is complex, the basic conclusions are clear:

> Among such institutions, we gave prime emphasis to the factory as a school in modernity. We also thought that urban living and contact with the mass media should have comparable effects. While emphasizing such modes of experience as more characteristic of the modern world, we did not neglect to study education, which earlier research had shown to be a powerful predictor of individual modernity, as well as other personal attributes such as age, religion, ethnic membership, and rural origin.
>
> (Inkeles & Smith, 1975: 325)

Although the dualist view of the transition from tradition to modernity is controversial (Zhou, 2010), Inkeles and Smith's study of "modern man" may also have the "ideological tint" of other modernization theories (Latham, 2003). This study at least reveals the indisputable fact that changes in the social environment bring about changes in people's values and lifestyles, which also have distinct social significance: They are not the marginal benefits derived from the process of institutional modernization, but the prerequisites for the long-term operation of these institutions (Inkeles & Smith, 1975: 455).

While we do not want to overstate the universality of these two studies, obviously they are all examples of how people observe the impact of social changes on the changes of human social psychology because they all reveal the spiritual shaping of their people by the special historical processes that took place in different countries or peoples at different stages of historical development. And the above general conclusion obtained by these two studies is also regarded as a general law of human behavior.

The Chinese feeling deserves our academic attention because, on the one hand, it endows the Chinese experience with complete value and significance on the spiritual level, and because, on the other hand, "its uniqueness may provide a social or psychological model for developing countries around the world to make the transition from tradition to modernity" (Zhou & Qin, 2010a). Indeed, the phenomenon of cultural reverse and its associated intergenerational disruption is part of the psychological experience of the Chinese people as a result of this dramatic change. We realize that because China's reform involves all aspects of society and touches upon the deepest problems of the latter, every researcher, no matter how intelligent or diligent he is, his concern may only touch on the very smallest areas of a changing society, and his discourse is also inevitably incomplete. However, no matter how small the power of individuals, we still hope that the research on the phenomenon of cultural reverse will leave an academic accumulation in the sense of knowledge sociology for the four decades of reform and opening-up and social progress.

Notes

1   Although Mao Zedong advocated cremation as early as the mid-1950s, the mandatory implementation of the policy appears to be related to the people's communes and the Great Leap Forward, which began in 1958. Because of the Great Leap Forward, the country needed to expand the area of arable land and thus persuaded or even forced farmers to square graves, which was very similar to the "square graves and restore farming" in Zhoukou, Henan province in recent years (Ye, 2012). At the same time, the state also began to promote cremation and the construction of crematoria in rural areas. However, after 1962, the failure of the Great Leap Forward led to the adjustment of a series of extreme policies, and the country began to adopt a more moderate policy on funerals, and the earth burial was restored to a certain extent. However, the arrival of the Cultural Revolution in 1966 once again intensified the disappearance of the original funeral methods. After the reform and opening-up in 1978, although many other policies had been restored, funeral reform was

basically adopted by the Chinese. This is discussed in Chapter 5 in *Longevity: The Old in China and Communism* (Davis-Friedmann, 1991: 61–67).

2 In daily life, people are very clear about the core connotation of filial piety and strictly divide it into two fields: "service" and "obedience". In my own case, I take great care of my mother in life, especially after the death of my father, but I often contradict many of her ideas. Thus, my mother often comments to me, "You are dutiful but not obedient." Whether I accept my mother's criticism or not, I have to admit that her division of the concept is quite accurate.

3 Interestingly, the gender of the child can sometimes be a barrier for parents, especially fathers, to accept "feedback". For example, BQF, a lawyer in a Beijing Telecom Company, said that if he had given birth to a son, he might have communicated with the child equally, but because he had only a daughter, he would be somewhat uncomfortable to listen to the child's guidance (BQF, 2005). However, mothers generally do not have this "psychological barrier"; they often have an appreciative attitude towards their children's "feedback".

4 In our interview in Guangzhou, the 12-year-old GAB, mentioned in Chapter 5 of the first volume of this book, also spoke grandly about this problem: "Although every time I know what my parents don't know, I feel a sense of pride, I still respect them the same. Because they are my parents, after all, the people who gave me birth, and I don't know much yet. I still need to consult them about most things, so I think I should be modest." Upon hearing GAB say this, grandma GAGM suddenly "broke the news" and said, "But once you said, 'You are retarded.'" Grandma's words made GAB's face turn red, arguing, "That's just a joke! I really respect them in my heart" (GAB, 2003).

5 This is the language of the Internet, which means "behind the times". It is the homonym of *Ultraman*, a Japanese animated film made by TYO (Tsuburaya), which is very familiar to young people born in the 1980s. However, Ultraman is an omnipotent hero with a perfect life form and historical responsibility, while the "outman" of the real world is an outdated person unable to adapt to this changing society.

6 Martin Whyte once compared Mao Zedong's China to the "empire of blue ants", thus corresponding to the "scattered sand" China of Sun Yat-sen (1924) and Chiang Kai-shek (1945) (Whyte, 1974: 2). Whatever other social features, monotony or uniformity was indeed one of the most striking features of daily life in the Mao era.

7 During the May Fourth new culture movement, the rebellious young generation's hatred of the older generation highlighted the sharp intergenerational conflict. As is known to all, Qian Xuantong, who was also the standard bearer of the new culture movement with Lu Xun, even said angrily, "A man should die at forty, or be shot if he is not dead." So on the 41st birthday of Qian Xuantong on September 12, 1928, Hu Shi wrote a song named "Anniversary song of my deceased friend Qian Xuantong" to mock his theory that "one should be shot at the age of 40" (Liu, 2011). In fact, since the beginning of the reform, there have been countless thoughts of "non-filial piety" that mock and even oppose the elderly. For example, the motto of Wu Zhihui, a reformist, is: "Stand on the side of the people to deny the monarch; stand on the side of the students to oppose the teacher; stand on the side of the youth to oppose the old" (Grieder, 1983: 177).

8 In 1999, for example, in the office of Professor Elizabeth Perry, director of the Fairbank Center for East Asian Studies at Harvard University, she and Professor Deborah Davis, the visiting dean of sociology at Yale, talked to me about this. The two professors also suggested that I use the term "culture reverse". In the conference "Understanding Cultures: The Use of Culture in China" held by the World University Union (WUN) in May 2011, Professor Gordon Houlden, dean of the School of Chinese Studies at the University of Alberta, Canada, and Professor David

Goodman, director of the Center for Chinese Studies at the University of Sydney, Australia, also asked the same question.

9   According to the latest statistics, the number of college students in China reached 8.20 million in 2019. In fact, what changes is not only the number of students admitted, but also the proportion of students admitted. In 1977, the number of examninees was 5.7 million, 270,000 were admitted, and the admission rate was 4.7%. But in 2019, there were 10.31 million examinees and 8.20 million students were admitted. The enrollment rate has reached 79.53%. In just 42 years, the two generations have different chances of going to college, which fully shows that the reform and opening-up initiated by Deng Xiaoping has created completely different life circumstances for the two generations.

10   Although it is called the "Chinese experience", I agree with Li Peilin that the phrase "not only refers to 'achievements', but also includes lessons, including all the special experiences along the development path" (Li, 2008).

11   In order to elaborate on the changes of Chinese people's social mentality and the marginal or polarized characteristics of what we call the Chinese feeling, I hosted a pen discussion entitled "Social mentality of contemporary Chinese people" in the fifth and sixth issues of *Journal of Jiangsu Administrative College* in 2014. In ten essays, the eight authors discussed five positive social attitudes, namely openness, mobility, competition, peace, and inclusiveness, and five negative social attitudes, namely anxiety, material desire (money worship), impetuousness, violence, and flaunting wealth (Zhou et al., 2014).

5 Conclusion

State, society, and intergenerational relations

> Youth, like spring, like the rising sun, like the budding flowers, is the most precious time in one's life. The youth to the society is the fresh and active cells to the body. Metabolism makes the stale and perishable to be always replaced by the fresh and lively. Health follows metabolism, and death follows decayed and dead cells; society flourishes if it follows the metabolic pattern, and it perishes if it is clogged with decrepit elements.
>
> Chen 1916

The metamorphosis of youth

Cultural reverse is a new phenomenon in Chinese society following the reform and opening-up in 1978—in Chapter 4, we used "only here" and "only once" to show its novelty, which reflects, from one side, the remarkable changes that have taken place in a country with a history of 5,000 years of civilization. On the micro-level, cultural reverse involves a change in the path and direction of cultural inheritance within the family and between generations. The offspring turns from the educatee to the educator in daily life or in the process of socialization, while the status of the parents changes in the opposite direction. On the macro-level, cultural reverse involves changes of the historical status of young people, changes in the relationship between young people and the state and society, as well as changes in the way of cultural innovation and inheritance in such an ancient country as China. Now, after we have made detailed analysis and discussion of cultural reverse and its microcosmic mechanism, it is necessary to further discuss at the macro-level the influence this phenomenon has on the contemporary change of Chinese social intergenerational relations and the future development of the whole nation.

In daily life, when people talk about "youth", they will naturally regard it as an age group associated with the growth of life and a social counterpart to adults. The continuous enlargement of the age range or boundary demarcation of this group, however, shows most clearly the social constructive significance of this group.[1] In other words, as an age group, the emergence of youth itself, as well as the determination and change of its specific age range, are all the products of social structure and its changes since the Industrial Revolution.

Before that, infancy and childhood were followed immediately by adulthood; in other words, there were only two age groups in traditional society: the underage and the grown-up, and there was no transitional period called "youth". Therefore, "youth" in the sociological sense can be, as Bourdieu put it, "just a word" (Bourdieu, 1993: 94–95), or, as John R. Gillis put it, a product of modern industrial society (Gills, 1974: 3).

Furthermore, since it emerged in the transition between the modern school system and the factory system, youth is endowed with an inherent dissociation from or opposition to the existing social structure, and thus becomes "a key point for social and political anxiety" (McRobbie, 2005: 175). As we have discussed in Chapter 1 of the first volume of this book, the emergence of youth as a result of the Industrial Revolution and its challenge to the older generation not only led to the rupture or discontinuity between generations, but also made the "generation" or intergenerational succession become a problem—which Simmel called the problem of modernity—for the first time in human history.

In traditional Chinese society, before the emergence of modern education, there was no youth in the modern sense; what's more, for certain reasons, young people were more attached to their households, families, and even society than those of other countries or nations. These reasons include the following. First, in traditional China, there was no clear age limit for education, marriage, property inheritance, or productive labor. In fact, generational or family hierarchy was of more importance than age. Second, Chinese traditional culture did not encourage young people to stay away from their parents: "When parents are at home, do not travel far" (Yang 1980) was the filial piety or virtue advocated by society. This, coupled with the fact that marriage was arranged by the parents and property was controlled by them, led to the attachment of the younger generation to the family or parents. Third, in addition to their own households, young males were also required to remain in the family to inherit the family genealogies after adulthood. Family membership was the most important identity of individuals, which also led to the family's de facto control of each individual. Finally, until the Qing dynasty, there was no peer group for young people, and such groups were in fact strictly prohibited in schools (Chen Yingfang, 2007: 2–12).

The change of Chinese society and the birth of youth as a result of it generally began when China was forced to cross the threshold of modernity due to the invasion of the West in modern times. While such an assertion, according to Paul Cohen, may sound more or less Western-centric (Cohen, 1989: 133), it indicates to some extent that the transformation from traditional agricultural civilization to modern industrial civilization caused by external forces is really the macroscopic background for the emergence of youth in the sociological sense. Further, Chen Yingfang divided this macro-background into two major opportunities: The national crisis caused by the impact of the West, and the educational reform that resulted from the eastward spread of Western learning. In Table 5.1, we can see the internal correlation between the two opportunities. The driving force behind the education reform was actually the national crisis,

Table 5.1 External strikes and educational reform

Events (Wars, etc.)	Innovations and Reforms	Modern Education	Studying Abroad
The Opium War (1840–1842)	"To learn from the developed countries so as to overtake them"		
The Second Opium War (1850–1860)	The Westernization Movement	Westernization schools	The government sends students to America
The Sino-French War (1884)	The Westernized Chinese style	Birth of modern schools (government, private, church)	The government sends students to France and Britain
The Sino-Japanese War (1894–1895)	The Hundred Days' Reform	Advocating educational reform	Studying in Japan
The Eight-Power Allied Forces' invasion of China (1900–1901)	New Policies	Abolishing the imperial examination and reforming the educational system	The rise of study-abroad fever
The Revolution of 1911		The rapid development of modern education	

which we explored in detail in the section "The dawn of revolution" in Chapter 2 of the first volume of this book. In the more than 70 years from 1840 to 1911, a series of wars, from the Opium War, the Second Opium War, the Sino-French War to the Sino-Japanese War and the Eight-Power Allied Forces' invasion of China, rocked the Chinese empire, which had thought it was mighty; but this led to reforms and innovations at a different level, among which modern education reform was key. We must not limit the significance of educational reform to the field of education. It is obvious that the establishment of modern schools, the reform of the education system, the sending of students overseas, and the abolition of the imperial examination system in 1905 shook the Confucian ethics that had dominated China for thousands of years and finally triggered the 1911 Revolution that led to the collapse of the Qing dynasty.

Compared with the national crisis caused by external forces, educational reform was more of a "midwife" that contributed to the birth of youth in modern China. It was the national crisis that led a large number of people with lofty ideals to realize the importance of transforming traditional Chinese education and cultivating scholars and students adaptable to the new era. As Zhang Zhidong said: "I believe that China is not poor in wealth but in talent, not weak in soldiers but in ambition" (Zhang, 1920: 1). At the same time when Zhang Baixi, Rong Qing, Zhang Zhidong, Yuan Shikai, and others

urged the government to "reduce imperial examinations and pay more attention to schools", led by Westernization schools, the upsurge of new education
appeared. By 1911, around the outbreak of the 1911 Revolution, there were
tens of thousands of new-style schools with 1.6 to 3.0 million students (Chen,
1992: 249; Xiong, 1994: 297), including 750,000 students above secondary
school. "As a new social group, the 'student class' has been formed in China"
(Chen Yingfang, 2007: 30–31), which was also the prelude for youth to step
onto the historical stage of Chinese society.

It has been more than 100 years since the official debut of youth in China.
This was also the centenary of the Chinese nation's rise from "being beaten"
and humiliated to struggling and then to becoming the world's leading nation.
In the course of the past 100 years, the youth of China has always been supporting our nation, experiencing suffering, but also gaining in temperance. In
"Youth" and Social Changes in China, Chen Yingfang described the transformation process of Chinese youth in the first half of the 20th century, and called
two successive generations of them "radical youth" and "revolutionary youth"
(Chen Yingfang, 2007: 180). In *The Fourth Generation*, Zhang Yongjie and
Cheng Yuanzhong divided the Chinese communists into four generations from
1921, when they "struggled to seize state power", up to 1985, and described in
detail the transformation process of Chinese youth following the "revolutionary
youth". The first generation were the revolutionaries of the older generation
headed by Mao Zedong, and the last generation were the increasing number of
students who swarmed into colleges and universities with the tide of reform and
opening-up. In between were "our fathers who are in their 50s, unsmiling,
solemn, reserved, and serious about everything—be it good or bad—they do",
and "those notorious rebels, the world-famous 'red guards', and the first batch
of candidates after the restoration of the National Entrance Examination"
(Zhang & Cheng, 1988: 61). Ten years later, in *The Fifth Generation*, Wu Jun-
ping extended the narrative of the metamorphosis of youth to the post-1970s
and post-1980s:

> They are different from the fourth generation in that they grow up in the
> environment of reform and opening-up, and have little memory of the trad-
> itional shackles, which distinguishes them not only from the fourth gener-
> ation, but also from the previous three generations.
>
> (Wu, 1998: 7)

The above intergenerational discussions on the transformation of Chinese youth
not only follow one another in time, but also hold basically the same narrative
position: the same generation "has experienced some major historical events
together, and produced the same ideas, values, attitudes, behaviors and interests"
(Li, 2013: 18).

In the construction of youth studies discourse, we are familiar with and agree
with the basic narrative of intergenerational theory. In Chapter 1 of the first
volume of this book, we have already stated that the theory of intergenerational

relationship from Mannheim to Margaret Mead is one of the three theories cited and discussed in this book. We agree that major historical events are the criteria for defining "generations", especially "social generations", but due to the homogeneity of a large number of historical events, even major historical events, we are more inclined to "package" some major historical events and discuss the influence of major historical periods rather than the historical events that occurred in them on generation division. Thus, we think that if we talk about the transformation history of Chinese youth over the past 100 years, following Chen Yingfang's "radical youth" and "revolutionary youth", the more characteristic intergenerational groups are "rebel youth" and "secular youth". From radical youth to revolutionary youth and rebel youth, to the secular youth formed by the post-1970s, post-1980s, and even the post-1990s, who grew up after the reform and opening-up—this should constitute the complete transformation history of Chinese youth over the past 100 years.

Radical youth were a generation of young people active on the stage of Chinese history in the first 30 years of the 20th century, including not only some from before and after the national revolution, but also Mao Zedong, Zhou Enlai, Deng Xiaoping, and other first-generation Chinese communists. The failure of the Reform Movement of 1898 and the May Fourth Movement in 1919 were the two important points in the gradual radicalization of the newly grown Chinese youth. The Qing dynasty's killing of the six gentlemen of the Reform Movement of 1898, such as Tan Sitong, and the Kuomintang's fascist rule after 1927, were the two major boosters that led to the radicalization of the young generation. Unlike Kang Youwei, Liang Qichao, and even Tan Sitong, the radical youth, though deeply influenced by the former, were no longer "reformers" but "revolutionaries" determined to overthrow the Qing government and even all the old systems. However, from 1898 to 1910, when failures followed and the sense of collective purpose became unsustainable, these values were translated into a certain level of individual behavior, and revolutionary heroism gradually controlled the imagination of the radicals (Grieder, 1983: 228). In 1905, 30-year-old Chen Tianhua jumped into the sea in Tokyo, and in 1906, 27-year-old Yao Hongye jumped into the river in Shanghai. Out of resentment toward the tyranny of their rulers and a cult of violent revolution, radical youths carried out a wave of assassinations and an uprising. In 1905, Wu Yue, 27, assassinated the "five foreign ministers" and was beheaded; in 1907, Xu Xilin, 34, and Qiu Jin, 32, died willingly for their failed uprising; in 1910, Wang Jingwei, 27, went north to assassinate Regent Zaifeng; in 1911, Peng Jiazhen, 25, assassinated Liang Bi, the leader of Zongshetang. The "radical" tendency of people to be heroes of the world at the turn of the century was expressed most vividly in "The assassination era" by Wu Yue:

To look to Europe in the west, and to Japan in the east, you can see that every revolution is preceded by assassinations. ... Today is the era of assassinations by my comrades, and tomorrow is the revolution time of our nationality. He that would reap the fruit of the future must sow the seed of today.... If there is a better reason to live than to die, then live; if death can bring hope to the living, then die. To live when you should live and to die when you should die, and this is called life and this is a real hero.

(Wu, 1907: 7–8; 27)

The outbreak of the 1911 revolution did not completely change Chinese social realities, but it did cause the Chinese society to fall apart. In 1919, after the May Fourth Movement, anarchism, nihilism, Marxism, socialism, nationalism, liberal democracy, and fascism, which were previously popular among young people, were further advocated and practiced by more youth intellectuals due to the decline of old ideas and old traditions. From then until the 1930s and even the 1940s, among emerging young people, especially young intellectuals, there was a growing trend of radicalization, which was manifested in the spread of Marxism and the rise of the communist movement, the development and radic-alization of the left-wing cultural movement, and the radicalization of the student movement (Chen Yingfang, 2007: 84). Although there were various reasons for the radicalization of Chinese youth, as Liu Zaifu said, the spread of Marxism and its class struggle theory in China was indeed an important motivation.[2] Furthermore, after 1937, due to the invasion of Japan, China, which was already in a state of turmoil, as it had been throughout modern times, was plunged into a catastrophe. As a result, the duet of "enlightenment and salvation" played by Chinese youth since the May Fourth Movement had produced a "variation": Not only did salvation for survival replace the cultural "enlightenment" with the theme of anti-feudalism, but in fact, as Li Zehou said, "traditional old ideology" "quietly infiltrated in a disguised way" (Li, 1987: 7), and finally "salvation overpowered enlightenment and peasant revolution over-powered modernization" (Li, 1994: 10).

In the late 1930s, "revolutionary youth" began to appear on the historical stage. On the one hand, it was the natural result of the above-mentioned theme of salvation for survival; on the other hand, it was also the product of the ideol-ogy of the Chinese Communist Party, which began to abandon the previous "closed-door" intellectual policy and became determined to systematically forge the younger generation. In terms of the former aspect, more and more young intellectuals entered the liberated areas to join the Chinese revolution led by the Communist Party of China (CPC) because they had devoted themselves to the Anti-Japanese War and the subsequent war of liberation for the purpose of saving the nation; in terms of the latter aspect, the CPC also made great efforts to attract young intellectuals to the revolution. Not only was the recruitment advertisement of the Chinese People's Anti-Japanese Military and Political Col-lege pasted on every lamp post from Yan'an to Xi'an, but also Yan'an made a promise of "freedom to come and go" to young intellectuals, and then improved their treatment in the border area under the extremely difficult eco-nomic conditions. The change of the policy further determined popular senti-ment. In just five years from 1938 to 1943, more than 40,000 intellectuals arrived in Yan'an, while in 1943, there were no more than 30,000 student Party members among the more than 1 million members of the Kuomintang. The latter were "obviously defeated in the great political battle for intellectual youth" (Pei, 2013). After the 1940s, the young intellectuals who went to Yan'an later became the most active grassroots cells and backbone of the CPC. They went deep into the vast Chinese countryside and effectively organized and mobilized millions of peasants, finally laying the foundation for the victory of the Chinese revolution.

It should be pointed out that, compared with previous radical youth, revolutionary youth not only had a lower educational and family background, but also no longer pursued the "individual standard" and "liberal orientation" that the latter once pursued at the cost of their lives as the enlightenment theme weakened. This made it possible for Mao Zedong and the Chinese communists to successfully discipline young intellectuals to conform to the Party's goals. In fact, after the "Yan'an rectification" in 1942, the political role of young intellectuals shifted from the organizer and mobilizer of Chinese workers and peasants to the "integrator", and then to the "recipient" or "transformed" of the workers' and peasants' culture after the 1960s. The historical role of the youth, at least that of the "leading role", was replaced by the young workers and peasants. Do not underestimate the political significance of "combining with workers and peasants" for the transformation or metamorphosis of Chinese youth from being radical to being revolutionary. In fact, during the whole 20 years from 1940 to 1960, the criterion for judging whether a youth was revolutionary or not was closely related to the political requirement set by Mao Zedong in his 1939 article "The direction of the youth movement", mentioned in Chapter 2 of the first volume of this book:

> To judge whether a young person is revolutionary, what should be used as the standard? How to identify him? There is only one criterion, and that is to see whether he is willing to integrate himself with the broad masses of workers and peasants and whether he will do so or not. Those who are willing and practice integration with workers and peasants are revolutionary; otherwise they are non-revolutionary or counter-revolutionary.
>
> (Mao, 1967b: 530)

The victory of the Chinese Revolution in 1949 did not change the criterion for judging the revolutionary youth, but the succession problems caused by the establishment of the revolutionary cause still endowed it with new historical connotations, especially after the 20th CPC National Congress in 1956. At that time, revolutionary youth were defined as "successors to the communist cause", and "the communist youth league of China", composed of revolutionary youth, was "a mass organization of advanced youth led by the communist party of China. It is the assistant and reserve army of the communist party of China" (Communist Youth League of China, 2013). In order to instill in the younger generation the political expectations of the state, and to help shape their imaginations or expectations of individual roles in accordance with the expectations of the state, after 1949, the state set out a series of examples of revolutionary youth such as Lei Feng, Ouyang Hai, Xing Yanzi, Dong Jiageng, and "Beijing youth commandos", supplemented by various political ceremonies (Cheng, 2008; Whyte, 1974) to prevent "peaceful evolution"[3] and to create "successors" to the proletarian revolutionary cause.

Although Mao Zedong took precautions to prevent "peaceful evolution", before the third and fourth generations of the CPC took over, he became deeply alienated from his own chosen successors in the party, and in 1966 vowed to launch a proletarian cultural revolution to replace Liu Shaoqi, the president he no longer trusted. Unlike Stalin's personal terror, as we explained in Chapter 2 of the first volume of this book, Mao Zedong used the Red Guards or "rebel youth" as a tool to bring down his political opponents, and received 11 million Red Guards in ten batches eight times between August 18 and November 25, 1966. Mao Zedong's eight interviews with the Red Guards, together with his previous letter to those of the High School Affiliated to Tsinghua University on July 30, "Long live the revolutionary and rebellious spirit of the proletariat" and "Again on the revolutionary and rebellious spirit of the proletariat", put the Red Guards on the political stage. Within two years, the Red Guard Movement shocked the world in a way unheard of in human history.

Although the movement marked by the "great rebellion" lasted for a little more than two years, its spirit of rebellion and its subsequent influence were continuously spread, and it has been revived again and again by the social ideals and political practices of Bo Xilai and his kind to this day. From the beginning of the Cultural Revolution in 1966 to the Tiananmen Square political turmoil in 1989, "rebel youth" with high political enthusiasm experienced the roller-coaster of political turbulence, and thus "turned their innocent hearts into a political block" (Zhang & Cheng, 1988: 98). As a result of the rupture of history, as well as the alienation of the subsequent "secular youth" from politics, and the consequent decline of their desire to live within the system—though this generation "born in the new society and growing up under the red flag" paid too much price for the "rebellion", especially the "going to the mountains and countryside"—some of them, especially the college-educated elites after 1978, actually extended their prime time. From the beginning of the 1980s when they came out of the campus to today, the reform and opening-up of four decades has become the background of their personal growth and social performance.

"Secular youth" entered the stage of history after Deng Xiaoping's "southern tour speech" officially launched China's transition to a market economy in 1992. Despite the numerous major historical events that have occurred in Chinese society during 1978–2020, from the point of view of this major historical period, with the gradual depoliticization of social life, market-oriented or pan-economic factors began to become the main axis of life. After 1978, economic construction replaced the class struggle of Mao Zedong's era as the focus of both official and civil concern; moreover, due to the direct correlation between such economic incentive policies and individual benefits, the exogenous "anxiety" of the leaders of the CPC who wanted to catch up with the world powers in a short period of time after 1949 was successfully transformed into the daily endogenous anxiety of individual citizens for the first time (Zhou et al., 2014). After the Tiananmen Square turbulence in 1989, strong political control and positive economic guidance made the focus of Chinese people, especially the younger generation, increasingly turn toward economic life. Chinese society began to transform from a politicized society to a secular one, and after 1992, it gradually became a society with a distinct mercantilism.

The secularization of social life has changed the social basis for generations of radical youth. The transformation of the whole society from traditional to modern, from planned economy to market economy, and from closed to open, also provides an opportunity for the transformation of the younger generation from radical to secular. To be specific, first, because of the progress of reform and opening-up, the young generation or secular youth who have grown up over the past few decades have become more and more rational. They believe more in science and replace the theological dogmas that governed daily life with the principles of reason; they doubt everything, have a critical spirit, and therefore become "alternatives" to the adult world. Second, because they have been familiar with the rules of the market economy since childhood and immersed in the atmosphere of that economy, they have developed not only an awareness of competition and risk, but also the mentality of utilitarianism and the code of conduct of pursuing sensory enjoyment. In the eyes of adult society, they are even "the most spoiled generation" or "the most selfish generation", in other words, the typical "beat generation". Third, because of the one-child policy launched in the 1980s, most secular youth, especially urban youth, are either the only child or at least live in families with few children. The inclination of the family intergenerational center nourishes their distinct personality, and the improvement of material conditions also indulges their pursuit of all kinds of fashion, which not only coincides with the noisy multicultural atmosphere that followed the 1980s, but also promotes the development of multiculturalism to a certain extent—from the "Super Voice Girls" who sing as they like, to Ma Nuo who said in the dating show *If You Are the One* that she would rather cry in a BMW than laugh on a bicycle, the diversity and eccentricity of cultures and values has reached a point that the adult world, which continues to dominate mainstream society, is amazed.[4] Finally, because of the endless emergence of various information communication technologies (ICTs) over the past decades, especially the development of electronic computers and network technology, the button has become the most realistic existence in the world of secular youth. This horizontal knowledge association has abandoned the traditional vertical accumulation of human knowledge, narrowed the distance between the world, expanded the horizon and activity scope of the younger generation, and, most importantly, provided an open space for self-expression for Chinese youth.

The reversal of the social image of secular youth occurred in 2008, when the post-1970s began to enter middle age successively, the first group of the post-1990s just entered youth, and the post-1980s became the backbone of secular youth. The Wenchuan earthquake and the Beijing Olympic Games provided a good opportunity for the post-1980s of secular youth to replace the previous confrontation and rebellion with cooperation and participation. Two years later, the Shanghai World Expo paved the way for the post-1990s to take the stage, so that the Olympic generation and Expo generation became the nicknames of secular youth. Even Li Zehou, who is always sharp, praised the post-1990s generation in his article "Answers to aesthetic education as a substitute for religion" written in 2006, saying that "the post-90s generation seems to be plain and indifferent, showing no affinity to others, and even being disobedient and playful, but they can stand up at any time, being tenacious and willing to take responsibility regardless of life and death" (Zheng, 2014). At this point, people finally see some hope in the transformation of Chinese youth over the past 100 years, although we will see that they still struggle to grow up in the crevice that exists between the state and society.

Growing up in the crevice between state and society

There are many historical and realistic ways to describe the transformation of youth, but as the transitional form between modern school system and factory system created by the Industrial Revolution, youth naturally has some tension of dissociation and opposition with social structure. If the social structure in reality is constructed by the interaction between the state and society, then young people in the modern sense exist in the crevice that lies between the state and society from the very beginning, and their growth space is to some extent endowed by the trade-off between the two.

In modern times, when young people appear on the stage of Chinese history, the Chinese empire they faced, though dying on the outside through harsh political rule and the social network woven with the traditional Chinese family system, became a powerful restraining force for the younger generation to play a historical role as an independent force. As we have explained in Chapter 2 of the first volume of this book, traditional Chinese society formed the habit of living together because of their dependence on the land; and because of the economic activity of farming, the family became the basic productive unit. Further, on this basis, the importance of the household, the family, and the clan based on blood relationship was formed. Because they lived in families, the patriarch or leader of the family was often the dominant one in the local society or community. In general, these dominators were not only experienced elders within the family, but also often those who understood that Confucian culture had the power to educate "and thus acquire knowledge of the management of social affairs" (Zhang, 1991: 1)—the so-called "gentry" class. The gentry at first consisted of two distinct social components: the scholars, who were composed of imperial officials, and the gentry, officials who had retired from their posts and lived in rural areas. However, in modern China, the gentry class has merged into one social class (Qiao, 1992: 170). Because this class acted as the spokesman or moral embodiment of Confucian culture, it was respected and trusted by the people within the group and its members often became the actual leaders in local society or the rural community. In the Ming and Qing dynasties, although the government was able to intervene in the life of the grassroots through the official system up to the county level, the basic social operation and governance functions were assumed by the gentry class. To borrow Fei Xiaotong's words, the consensual power of local society embodied by the gentry connects the violent power represented by the state with the patriarchal power generated by the succession of the family (Fei, 1998: 76). Therefore, in traditional China, "the suppression of young people is not only based on the organization, system and ethics of the family, but also on the background of gentry domination and the political system of the country based on it" (Chen Yingfang, 2007: 22). It can be said that it is the family organizations controlled by the gentry that successfully transformed the filial piety within the family to loyalty to the monarch. After the 1911 Revolution, not only did Yuan Shikai still respect Confucius and read scriptures and dream of restoration, but even after the Kuomintang formally took over state power in the 1920s, based on the need to maintain rule and resist the increasingly fierce communist tide, the national government did not actually touch the old social structure. Not only did the triad of clan power, gentry power, and political power, which had been the basis of political governance since the Ming and Qing dynasties, remain the same, but the Bao-Jia system of "households", which had been practiced for a long time in feudal times, was still in use. And the Confucian family ethic was still used to rule and educate young people; as we pointed out in Chapter 4, loyalty and filial piety was still the foundation of the country.

The isomorphic pattern of family and state of traditional Chinese patriarchal society makes the first old wall encountered by the younger generation who had just stepped onto the stage of history at the beginning of the 20th century was their own family and its related old systems including filial piety. In this way, it is quite normal that the rebellion against parents and family naturally became the common action of logic of the generation of radical youth. Although love, marriage, and family constituted the main contents of the so-called "troubles of youth", they essentially reflected the contradictions and conflicts between generations, behind which was the difference between the old and the new ages. The emergence and rapid growth of modern schools, and the continuous emergence of such public spheres as newspapers, radio, trendy publications, business associations, civil society groups, parties, shopping malls, cafes, museums, public hospitals, and racecourses, gave birth to a growing number of young intellectuals who were receptive to new cultures and ideas, while the social structures, including the family, became increasingly intolerable. In this way, the young generation's resistance to the old system naturally focused on the pursuit of freedom of marriage, and an indictment of the feudal patriarchal system including the patriarchy and the "cannibalistic ethics" centered on filial piety. In a word, from "resisting the family to reforming the society". In fact, whether it was Wu Yu, Shi Cuntong, Mao Zedong, or Ba Jin, the discontent with society and the state of their generation of "radical youth" was initially born out of contradictions and conflicts with their own families and with their fathers or the patriarchs of their families.[5]

Furthermore, if the traditional Chinese family doctrine advocates patriarchy and filial piety, which has a distinct authoritarian tendency, it is not only consistent with the autocratic rule of the state that has lasted for thousands of years, but also the breeding place of absolutism. All these have determined that all the actions of radical youth are characterized by a distinct anti-authority. In a sense, the radicalization of radical youth is not only manifested in the worship of violence, such as assassination and riot, but also in the denial and contempt of all authority. In his book *Intellectuals and Modern China*, the American historian Jerome Grieder said of another anti-Confucius pioneer, Wu Zhihui, that

> the events of that year, and the Boxer disaster two years later, brought him to an outspokenly antiauthoritarian position: side with the people in any dispute with the monarchy, was his motto; side with the students in any dispute with their teachers; side with the younger generation in any dispute with the older generation. Such opinions were a trifle advanced for turn-of-the-century Shanghai.
>
> (Grieder, 1983: 155)

It is hardly an exaggeration to say that this is the attitude shared by the generation of radical youth.

After 1937, although the Kuomintang was still the ruler of Chinese society in the non-occupied areas, especially in the national-controlled areas, the "holy land" in the mind of Chinese young intellectuals was Yan'an. For the Chinese Communist Party headed by Mao Zedong, on the one hand, after the outbreak of the War of Resistance against Japanese Aggression, not only the extreme demand for talent made them realize that "whoever gets the intellectuals gets the world", but also the formation of the situation of "national resistance against Japanese aggression" after the "Xi'an incident" also gained legitimacy for the competition for talent, so, attracted and inspired by various positive policies,

> thousands of intellectuals fled to Yan'an from all over the world, the youngest being 12 or 13 years old ..., including university professors, engineers, and journalists of all parties and factions, and even miss Shanghai, who loves to eat and dance, pregnant young women, and overseas Chinese returning from southeast Asia.
>
> (Pei, 2013)

This naturally prepared a talent pool for the expansion of the Communist Party's influence and the subsequent success of revolution. On the other hand, the influx of so many young intellectuals into Yan'an and other base areas not only brought security risks and financial pressure, but also brought difficulties in education and discipline. Not mentioning liberal writers like Wang Shiwei, Xiao Jun, and Ding Ling and general intellectual youth, even Zhou Yang, the leader of the left-wing writers, who always paid attention to keeping in line with the Party and its leaders subjectively, initially had strong anti-authority and personal freedom tendencies as the spiritual successor of the May Fourth generation. Xiao Jun thought that there was a sense in Tolstoy's character of rebelling against established authority and wanting to be a "king", "very much like himself" (Yang, 2014). Zhou Yang was also fascinated by Nietzsche's philosophy when he was in college. In his own words, Nietzsche "taught me to boldly deny all conventionalism, tradition and authority" (quoted from Xu, 2010: 36). Although the leaders of the Chinese revolution, including Mao Zedong, were at first radical youths who opposed authority, now, based on the organizational need to compete with the Kuomintang for the world, and the individual need to establish his own prestige in the party, educating and disciplining the younger generation, especially the young intellectuals, to obey the organization and its leaders became the primary task of the surging revolutionary cause. Against this practical background, Mao Zedong was naturally convinced that young intellectuals "should be well educated and guided to gradually overcome their weaknesses in the long-term struggle so as to make them revolutionary and become mass" (Mao, 1967c: 582).

The intention of forging or disciplining the revolutionary youth coincided with the mass production movement that began before and after, and thus achieved a perfect form of expression. The large-scale production movement, which started from the production mobilization meeting of the Party, government, and army in Yan'an in February 1939 and reached its climax two years later when the 359 brigade entered Nanniwan for reclamation, was originally aimed at breaking the economic blockade of the Shanxi–Gansu–Ningxia border area by the Kuomintang, but it was quickly transformed into a way to reform and discipline the population in the liberated areas, especially the young intellectuals who poured in from the nationalized areas, by means of "labor". We have mentioned that since the May Fourth Movement, young intellectuals had always taken it as their duty to save the old China from fire and water, and formed a tradition of "enlightenment" aimed at opening up people's wisdom, but this was completely overturned by Mao Zedong's recipe of "combining with workers and peasants". The mass production movement reinforced the idea that no one can eat unless he or she works.

However, by limiting labor to manual labor, the value and power of knowledge was denied, and, as a result, a large number of young intellectuals who once regarded themselves as very high lost their original self-identity and became self-deprecating, while accepting the arranged destiny of transformation through labor (Zhou Haiyan, 2013: 163).

When discussing the discipline of power on the body, Foucault wrote, "the body becomes a useful force only if it is both a productive body and a subjected body" (Foucault, 2012: 26). In the early 1940s, when the mass production movement forced the young intellectuals to be "reborn" through physical labor, the rectification movement had just begun in time to reform the minds of leaders at all levels and young intellectuals through a series of ways to forge "new people". Although the core of Yan'an rectification was to destroy the foundation and influence of the "dogmatic sect" headed by Wang Ming and others in the Party, its essence was "to carry out ideological transformation of the majority of party members and cadres—to transform their ideological consciousness with Mao Zedong's theories and concepts" (Gao, 2010: 177). In addition to gentle means, such as studying documents, writing introspective notes, and filling in "small broadcast questionnaires",[6] the rectification also rapidly promoted violent means as the movement was carried out further, such as political review of cadres, anti-espionage campaigns, accounts of personal history, and the "pants off and tails off" movement for self-disclosure and self-prosecution. Strong group pressure finally made all the participants, especially the young intellectuals who were touched the most, convinced and began to unconditionally agree with the Party's principles and leadership authority. As Wei Junyi reflected more than 50 years later: After that, "I gave up everything I got from reading. I preferred to be a fighter with superficial knowledge and firmly believe everything Lenin, Stalin and Mao Zedong say, because it is the doctrine I worship" (Wei, 1998b: 3).

With the transition from radical youth to revolutionary youth, the attitude of the younger generation to authority also changed from denial and rebellion to submission or worship; of course, it was the new communist authority—Mao Zedong, who became the irreplaceable symbol of this authority, and increasingly, the only one. According to Franz Schurmann, after the victory of the Communist Revolution in 1949, the gentry or landlord class was completely destroyed on the basis of the collapse of Confucian values, and the new marriage law symbolized the liberation of women and the total collapse of paternalism (Schurmann, 1971: 7). At this point, the old social system completely collapsed, and the CPC rebuilt the new China according to its own ideology and rational organization mode, and realized the state's "political conquest of society" (Madsen, 1999: 42).

After 1949, based on the appeal to legitimacy of the Communist Revolution and the hope of eternity for the revolutionary regime, the social status and historical significance of young people or revolutionary youth were highly affirmed. Obviously, as a generation of dynastic change, the young people, especially the young revolutionary cadres, were the representatives of the new social order, the leaders or actual dominators of China's vast grassroots society, and of course, the successors of the future cause. Therefore, Mao Zedong did not forget to continue to reaffirm the political mission and historical role of youth on all possible occasions:

> The world is yours and ours. But in the end it's yours. You young people, full of vigor and vitality, are in full bloom, like the sun at eight or nine o'clock in the morning. ... The world belongs to you and China's future belongs to you.
>
> (Mao, 1965: 14–15)

Although Mao Zedong bestowed warm praise on the role of youth or revolutionary youth, their dominant position had been lost and their independent growth space was squeezed. While before 1949, the Kuomintang government still practiced authoritarian state rule at home, due to the extensive influence of Western society, the existence of liberated areas holding the banner of democracy, a certain degree of rural autonomy implemented by the gentry class, and the development of modern education, media, and other public fields in the metropolis, and even the existence of concessions, there was still a certain social space for the independent growth of young people. After 1949, this already tight space became even narrower. The one-sided international policy towards the Soviet Union and the outbreak of the "war to resist U.S. aggression and aid Korea" completely blocked any possible influence from the West; the overthrow of the gentry class and the subsequent land reform and collectivization of agriculture, as well as the simultaneous socialist transformation of industry and commerce, strengthened the state's control over urban and rural society; the "department readjustment" plan implemented from 1952 to 1953 reconstructed China's university education system in accordance with the Soviet model—private schools, especially missionary schools, were abolished, and departments related to ideology, including political science, sociology, law, journalism, and communication, were largely eliminated, on the one hand, and the ideological reform movement of university teachers was carried out in an all-round way, thus "the school, once a haven for anti-system radical youth has been transformed into the breeding institution of 'revolutionary youth'", on the other hand (Chen Yingfang, 2007: 186). While the state and the Party achieved overall control or conquest of the society—the total control of the media, the disappearance of social groups that were relatively free from the state, the establishment of the household registration and personnel file system, the regularization of ideological transformation, the establishment of the occupational distribution system, and the implementation of the complete political socialization ceremony—the youth, or the "revolutionary youth", completely lost their independence and became the assistant or subsidiary of the state, especially the Party. At this time, the word "revolutionary" in revolutionary youth had completely lost its original meaning of "resistant" and become a synonym for obeying the new order, namely revolutionary order, and following the rules in daily life. In this context, the "spirit of screws" represented by Lei Feng, a model of revolutionary youth highly respected by the state—that is, the individual is just a screw in the big machine of the state and the collective—naturally became the basic role-positioning of revolutionary youth.

The transformation from revolutionary youth to rebel youth in 1966 took place without any changes in state and social relations. However, when the country was divided into two parts—two opposing social systems of the Party and the government (Zhou, 2000b), and the latter system led by Liu Shaoqi was regarded as a symbol of capitalism—by its founder Mao Zedong, the rebellious youth who appeared at this time could either continue to worship authorities feverishly, or turn their heads to crazily fight against the authorities that contradicted this, so that they generally had the typical dual personality of "authority personality" according to Chen Peihua (Chen Yingfang, 2007: 15–16). It is true that most of the young rebels "were born in the new society and grew up under the red flag" and they should have followed the path of their predecessors, the revolutionary youth, and grown into dedicated and authoritative builders of socialism like Lei Feng. However, in the process of political socialization of young people after 1949, the so-called "revolutionary heroism" education composed of radicalization and resistance still lurked in the daily cultivation of Lei Feng's traits of loyalty and obedience. In daily life, this kind of education on radicalization and resistance was included in the following aspects. First, although in the new social order, "chairman Mao can only be worshiped, not imitated", the rebellious image of young Mao Zedong was still deeply rooted in the hearts of the younger generation and had a large number of fanatical followers for a long time. Second, the legitimacy of "violent" revolutions had been lauded for its appeal to the legitimacy of communist revolutions, which was especially true for those children of the "five red categories" of people (i.e., revolutionary soldiers, revolutionary cadres, workers, poor and middle peasants after 1949), or today's so-called "red second generation" (the earliest Red Guards in the Cultural Revolution). Finally, after 1949, Mao Zedong emphasized class struggle and never yielded in the fight against "imperialism, revision and counterrevolution" (Chen Peihua, 2007: 82–93; Chen Yingfang, 2007: 201–202). It can be seen that under the long-term immersion of such education, when the Cultural Revolution launched by Mao Zedong himself provided the stage for rebellion, out of loyalty to the great leader and worship of violent revolution, the revolutionary youth would naturally turn into rebel youth overnight.

To be frank, as we have mentioned in the discussion of the youth revolt in the Cultural Revolution and the subsequent "going to mountains and countryside" movement in Chapter 2 of this book, although the movements in the late Mao Zedong era caused irreparable damage to the growth of China's youth, as 17 million intellectual youth were suddenly left at the bottom of society, where social control was relatively weak and even the rural society alienated them, in addition to the strong homesickness composed of depression and disappointment, independent thinking also began to sprout within the educated youth group. The relatively independent and relaxed environment created by the lack of control, coupled with the realization of the absurdity of coming to the countryside from thousands of miles away and receiving "re-education" from the poor and middle peasants after close contact with them, made it possible for them to reflect on the "going to the countryside" movement and even on the class struggle and Cultural Revolution advocated by the Great Leader.[7] Therefore, since 1968, the boom of underground literature, educated youth literature, and various "gray-cover books" and "yellow-cover books" published to criticize revisionism before the Cultural Revolution became popular among urban youth, especially among the educated youth who went to the countryside.[8] These underground reading and reflection activities later not only "eventually developed into open forms of political expression" (Bonnin, 2004: 343; Leese, 2011: 243)—the April Fifth Movement in Tiananmen Square in 1976 and the large-scale "returning to the city" movement of educated youth after 1978 (Liu, 2009:

451–498)—but also laid a foundation for the development of the "ideological liberation movement" centering on the discussion of truth standards and the large-scale reform and opening-up afterwards.

If we continue to talk about secular youth from the worship of authority, the so-called generation born in the 1970s to the 1990s who grew up with the reform and opening-up, perhaps the most typical change was the rapid secularization of the objects of worship in their vision—from political authority to consumer authority or the idol of the masses. Two of the most striking features of this shift are first the political figures of the revolutionary era were replaced by singers, movie stars, or sports stars. In Chapter 4 of the first volume of this book we have stated that these new secular icons showed a bright populist trend and were no longer charismatic politicians. Second, even those statesmen worshipped by the younger generation no longer had a divine aura. From the "Hello, Xiaoping" banner on the National Day parade of the 35th anniversary in 1984, to network users "Shi*jin* Ba*bao*fan" (literally meaning "the mixed rice pudding", practically, "the fans of Chinese President Hu *Jin*tao and Premier Wen Jia*bao*") and "Xue*xi* Fensi Tuan" (literally meaning "the fans who learn from their idols", practically, "the fans who learn from Chinese President *Xi* Jinping"), the young people, who used to look up to the political leaders as divine, now placed them at their own level.

As we have mentioned before, the best of the rebel youth, those who poured into the universities in 1978 under the tide of reform and opening-up, have been socially active in Chinese society for over 30 years after graduation, and history excessively repays the deprivation of this generation to this small elite. In my view, their success is partly due to their "interrupted life course and hard rural life experience, which may lead them to abandon some illusions and inspire a pragmatic orientation more suitable for the market economy" (Zhou & Hou, 1999), but at the same time, it is more likely that the secular youth behind them, the so-called post-1970s, post-1980s, and even post-1990s have completely left the planned economy, the original system, and even the lifestyle of their predecessors, which leaves the 77-graders and 78-graders, who are at best half-educated, with no challengers or rivals on their accustomed paths. In other words, the younger generation has a different way of life, making them and their predecessors two-track cars that would never meet each other, leading to long periods of brilliance for the 77-graders and 78-graders.

Although China's civil society has not yet formed, let alone formed a challenge to the country, it is acknowledged that the state's control over society has been gradually weakened over the past four decades; social mobility has been greatly strengthened in space, occupation, and status; and cultural diversity and heterogeneity have also been significantly enhanced. All these have created conditions for the free and spontaneous growth of secular youth. From 1978 to 2020, outside the country, there have been three spaces for the growth of secular youth: the market, society, and the Internet.

The market was gradually formed in the reform and opening-up after 1978. Before that, the state eliminated the status and role of the market through the planned economy, which also made young people rely on the state for their livelihood. Take occupational acquisition as an example. In Western countries, occupational segmentation mainly relies on diplomas, training, and a market access system (Weeden, 2002), while in the Mao Zedong era, it was mainly achieved through the identity and household registration system. As we have mentioned before, the household registration and personnel file system, together with the identity system, eliminated the possibility of young people seeking jobs by themselves, and naturally achieved effective control over them to a considerable extent. After over 40 years of reform, although the occupation acquisition system formed in the planned economy era still exists in government agencies, public institutions, and public enterprises, the impact of the urban–rural split household registration system on occupational acquisition continues, differences in wages and social security of laborers with different status are sometimes obvious (Bian & Zhang, 2001), a relatively free labor market has been formed and perfected. Not only did 260 million rural workers find their jobs in cities and industrial and commercial enterprises through the market, but also the improvement of the rate of return on education (Li & Ding, 2003), which we mentioned in Chapter 1 of the first volume of this book, made the relationship between human capital and labor price more market-oriented. All these make the dependence of secular youth, starting from the post-1970s, especially the post-1980s and post-1990s, on the state for career acquisition and even breadwinning to have been significantly reduced. According to the statistics of "Comprehensive survey data of China's social conditions" in 2006 and 2008, Li Chunling et al. confirmed that not only did the proportion of agricultural employment of the post-1980s group drop sharply, but also their proportion of employment in non-public institutions was much higher than that of other generations (Li, 2013: 102–103, 346–348).[9] It can be said that the existence of a relatively free market not only provides secular youth with the possibility to seek life outside the state system, but also provides them with the possibility to freely express their personal opinions, actively participate in public affairs, and even to be maverick and deviant in their personal life.

Although the excessive promotion of the market economy and the promotion of the related principle of priority of growth are generally believed to affect the healthy development of society, so that China, as a socialist country, has formed a market economy which Polanyi called "disembedded" in society (Polanyi, 2001), the expansion of the scale of freedom corresponding to the nature of the market expands the space for the growth of society and the growth of the young generation. In the 1990s, especially after 2000, based on the partial transfer of the state to society, citizens or social organizations were encouraged to manage their own affairs in an autonomous way, "enhancing the vitality of social development" (Central Committee of the Communist Party of China, 2013: 69–70), and the originally cramped social space expanded to a certain extent. For secular youth, the social space they live in mainly consists of the following. On the one hand, with the implementation of the college enrollment expansion policy in 1999, higher education has expanded rapidly in the past 20 years, with the gross enrollment rate approaching 50% and the number of college students reaching 30 million. As the largest group of college students in the world, Chinese college students have become a social group with a certain degree of freedom, which also provides social soil for the breeding of various new ideas and behaviors. On the other hand, after the 1990s, a variety of voluntary civil organizations, especially grassroots organizations, began to emerge, including various officially registered civic organizations (NGOs or NPOs), informal grassroots organizations, student societies, consumer and entertainment clubs (including the fraternity), reading parties, business associations, and other mutual aid groups. Although both the registration and the activities of them are strictly controlled by the state, the emergence of these main "organizations aiming at social service and social change" (Yang, 2013: 138) provides the possibility for independent activities of the younger generation, especially for influencing the direction of national policies. For example, the post-1980s generation basically presented themselves as volunteers at the disaster relief site of the Wenchuan earthquake and during the Olympic Games in Beijing, showing their ability of self-organization and self-participation for the first time.

In fact, in addition to the market and society, the rise of the Internet society after the 1990s also provided free space for the growth of Chinese youth. Although in the relevant sections of Chapters 2 and 3, we have discussed the influence of the emergence of the Internet in China as a social force on the formation of the public sphere, here we are willing to discuss it as a relatively independent factor affecting the growth of young people. The significance of the network to the expansion of social space lies in that, on the one hand, this online mode itself is a public space where citizens can participate, form public topics and public opinion forces, and influence national policies and actions (Hu, 2008: 312). On the other hand, not only do many public societies and NGOs depend on networks, but in fact their ability to use the network directly affects the nature and vitality of these communities or organizations, because the horizontal communication and information sharing of public goods through the network are just two important characteristics that civil society organizations must have. In addition, it must be pointed out that the discussion on the use of the Internet and its significance should not be limited to young intellectuals. Today's large number of migrant workers who enter the city directly from the countryside are actually the generation using electronic technology. "The Internet, mobile phones and QQ grew up with them. At least among the migrant workers in the eastern coastal areas, an active electronic culture of the working class has been formed" (Yang, 2013: 239). If we say that there has always been a great difference between young intellectuals and ordinary people in modern China, today, thanks to the emergence of the Internet, for the first time, they share similarities in the use of media. It can be assumed that this will further affect their similarity in values, life attitudes, and social behaviors, and make cultural reverse a new way for the whole society to reforge intergenerational relations.

Cultural reverse: forging new intergenerational relations

The reason why we spend considerable space describing the growth path of Chinese youth in the past century is to explain that, as a relatively free social force, the growth of young people has always been under the control of society, especially the state. Comparatively speaking, in the two periods before 1949 and after 1978, especially after 1992, young people obtained a larger space for growth and their independence became stronger. Before 1949, in the confrontation with the Manchu dynasty and Kuomintang rule, youth, including radical youth, the backbone of them, not only grew up, but actually rewrote the history of China with their radicalism and tenacity. After 1978, China's reform and opening-up, especially the efforts towards marketization after 1992, provided the possibility for secular youth to get rid of the overall attachment to the state, especially state power. The expansion of various social space also provided a broader stage for the participation of the younger generation.

When Chen Yingfang analyzed the division of May Fourth youth after the 1920s, she proposed the role or significance of intergenerational opposition in the subsequent political opposition between the Kuomintang and the Communist Party. Although Chen Yingfang carefully stated that this "is not to prove that the opposition between the Communist Party and the Kuomintang is only an inter-generational opposition" (Chen Yingfang, 2007: 92), relevant data can still prove that intergenerational opposition does constitute some element of political or general social opposition. In the 1920s, most of the powerful faction of the Kuomintang were born in the 1860–1880s, and they had little direct contact with the May Fourth Movement and the new culture movement. On the contrary, except Chen Duxiu, most of the founders and early leaders of the CPC, including Mao Zedong, Li Dazhao, and Zhang Guotao, were born after the 1880s. They basically belonged to the new youth or May Fourth youth generation. This may indicate that significant historical phenomena such as wars and revolutions can probably create a generation, and may in turn become tools for understanding historical rhythms in accordance with the intergenerational turnover (Atiyah, 1993: 144–145). Further, if one considers that in normal intergenerational transitions, the older generation often controls the power of the state, then the relationship between the growing younger generation and the state may also project intergenerational relationships among different generations of society. In this way, perhaps the state's shaping of youth and youth's compliance or resistance to the existing order are just a more realistic magnification of intergenerational relations within families at the macro-level.

As we have argued in Chapter 1 of the first volume of this book, generation and intergenerational relations are not only biological facts or natural continuations of biological facts, but also social facts. On the one hand, generation itself is the basis for the existence of society, a community of people, while the intergenerational relationship is a conventional social relationship. On the other hand, the problem of generation or intergenerational relationship is caused by the fracture or discontinuity between generations arising from the transition from traditional society to modern society in modern times. In other words, it is the rapid social changes in modern times that make biological generation turn into a real social generation. Considering that intergenerational relationship, as a social fact, is constructed by members of social groups, especially the elders, according to the values or life meaning of their times, its fragmentation or discontinuity is almost reflected as the fracture or change of the previous construction mode.

From this point of view, the construction of intergenerational relations in traditional society is continuous and smooth. Take China as an example. The core of the intergenerational relationship in feudal society—filial piety and seniority—became a sacred tradition through inheritance of rites and customs. Rites and customs involved all aspects of the daily life of villagers, which were not only collective habits and local rules, but also the product of the collective memory of the elders. According to Halbwachs's point of view, in the process of rites and customs inheritance, "collective frameworks are, to the contrary, precisely the instruments used by the collective memory to reconstruct an image of the past which is in accord, in each epoch, with the predominant thoughts of the society" (Halbwachs, 1992: 40). It is the social responsibility of the older generation to establish a historical identity of one's family, nation, or group through the intention to reconstruct the past for the younger generation through their own memory, or to establish a contemporary connection with the past or even the ancient one. Although as a social construct, it is not difficult to falsify or distort collective or social memories since they can be reconstructed, in traditional society where today and even tomorrow is nothing but the natural continuation of yesterday, because current events are not definitely different from previous events, and current values are not different from previous values, in most cases, this pseudo-construction or distortion is only the result of individuals' attachment or ostentatious motivation (e.g., as Halbwachs says, falsifying one's aristocratic identity by compiling a family tree; Halbwachs, 1992: 225), and it will not become the common behavior of the whole group or society, whether intentionally or unintentionally.

The rapid social changes that have taken place since modern times have produced many unprecedented things and changed or even overturned the values of the younger generation in judging the meaning of life. As a result, the reconstruction of collective memory has become an increasingly challenging form of social engineering. The greatest difficulty in social memory is how to reconcile the reconstruction or narrative of the past with the values or beliefs of today. From the perspective of the changes of Chinese society over the past hundred years, in the four generations in the long period we discussed, the reconstruction and inheritance of collective memory between generations basically did not have too much of a barrier between the following three generations, which effectively molded the intergenerational relationship between them. One is between radical youth and revolutionary youth. Although the latter inherited two elements of memory from the former's narrative—"sacrifice" (devotion) and "anti-authority"—after the 1930s, Mao Zedong transformed anti-authority into loyalty to the Party, the state, and the leader himself by the need to save the nation, thus successfully realizing the continuation of the collective memory. The other is between revolutionary youth and rebel youth. Although the latter responded to the Great Leader's call in the Cultural Revolution and directed the struggle against the former, as successors in their growth process, they directly received the revolutionary education or historical narrative from the former—including the worship of violent revolution and their unconditional obedience to the Party and leaders. In other words, although they beat their predecessors in the Cultural Revolution, they still accepted the collective memory of their narrative.

The crisis of the construction and inheritance of intergenerational collective memory mainly occurred during the two great changes in Chinese society in modern times. The first crisis occurred in the late 19th and early 20th centuries between feudal scholar-officials and radical youth. At this time, no matter how hard Li Hongzhang and his kind tried to instill into the younger generation the "confidence in system"—"both China's civil and military systems are much superior to those of the westerners", numerous failures and dilemmas forced the young people with lofty ideals to seek otherwise for solutions, resolutely waging war against the Qing dynasty and Confucian ethics. The second crisis came in 1978 with the opening-up and especially after 1992 when secular youth came of age. At this time, the change of social environment, especially the change towards the market economy, changed the mainstream of values, and the parents and grandparents of the generation born in the 1970s, 1980s, and 1990s—the middle-aged rebel youth and the aging revolutionary youth of the past—found themselves in danger of being wiped out almost overnight. They were not only at a loss over the new era composed of consumption and the Internet, but more importantly, they found that the social changes had ruined the inheritance value of the revolutionary or insurgent culture they represent, and also reversed the intergenerational relationship between them and their offspring.

Take "youth without regret" as an example. This is a common historical narrative of the rebel youth in recent years, that is, the educated youth generation who went to the countryside and went to the mountains in the Mao Zedong era. At this time, most educated young people began to retire from work or from the social stage after experiencing a series of hardships in life, such as going to the countryside, returning to the city, seeking jobs, being laid off and making a living again, and the small number of "elites" of 77-graders and 78-graders who later became "worker-, peasant- and soldier-students" or caught the last opportunity to get into college in Deng Xiaoping's reform also began to reach the peak of their life—becoming the backbone of society or even the leaders of the Party and the country. In almost all historical narratives of educated youth, the "bitterness" of going to the countryside is the common feeling of people and also the "main melody" of their narration. However, there is a sharp internal contradiction between such narration and the life summary of "no regret" (Liu, 2003). Obviously, a painful history has created a wasted youth, but its participants have all said "youth without regret" after more than 30 years. You can feel that social forces play an important role in the construction of individual memories.

In the analysis of "youth without regret" of the educated generation, Liu Yaqiu sets two levels of "individual memory" and "collective memory". On the first level, "no regret" is attributed to the experience of "suffering" as a wealth of life, or the sharpening of personal character; on the second level, "no regret" is attributed to "suffering with the republic"; in other words, through the collective transformation of the suffering of individuals, it explains the theme of no regret because they have suffered for the republic (Liu, 2003). Although we acknowledge that the collective memory of each generation is mainly influenced by their life experiences when they were relatively young (Coser, 2002: 52), and the collective memory of each generation is largely about knowing oneself or self-identity, if we put this "no regret" narrative into the context of intergenerational relations, we will immediately find that the narrative object of educated youth or rebel youth is their offspring, that is, the secular youth born in the 1970s, 1980s, and 1990s. If we regard the collective memory of "youth without regret" as an intergenerational expression or exchange, even if there is some distortion in this collective feeling, its original intention is just that: On the one hand, they establish their own meaning in the eyes of the next generation—we are "not the 'suffering' weak, but the strong fighting against adversity, the backbone of the society" (Wang & Liu, 2006); on the other hand, they want to tell the next generation that it is precisely because "we have endured the sufferings of the republic that you have had the good times of reform and opening-up".[10]

> We have experienced about half a century of history ourselves. At the dawn of the new century, history has sent us into today's turbulent, multipolar world. A world with diversified beliefs and values; a fast-moving, restless, competitive world. As we look back, we marvel at the sacrifices this generation has made, the hardships it has endured, the contributions it has made, and the spirit of constant struggle. ... No matter in which kind of ordinary post, facing the reality, struggle, and search is always the theme song of this generation. I think, in the face of the motherland, in the face of the future, in the face of parents, lovers and children, we are fully qualified to say: we have tried our best.
>
> (Qu, 2002: 123)

This oral account by educated youth entitled "Struggle and search is always the theme song of this generation" tries to affirm the meaning of life and the value of struggle, but also more or less shows some hidden helplessness. If this helplessness in the face of parents is a kind of guilt of "having failed to stick to family possessions", then in the face of children or of the future, it is filled with a sense of inadequacy. From our discussion, we can see that whether from the twin sense of "guarding the home and protecting the possessions" or "expanding the territory", rebel youth or educated youth generally are not successful in life. They have inherited the past from the revolutionary youth, but may lose the future in the face of rapid social changes.

Of course, the loss of dominance by the older generation over the younger generation is not the whole story on the Chinese intergenerational stage; the other part of the story is composed of intergenerational dialogue and symbiosis; that is, through cultural reverse discussed in this book, intergenerational relations in contemporary Chinese society are achieving a dynamic new turn. Twenty years ago, when I returned to the research on this topic, I wrote clearly and definitely:

> "cultural reverse" is the product of a changing society, which indicates that the one-way cultural inheritance mode of traditional society is changing to the two-way or even multi-directional cultural inheritance mode of modern society. In fact, the emergence of this cultural inheritance model not only provides the possibility for the older generation to conform to social life and keep up with historical trends, but also increases the younger generation's sense of historical responsibility. The symbiotic complementarity between general socialization and reverse socialization or "cultural reverse" indicates that the cultural continuity on which the development of society depends has never been so evident as today in the rise and fall of the older generation and the younger generation.
>
> (Zhou, 2000a)

Because the parent–child relationship or intergenerational boundaries within the family are very clear—in this community of people, the father is the father and the son is the son—it is easier to compare values and lifestyles between generations. Compared with rural areas in China, cities, especially coastal cities, have undergone more significant social transformation in the past four decades after the reform and opening-up, and correspondingly, there has been more significant cultural reverse between generations of urban families. At the beginning, we explained that the research objects described in this book are mainly limited to the parent–child or intergenerational relationship within families, and the families interviewed, except in Chongqing, are also mainly limited to coastal cities. However, it must be pointed out that this does not mean that cultural reverse is only a reverse inheritance phenomenon within the family, nor that it is only found in the most developed coastal cities or metropolises in China. In fact, after the reform and opening-up, when China opened its door after years of imprisonment, especially after the rapid transformation of society and the growth of the younger generation promoted by globalization and the Internet, as a new way of cultural inheritance, cultural reverse is changing and remaking the intergenerational relationships throughout the whole of China. While it encourages the older generation to lose absolute control and educational power over the younger generation, it also helps it to better adapt to an increasingly modern society through dialogue and communication. As a result, society has become increasingly youthful and vibrant.

Cultural regurgitation not only occurs within families, but also is the most common cultural phenomenon among generations in China. It occurs in all aspects of social life: from values to life attitudes to behaviors, from elites to the middle class to the grassroots. Almost every stratum, every group in every stratum, every person in every group, as long as you are old you will feel the influence or reverse from the younger generation. Whether you accept it or not, however much, you will feel that by not accepting it, not only will you struggle to navigate a China you are no longer familiar with, but you will, in fact, lose one last bit of your ability (not power, I'm afraid) to "educate" the younger generation. In this age of dialogue and symbiosis, the ability to educate others is closely related to tolerance and acceptance of others.

Therefore, in this era, those few "tide surfing" elders who are still able to do well on the social stage are all experts who are willing and good at learning from the younger generation, and thus finally retain an influence on or educational ability for the younger generation.

In modern life, general social relations that have the most distinctive intergenerational characteristics occur in the mentorship system in the factory and in the relationship between graduate students and mentors in universities. Although after the founding of the People's Republic of China, when the East China Normal University opened the "First Education Seminar" with the help of Soviet experts in 1955, it adopted their training mode of teaching and collective guidance (Yi, 2012); generally speaking, no matter whether before or after 1949, especially after 1978, the one-to-one tutorial system has been the regular training mode of graduate education in Chinese universities and research institutions. Because of the extraordinary development of graduate education,[11] especially doctoral education, the binding and interweaving of the interests of teachers and students and their frequent daily interaction, combined with the traditional Chinese saying "Once a teacher, always a father", not only is the relationship between a mentor and a disciple (student) now very common and close, but the teacher–student relationship in Chinese society has also become a kind of pseudo-blood relationship very similar to parent–child relationship.

After the resumption of China's postgraduate education in 1978, a large number of intellectuals, who had previously worked in the cowshed or in the May Seventh cadre schools toward "reform through labor", returned to institutions of higher learning to teach in laboratories and classrooms, and enrolled graduate students. However, years of class struggle and political movement had hollowed out their brains and made them feel deeply unfamiliar toward the academic world, especially the Western academic world.

Even Professor Fei Xiaotong, who studied in Britain as a young man and was well-educated, once lamented that because of his long isolation from Western academia, "I can't keep up with their changes in the past thirty years" (Fei, 1985: 279). Compared to these academic titans, more professors who graduated after 1949, the so-called professors "trained by new China", were unable to cope with the influx of students after 1978, especially those with rich social experience and a strong thirst for knowledge. Although the boundaries between teachers and students were clear and the rules could not be crossed, the question of who instructs whom remained an unspoken topic in universities for quite a long time. In the early years, professors lived in poverty and funding for research was tight, which led to mentors developing unambiguous aspirations for fame and wealth and the possibility of tension between teachers and students.[12] Decades later, when the first generation of graduate students after the reform and opening-up became mentors themselves, thanks to 42 years of reform and opening-up and the country's progress, their education, vision, ability, and even economic status are generally better than their teachers, but the progress of science and technology in these decades, especially with the emergence of the network society, still requires them to face the challenges of the younger generation. Without the help of the younger generation, that is, their own graduate students, many mentors have difficulties in project application, data search, data collection, experiment design, model construction, and paper writing, especially in English. It has also made the question of whether and how mentors should sign papers completed by their students (such as whether they should be the first author) a common subject of debate at colleges and universities, which has ensued even for prominent and respected scholars.

Professor Jin Shenghua, from the school of psychology of Beijing Normal University, is a 77-grade college student who entered the university after the reform and opening-up. In the late 1980s and early 1990s, he successively studied for his master's degree and doctor's degree in psychology. Recalling his graduate days, Jin Shenghua affirmed that at least when he was studying for a master's degree, he was not influenced by the teacher in his studies. On the contrary, he influenced the teacher in many aspects:

> When we were students, although the teacher was still a teacher, generally speaking, because the social psychology had just recovered, the teacher didn't know much, but my English was better, so I helped the teacher a lot. For example, I helped my teacher frame some of his books.
>
> (Interview with Jin Shenghua, 2005)

Compared with those PhDs and masters under his guidance today, on the one hand, Jin Shenghua affirms that he has good theoretical and statistical skills, and his interests range from social psychology to education to human resources, so it is impossible for students to immediately replace him even if they are only one or two years younger than him; on the other hand, he admits that students have helped him a lot, at least in some ways:

> This kind of help is mainly in two aspects: One is in the use of the network. For example, we were going to build a human resources website, which contained a lot of technical work, including the use of software and so on. I tried to do a few things at first, only to find that I couldn't compete with my two students, because they originally majored in information engineering, so I kind of gave it up. Now such work is simply handed over

to my graduate students. The other is in researching specific topics. Some of the topics were new to me, so what I had was a clear theoretical framework and knowledge system, but the details were not clear. So I would give it to three to four doctors or masters, who were responsible for collecting information and making presentations, and I would use their data to modify the original research framework. As a result, my research framework was enriched, their desire for self-expression was satisfied, and both of us improved our knowledge.

(Interview with Jin Shenghua, 2005)

Just as cultural reverse has affected the intergenerational relationships of China's urban families and society as a whole, this revolutionary approach to cultural transmission has also affected the broader population and families of rural areas over the past few decades. We know that the victory of the Chinese revolution depended on the participation of millions of peasants. However, after 1949, a series of rapid and violent campaigns were carried out in the rural areas—from land reform, unified purchase and marketing of grain, cooperation, and people's communes, to the socialist education movement of "four purifications" in the fields of politics, ideology, organization and economy and "emulating Dazhai on agriculture", which did not change the poverty and backwardness of the rural areas, but plunged Chinese agriculture into a deeper process of involution—that is, "with extreme labor intensification … It inevitably leads to diminishing marginal returns". Not only was society in the process of "growth without development" for several decades (Huang, 2000: 241), but also around 1960 there was a large-scale famine and the tragic death of tens of millions of people.

After 1978, reforms began first in the countryside. The system of contract responsibility linked to production and the establishment of township enterprises began to change the poverty in rural China. After 1980, farmers began to get rid of the shackles of the land and went to towns or cities, either for business, work, or to engage in other non-agricultural occupations. After 2000, this wave swept inland from coastal developed areas, spread from males to females, and expanded from individuals to family groups and whole villages. By the time of the Sixth Census in 2010, the total floating population in rural areas had reached 260 million, among which the new generation of the post-1980s accounted for more than half (Ma, 2011). Despite the fact that large numbers of migrant workers brought China's urban and rural development some problems, such as land abandonment, rising crime rates, and governance crises (He Xuefeng, 2013: 162), the hollowing out and economic decline of China's rural areas (Li, 2004: 1), the increase in the number of left-behind children, the decline of family stability, and the dislocation of values and consumption concepts among young farmers (He et al., 2010: 243), this "third great creation of Chinese farmers" (Huang, 1996: 65), which was completely comparable to the contract responsibility linked to production and the establishment of township enterprises, brought more positive influences to Chinese society. It not only drove China's economic development and urbanization process, promoted the population flow and market circulation between urban and rural areas, and enabled farmers to acquire the modern growth of values and social psychology through flow and urban experience (Zhou, 1998b), but it also impacted the urban–rural dual partition system with strong barriers formed after the 1950s (Solinger, 1999). If we return to the topic we have discussed, the influence of young farmers, who acquired varying degrees of modernity through mobility and urban experience, on their parents, their fellow villagers, and their hometown was also immeasurable. When Deng Xiaoping retired from politics, a large number of young people who had worked on the coast for years returned home, bringing not only goods, but ideas and lifestyles that enabled them to run their own businesses and set new standards for inland areas. This process accelerated the spread of the national urban culture (Vogel, 2012: 652).

In *Deng Xiaoping and the Transformation of China*, which was first published in 2012 with 500,000 copies, Ezra Feivel Vogel, a lifelong studious and wise Harvard professor, saw the multifaceted cultural back-feeding effects of young migrant workers on their homes and fellow citizens. Thus, in the eyes of this American sociologist who is a China expert, the mobility of farmers has not only the simple economic significance of getting rich and getting rid of poverty, but also the revolutionary role of driving cultural and social changes. In fact, just as the sudden opening-up and reform in 1978 created a precipitous gap between the decades that followed and the decades that preceded it, so the rigid urban–rural divide that emerged after 1949 also created a huge regional gap. If it is the former that gave the younger generation the ability to "feed back" to their parents, then of course the latter also enabled those young migrant workers who were the first to step into the developed coastal areas, step into the urban life, and thus lead the trend to feed back to their hometown and their people.

Back in the mid-1990s, more than a decade before Vogel published *Deng Xiaoping and the Transformation of China*, along the lines discussed above, Rachel Murphy, a PhD student at Cambridge University, was studying the broader impact of returning migrant workers on rural China and its farmers, in Wanzai, Xinfeng, and Yudu counties in Jiangxi, the big labor-exporting province in central China. In her doctoral dissertation titled "How migrant labor is changing rural China", the impact of returning farmers on the local economy, society, and culture was reflected in many aspects. For example, returnees bring back civility, hygiene, law, and modern culture to the countryside. They use their savings and skills to find non-agricultural employment opportunities in the local areas. Another example is that some of the remittances workers send back to their hometown will be used for production purposes, thus improving the family's ability to obtain income from the land and facilitating their participation in urban and rural social and economic life. Also, although working for money may inhibit some people's motivation to study, it also encourages other parents to invest in their children's education because of its contribution to the family economy. Finally, returning migrant workers bring about changes in management practices for rural enterprises, and even influence the government to change the traditional management mode formed under the planned economy system (Murphy, 2009: 48–72, 81, 95, 179). Considering that compared to the older people who stayed at home, whether it is the first generation of migrant workers or the second generation of post-1980s migrant workers, they are generally young people when they seek their dreams in the city. Therefore, we can fully regard the impact of migrant workers on their hometown and fellow villagers as a kind of intergenerational influence similar to the cultural reverse we discuss here.

It is conceivable that the concrete practice of this influence in rural China must be mixed with the excitement of the pioneers and the loss of the laggards, but in the end it must also lead to the joint progress of two or more generations.

The greening of China, or the rebirth of an ancient people

So far, we have spent more than 160,000 words discussing the dramatic differences between two or several generations caused by the huge fission in Chinese society since the reform and opening-up, as well as the subversion or revolutionary change of the traditional cultural inheritance mode caused by it. We are not making a mountain out of a molehill, spending too much intelligence and energy, too many days and nights, in this small area we call "cultural reverse." While the conclusions are far from shocking, it is undoubtedly worth spending the most creative 25 years of our life trying to figure out the patterns and details of it.

So the question is: Are our personalities too sensitive to social change? Or is it because of the discipline in which we have been immersed that we have, consciously or unconsciously, sharpened the so-called "sociological imagination" that keeps us active in the discipline we explore? Or is it true that our society today is undergoing unprecedented changes that are affecting or reshaping not only the intergenerational relationships of Chinese society, but also, most likely, a different future for our ancient country?

Before the reform and opening-up in 1978, although Mao Zedong was obsessed with whether the revolutionary cause could last forever, the intergenerational problem was not a serious concern of the whole society, for the younger generation or youth was only the "alternative" of the adult society, a product that the elders were trying to forge—its eligibility was determined by the judgment of the elders. However, after 1978, the sharp social changes altered the intergenerational power pattern, and the older generation lost its power of discourse, leading to a shift from the one-way intergenerational dominating relationship to the multi-generational coexistence relationship. In reality, the intergenerational relationship ranges from intergenerational separation, intergenerational conflict, and intergenerational symbiosis, to intergenerational reverse, to, of course, the traditional intergenerational domination. The complexity of intergenerational relations has not only triggered the collective anxiety of the older generation about their future, but also prompted the younger generation to think about the living conditions of the present. Therefore, as the French sociologist Jean-Charles Lagree puts it, "there has been an explosion of works around the world that have been labeled 'intergenerational'" (Lagree, 2007: 328). In China, where generation or intergenerational relationship was no longer an issue after 1949 at least, this concept has once again become an important word in people's daily life and academic discussions. If we search the National Journal Full-text Database (CJFD) with "intergenerational" as the key word, we will find that the number of relevant papers showed a distinct upward trend during the 37 years from 1983 to 2020: from 3 in 1983, to 75 in 1993, to 1,153 in 2003, to 5,523 in 2013, finally to 9,240 in 2020 (CNKI, 2020). Not only that, but the subjects of concern have become increasingly diverse: the intergenerational elite transformation in cities, class reproduction, intergenerational income flow, the intergenerational transmission of poverty in rural China, generational differences in household consumption, intergenerational inheritance of family capital, the generation difference between collective action and the protection of workers' rights in Pearl River Delta, generational differences and the net generation, intergenerational criticism of literature, only children and intergenerational relationship, cultural reverse between generations, as well as the generational change and its power. Almost all social science issues can be addressed from the perspective of generation or intergenerational relations, and the generational or intergenerational perspective has become a realistic research approach comparable to the once-popular class or class struggle perspective.

In this sense, it is not that we are over-sensitive or over-imaginative, but rather that the complex and multi-dimensional social changes described in this book contribute to generational change and, in turn, to the modern direction of the ancient country of China. This trend, both subtle and silent and grand, reminds us of a scene in 1970. At the end of the American Youth Movement in 1968, around the time that Margaret Mead, the anthropologist described in our first chapter, wrote the seminal book *Culture and Commitment: A Study on Generation Gap*, in the small town of New Haven, a little more than an hour's drive from New York, Charles A. Reich, a professor at Yale law school, produced another account of American Youth Culture, *The Greening of America: How the Youth Revolution Re-valued America* (1970). Like Margaret Mead, Reich not only praised youth culture, but also discussed it in a similar syllogistic historical pattern. For this reason, Reich used the concept of "consciousness" to describe the intergenerational inheritance of American society. He firmly believed that the concept of consciousness gives us diverse materials, by which we can discuss in a timely fashion what has happened in America and what is happening now (Reich, 1970: 24). According to Reich, there are three types of consciousness that dominate contemporary America:

One was formed in the nineteenth century, the second in the first half of this century, the third is just emerging. Consciousness I is the traditional outlook of the American farmer, small businessman and worker who is trying to get ahead. Consciousness II represents the values of an organizational society. Consciousness III is the new generation. The three categories are, of course, highly impressionistic and arbitrary; they make no pretence to be scientific. And, since each type of consciousness is a construct, we would not expect any actual individual to exhibit in symmetrical perfection all the characteristics of one type of consciousness.

(Reich, 1970: 22)

Obviously, the first consciousness is the "American dream" that serves as the core of traditional American middle-class values and inspires generations of Americans. If the first consciousness encourages people to be self-made men, then the second consciousness, the values advocated by the American authorities, regards the United States as a country of organization and domination, and individuals must find their own way in the world created by others (Reich, 1970: 63). Furthermore, unlike the first two kinds of consciousness, Reich believes that the younger generation has formed a different kind of consciousness from their parents'—the third consciousness. The young people of the third consciousness have no difficulty in seeing the political falsehood and dishonesty, the ugliness and superficiality, of architecture and urban planning. Therefore, older generations should be re-educated so that they have the same insight (Reich, 1970: 283). Reich predicts that because of the third consciousness,

there is a revolution coming. It will not be like revolutions of the past. It will originate with the individual and with culture, and it will change the political structure only as its final act. It will not require violence to succeed, and it cannot be successfully resisted by violence.

(Reich, 1970: 11)

This is a silent revolution in values, and with the emergence of the third consciousness dominating society, the United States will experience a common greening.

We acknowledge that the United States and China, two of the great powers in the world today, have many differences, including history, culture, population, resources, patterns of economic operations, and entire political systems, but the theme we are talking about today—the transformation of intergenerational relations in Chinese society, or cultural reverse—is emerging in a context very similar to the crisis in American culture nearly half a century ago that Charles Reich and Margaret Mead discussed. To borrow Reich's language, for Americans living in the 1960s and 1970s, "the great question of these times is how to live in and with a technological society" (Reich, 1970: 22). We have explained at length in this book that since the reform and opening-up in 1978, due to the rapid economic growth and great social changes, China has also begun to be a technological society constructed by the rapid development of electrical appliances, manufacturing technology, and the Internet. It is the development of technology, especially Internet technology in daily life, that has made the growth of GDP, the advent of consumerism, and globalization no longer of mere material significance to the 1.3 billion Chinese people, making it possible to change the way two generations behave and live, and making it possible for the younger generation to display values and social behaviors that are radically different from those of their parents, not to mention their grandparents, and thus ultimately rewrite the history of this deeply traditional nation.

At the end of this book, we will discuss a specific example of cultural reverse that happened around me. In August 2014, Nanjing hosted the Second Youth Olympic Games on the basis of the Tenth National Games held in 2005. For Nanjing, the former capital before 1949, this was one of the few major political tasks it took on after becoming the "abandoned capital" in 1949, and a rare opportunity to show its face, or show the city's charm. Although the Youth Olympic Games ended with many disappointments, such an international event was, on the face of it, a once-in-a-lifetime opportunity for a second-tier Chinese city like Nanjing to raise its international profile.[13] However, a story related to the topic discussed in this book took place during the preparation of the Youth Olympic Games, which will give you a real picture of intergenerational relations in Chinese society, and will convince you that only when the older generation can truly listen to the younger generation, accept their values, and the way they see society and the world can today's China finally change its rigidity and decay; in other words, only in this way can the nation be as green as the withered seedlings that thrive on spring rains.

NMB, the protagonist of this story, was a senior in Nanjing Foreign Language School in 2012. NMB was born in a family rich in business talent but with an unseverable affection for the campus. His father NMF and mother NMM were math classmates at Beijing Normal University before graduating in 1989 and were assigned to teach in their hometown middle school because of the far-reaching political turmoil. They both went to graduate school, and after their master's degrees, both of them made good starts in their business careers. Then they both gave up bright business prospects to pursue doctorates in university. After receiving a doctorate in management, NMF engaged in advertising research, which led to his involvement in the early planning of the Youth Olympic Games. It was this plan that pushed NMB, NMF's son who was preparing to go abroad in his third year of high school, to the front of these Games:

> At that time, I had decided to study abroad, so I didn't have to prepare for the college entrance examination, and had time to follow my father to the Youth Olympic Games "promotion slogan" review meeting. Two of my classmates and I went to the meeting and found that all the people present were members of the so-called Organizing Committee of the Olympic Games, except the three of us. There were a few foreigners among them, but most of them were Chinese, and all of them looked big and fat to us children. They put us in a corner and then rambled on, sometimes in English, sometimes in Chinese. Because the three of us were foreign language school students and our English

was good, their speech sounded quite funny to us. So I raised my hand and said to the officials in English, "This won't work. Now that it is a great event for young people, why don't you get more young people? Why not let the young people decide the slogan?" "Didn't we invite you here?" they answered. I said, "Just the three of us, sitting in the corner." When I finished, the adults laughed, and I sensed some awkwardness in their laughter. It happened that I was wearing a T-shirt that read "Can anybody hear me?" I didn't know if anyone noticed, but I think it just reflected my state of mind at that time.

(NMB, 2013)

To be fair, NMB's questioning, though uncomfortable for the adults, made them think that there was some truth in it, and that NMB was clever and good at English, so they continued to seek him out for various activities in the following period of time. NMF teased that his son had become a "middleman" during that time—taking a group of classmates, many of them foreign, to participate in various Youth Olympic Games preparation activities. NMM participated in one such event, in which NMB took the class's international team—Chinese students, as well as students from the United States, France and Chile—to talk to the Youth Olympic Games organizing committee. These children from all over the world had never been immersed in such officialdom culture as China's, so they were frank with those officials of the Youth Olympic Games, never thinking that they were officials or leaders. At first, the Chilean boy refused to speak. He had never been happy since he came to China, because in his opinion, Chinese children lived every day like they were in prison—doing nothing but homework. But then he spoke up, and despite his anger at Chinese parents, he said that the children in Chile play soccer for four hours a day (even that sweet-natured French girl chimed in, saying they played soccer for at least two hours a day), and you are making Chinese children like this!

> I could tell that the Chilean boy was really angry, and he felt sorry for the "abuse" of his Chinese classmates by their parents. At that moment, I felt the Chinese members of the Youth Olympic Games organizing committee were a little touched, as they realized that children aged 13–19, the so-called teenager, were the main audience of the Youth Olympic Games, and their thoughts might be their real expectation of them. In other words, you can't see the Youth Olympic Games as a sports meeting. For children, sport is something that permeates their lives, or sport is life; it's not that we are bringing the kids together and having a sports meeting at that time.

(NMM, 2013)

Although the international team of the Foreign Language School led by NMB made many contributions to the youth Olympic Games—NMB was "working hard" for the international event in his city, and at one point he even wanted to enlist dozens of students from around the world who had studied at the university before returning home—the handsome boy in the end felt cheated by the adult world. It is not that the elders of the organizing committee did not want to listen to young people, or that they did not have any ideas at all, but their true purpose of involving children in the "youth show" was neither to listen nor to learn, but just to give the event in this semi-marginal city some international flavor. Apart form NMB, even his PhD parents were initially unaware of the hidden intentions behind the smiling faces. Even when NMB was asked by the accreditation committee to bring children from as many countries as possible, it was kindly interpreted by the children that the adults wanted to listen widely to opinions and suggestions. But when the organizing committee was about to launch a promotional slogan press conference, the real reason the "seniors" valued NMB and his team was finally made public. The organizing committee called NMB and asked him to get some students to come to the televised press conference, but the seniors repeatedly stated that they would mainly look for foreign students, preferably American and European students with blond hair and blue eyes, and promised to put his international team in the front row—as they say, "It looks good."

"It looks good" was the real motivation why the organizing committee of adults was so interested to deal with NMB, and it was this fatal motivation that hurt the innocent and emotional NMB and his kind. In other words, children led by NMB with a sense of participation in their dreams ended up as props for seniors to construct the "international style", like their scripts, stage lighting, SONY MSW-930p or 5DMarkII, or whatever. China's reality, or "national conditions", educated NMB, who decided at the last minute to withdraw, and the planned international mobilization would not happen. Of course, NMB's departure did not affect the Nanjing organizing committee's enthusiasm for publicity—"Share the games, share our dreams", the slogan of the Youth Olympic Games co-developed by NMB, still made their younger followers confident and ambitious.

Do not assume that the loser in this intergenerational interaction or contest is NMB who finally quit, or that the elders or seniors who experienced this youth show were unscathed. No, the countless complaints we hear today about how the younger generation is apathetic, uninvolved, or simply rejecting the adult world (Chen Yingfang, 2007: 224–229; Li, 2013: 75) are actually the inevitable result of the older generation interacting with the younger generation in the same false way. Children or the younger generation are not reluctant to participate, but they are responding in a unique way to the hypocrisy and affectation of the older generation. What we adults fail to realize is that by "sharing" the youth of the younger generation in a false way today, we are depriving ourselves of our future altogether. But if you, like the countless others we have written about in this book, sincerely accept the advice, opinions, and criticisms of our children, in short, accept their cultural reverse, not only will you be able to fit into this new world and win the future, but our old country will be rejuvenated.

We are not the first to think that young people or teenagers represent tomorrow or the future more than older people. As early as 1900, the year of the new century after the failure of the 1898 reform movement, when the whole country was in a state of low spirits with the intelligentsia, and the boxers of the Yihetuan were under the double spell of nationalism and invulnerability, Liang Qichao, a famous thinker at the end of the Qing dynasty, wrote his article "On young China" with great enthusiasm. The article uses "the old man" as a metaphor for the "great empire" of the Qing dynasty, which had entered a doomsday dusk, and "the young man" for the vigorous and eclectic "young China":

> Old men think of the past, young men of the future. Nostalgia comes from thinking of the past, while hope from the future. Nostalgia leads to conservativeness, and hope to progress. Conservativeness keeps one old, and progress new. Those who are thinking of the past think they have experienced everything, so they do not bother to change; those who are thinking of the future think they have experienced little before, so they dare to break the rules. Old men are full of worries, and young men of joy. Worries make one frustrated, and joy makes one vigorous. Frustration leads to cowardice; and vigorousness to the heroic. Cowardice makes one drift along, but the heroic makes one adventurous. The former can destroy the world, while the latter helps build the world.
>
> (Liang, 1999, Vol. 2: 409)

To make a new world, of course, we must first make a group of new people worthy of this job. After the 1911 revolution, both Yuan Shikai's reign as emperor and Zhang Xun's restoration deeply impressed Lu Xun, who had been extremely excited before, with the idea of "tyranny will last forever, and rejuvenation is hard" (Lu, 2005, Vol. 8: 42). Therefore, on the one hand, he called for "saving children" through the *Diary of a Madman*; on the other hand, he was determined to start from the children's education to transform the national character, to solve the problem of "rearing people" in Chinese society. In Lu Xun's opinion, there were many Chinese children who were "lively, healthy, tenacious, with their heads and faces held high" or "looked foreign" at the very beginning, but the "good children" favored by families and society were "low-browed, agreeable and submissive". In view of his abhorrence of the national character of China and the social system that created it, Lu Xun firmly believed that:

> Among the so-called "foreign styles", there are many advantages, which are also inherent in the nature of Chinese people. However, due to the repression of various dynasties, they have shrunk down. Now they are even given to foreigners without any reason. It must be brought back—be recovered.
>
> (Lu, 2005, Vol. 6: 83–84)

If "what happens in childhood is what happens in the future" (Lu, 2005, Vol. 4: 581), then a weak childhood naturally will not have a vigorous youth, let alone a strong prime of life.

In fact, what Lu Xun said, namely "what happens in childhood is what happens in the future", does not only refer to the situation of individuals, but also the situation of a nation or a country. In other words, what kind of children we have now determines what kind of nation and country we will have in the future. In this sense, the old Chinese saying "You may predict one's future when he is very young" can be interpreted to mean that the future of our nation or country is determined by the ambition, character, cultivation, and ability of today's young people and even babbling children. We have repeatedly discussed in this book the life course theory of the American sociologist Glenn Elder, in his book *Children of the Great Depression*, which "on the shelves of social scientists such as Japan, China and Germany who are concerned about the consequences of rapid social change for individuals ... there may be a place for it" (Elder, 2002: 422). Elder elaborates on the shaping of individual personality and the whole history of life by past historical times and the historical events in them. Instead of marveling at the power of the creator in the face of the oddities of individual lives, you might as well acknowledge that "changing times are shaping our lives" (Elder, 2002: 420). Furthermore, the "carving" or "shaping" of people by the times has different meanings in different life courses of a person. Even the same major historical event does not exert the same influence on all living individuals at the same time; it depends on one's class status, educational background, career and learning ability, and, of course, as the theme of this book suggests, it equally or even more depends on the stage of one's life—that is, how old one is at the time of this or these major historical events. Obviously, our memories of important political and social events are structured according to age, especially when we are young (Coser, 2002: 51). Therefore, "one's basic values reflect the conditions that prevailed during one's preadult years" (Inglehart, 1997: 33). Take the four generations of Chinese youth discussed in this chapter as an example. If the major historical event for the radical youth was the expulsion of the Manchus or the overthrow of the Qing dynasty, for the revolutionary youth was saving the nation from subjugation, and for the rebel youth was the great proletarian cultural revolution, then the most important historical event for contemporary secular youth is the economic growth and marketization against the background of globalization.

Never underestimate the impact of economic growth and marketization on the evolution of Chinese people's values and social behaviors. In the past 100 years, Weber, Ingles, and Inglehart all discussed the relationship between economic development or modernization and the evolution of people's social psychology. For China's younger generation, what we call the secular youth, or those born in the 1970s, 1980s, and 1990s, the most important change in their personal growth history is that as China's economy has grown, basic survival has become less of an issue for most Chinese. This change makes it possible for Chinese people, as Inglehart said, to shift from the value of subsistence to the value of self-expression of happiness, which leads to the emergence of the so-called value of post-materialism. Taking into account the reality of China, Inglehart also affirmed clearly:

China has made remarkable economic and technological progress in the past 30 years … In the following decades, China will experience a process of intergenerational value transformation, in which younger groups tend to be more inclined to gender equality, tolerate foreign groups and attach more importance to freedom of speech than their elders.

(Inglehart, 1997: 1)

In fact, from the perspective of the issues we have discussed—the greening or rejuvenation of China or the Chinese nation, in addition to the transformation of the values of the younger generation—through cultural reverse they can also transfer their understanding of the new world to their elders, and facilitate the latter's transformation to the new era. So, as Liang Qichao says:

If the young people are intelligent, China will be intelligent; if the young people are wealthy, China will be wealthy; if the young people are strong, China will be strong; if the young people are independent, China will be independent; if the young people are free, China will be free; if the young people are progressive, China will be progressive; if the young people can get ahead of Europe, China will get ahead of Europe; if the young people are best in the world, China will be the best in the world. The morning sun is rising in the sky, bright and brilliant; the Yellow River is running to the sea, mighty and magnificent. A hidden dragon leaps out of a deep pool and fishes flee; a tiger cub roars in the hollow valley and beasts creep; a proud eagle springs off the vast land and dust reels. Exotic buds are bursting in the trees, pretty and vigorous; double-edged swords are sharpened on the stones, icy and glorious. Blue heaven over our heads, yellow earth below our feet, profound history in our hearts, and extended roads before our eyes, we look forward to our future as wide as ocean, great and grand. So majestic is our young China, forever with the universe; so robust are our Chinese youth, eternal with our motherland.

(Liang, 1999, Vol. 2: 411)

Finally I again quote "On young China" by Liang Qichao as the end of the book, because I, like countless ancient sages who wanted to realize the great rejuvenation of the Chinese nation, have deep expectations for a young China with eternal youth:

We will grow old, but our motherland will remain young.

Notes

1 Until around World War II, the age of youth was mostly defined as 15–20 years old. In France's postwar census, for example, youth was defined as between 14 and 18. Since then, the age range of young people has been pushed back again and again, from 15–25 years old to 20–30 years old and even 35 years old. As a criterion for

comparison, the *Constitution of the Communist Youth League of China* stipulates that young people are aged from 14 to 28. The most important change is the latest youth standard established by UNESCO in 2013. Anyone under the age of 44 can be called "youth", which reflects the two changes caused by the development of education, especially higher education, worldwide since the Industrial Revolution: (a) the number of years of individual education is getting longer and longer; and (b) the number of people receiving education, including college education, is increasing. These two changes eventually lead to the widespread disengagement of young people from society in order to obtain education, knowledge, and qualifications (Lagree, 2007: 3).

2 According to Liu Zaifu, since the end of the 19th century, Chinese intellectuals have experienced the awakening of three major consciousnesses: The awakening of "nation-state" consciousness in the late 19th century to the early 20th century, the awakening of "man–individual" consciousness in the May Fourth Movement, and the awakening of "class-state" consciousness in the 1920s to 1930s. These three awakenings profoundly influenced the appearance and destiny of Chinese society in the 20th century (Liu, 2011). The awakening of the consciousness of "class-state" is a direct result of the popularity of Marxism and its class struggle theory in China after the Russian October Revolution in 1917.

3 The issue of preventing "peaceful evolution" appeared in the secret report of Khrushchev, the 20th leader of the Soviet Communist Party in 1956. Later, after the Soviet controversy in the 1960s, Mao Zedong gradually formed the idea of opposing revisionism, preventing peaceful evolution and training successors. In 1964, Mao Zedong made a special speech on this issue, and the *People's Daily* also published an editorial on the issue of "cultivating successors to the revolutionary cause of the proletariat. It is the great plan of proletarian revolution for one hundred years, for one thousand years, for ten thousand years. According to the changes that took place in the Soviet Union, imperialist linguists also placed their hopes for 'peaceful evolution' on the third or fourth generation of the Chinese communist party. We must put this imperialist prophecy to ruin. We must train and bring up successors to the revolutionary cause from the top to the bottom in a universal and constant way" (Editorial Department of *People's Daily* and Editorial Department of *Red Flag* magazine, 1964).

4 Although Ma Nuo was widely criticized for her daring performance and earned the title of "gold digger", tolerance in today's society is: On the one hand, people admit that Ma Nuo's "worship of money" is the projection of our era, rather than the "sin" of Ma Nuo herself. On the other hand, people agree that while sitting in a BMW does not necessarily make you smile, sitting on a bicycle definitely doesn't. This shows that the younger generation living in today's secular society has understood the meaning of material life and will no longer believe in absolute ascetic values.

5 In Chapter 2 of the first volume of this book, we described the contradiction between the young Mao Zedong and his father and the private school teacher, and how his rebellious spirit against tradition was born. For the radical youth of the May Fourth generation, this is not an individual case, but a phenomenon of universal significance. As Li Wenhai and Liu Yangdong said, "The May Fourth elite who criticize the old family system particularly fiercely often have personal backgrounds. Wu Yu is an example" (Li & Liu, 1992: 223). When Wu Yu was young, he was loved by his grandfather and his mother, but as he grew older, he clashed with his father and other family members over who owned what. In Wu Yu's own words, "I was framed by the society outside and stung by the elders inside" (Wu, 1985: 335), which triggered his words and deeds in the year of 1911 that were neither filial nor Confucian. Coincidentally, in 1919, Shi Cuntong, a student of Zhejiang First Normal University, caused a great uproar because of his article "No filial piety". His hatred of traditional

Chinese culture, his yearning for free and equal anarchic communism, and finally his determination to become a warrior to fight the old system to the end, also originated from his conflict with his indifferent father regarding the treating of his sick mother (Jiang, 1997). Finally, Ba Jin always compared his large family to "an autocratic kingdom", where "many lovely lives struggled, suffered, languished, moaned to death in the prison of false ethics". "I am beginning to feel that the current social system is unreasonable. I used to think arrogantly if we could change it and arrange everything better" (Ba, 1982: 94–95).

6 "Small broadcasts" refers to private discussions among comrades about the Party's political and personnel relations and personal lives, which correspond to the "big broadcasts" like Party propaganda. On December 6, 1942, the General Learning Committee of the CPC Central Committee, which was in charge of the rectification movement, issued a notice on the elimination of small broadcasts in Yan'an. Filling out the small broadcasts questionnaire was a way of organizing and motivating people to explain their daily behavior, which shows that since then, the Party would pay more attention to the thoughts and behaviors of party members and effectively control them.

7 Every educated youth, including me, who went to the countryside, was deeply disappointed to find that the farmers by whom they were supposed to be educated were vastly different from the "poor and middle peasants" that the authorities promoted as their ideal. Richard Madsen mentioned this in his book *Morality and Power in a Chinese Village* and Michel Bonnin in his book *The Lost Generation* (Bonnin, 2004: 264–268; Madsen, 1984: 118–125, 145–148).

8 After the 1960s, in order to fight against Soviet revisionism, the CPC Central Committee decided to publish a number of works and literature involving revisionists and Western social theorists in the form of "internal books". The covers of these books were mainly pure gray, but there were also other colors such as yellow, white, and black. Among them, gray books were mainly theoretical books, such as Bernstein's *The Premise of Socialism and the Task of the Social Democratic Party*, Kautsky's *Terrorism and Communism*, Trotsky's *The Revolution Betrayed*, Plekhanov's *On the Role of Individuals in History*, and Djilas's *The New Class*. Yellow books were dominated by literature, especially Soviet literature, such as *Thaw* by Ehrenburg, *The White Ship* by Aitmatov, *One Day in the Life of Ivan Denisovich* by Solzhenitsyn, as well as Western literature such as *The Catcher in the Rye* by Salinger, *La Nausee* by Sartre, and *L'Etranger* by Camus. Finally, there were fewer black books, that is, books related to the history of the Communist Party published by the People's Publishing House in 1980 under the name of "Modern Historical Materials Publishing House", such as Zhang Guotao's *My Memory*, Wang Ming's *Fifty Years of the Communist Party of China*, and Chen Gongbo's *Bitter Smile*. According to incomplete statistics, the total number of such "covers" reached 2,000 in over 20 years (Shen, 2007). The odd thing was that Mao Zedong, who agreed to publish these books in order to strengthen his critique of revisionism, to strengthen the legitimacy of his theory, or to train the revolutionary successors of the proletariat, actually led a whole generation down the path of "alienation" or reflection.

9 According to Li Chunling et al., among the post-1980s employees, 32.5% are employed in private enterprises, 5.4% in foreign-funded enterprises, and 17.8% are employed in individual industry and commerce or are self-employed. In total, about 55.7% of the post-1980s employees work in non-public institutions (Li, 2013: 347).

10 Of course, the above language is the conventional way of narration for most people who were educated in the countryside or feel frustrated in life. For those few successful people, especially those in politics, emphasizing their experience of going to the countryside, "alliance with workers and peasants", and expressing "no regrets about youth" is not only a political qualification in the past, but also a political

expression in the present. As far as collective memory is concerned, since, in every era, this intention is consistent with the dominant thought of society (Halbwachs, 1992: 71), and our dominant ideology today still affirms the importance of this alliance, the vast majority of educated youth, whether frustrated or satisfied or even successful, will naturally continue to construct their collective memory along this dimension.

11 In China's modern education, although as early as 1935, the national government promulgated the law on the conferment of academic degrees, only nine academic degree examinations were held, and 232 master's degrees were awarded up until 1949, due to the war. After the founding of the People's Republic of China, East China Normal University, with the help of experts from the Soviet Union, established the first educational history research institute in 1955. In 1978, after a 12-year hiatus in postgraduate recruitment, the mainland reopened the postgraduate recruitment examination, and in the nearly a quarter century after the promulgation of the regulations of the People's Republic of China on academic degrees in 1980, postgraduate education developed rapidly. By 2011, China has trained 400,000 doctors and 2.4 million masters (Yang, 2013). Since 2008, China has trained 50,000 doctors every year, surpassing the United States and becoming the world's largest doctor-producing country.

12 In the two famous universities in Nanjing, there were disagreements and even conflicts between teachers and students in the 1980s over the signing of books and unfair distribution of royalties. The most common version of teacher–student conflict is: The tutor thinks that you are my graduate student and it is natural for you to help me. Graduate students complained, "We write the books, but the teacher is the first author or even the only author; not only that, he scoops up all the payment of the books." Students never think that their tutors are still associate professors in their 50s and 60s because of the Cultural Revolution. The professors may even not have published any monographs, and be constantly in financial difficulties.

13 In the "Report on the cultural influence of Chinese cities" recently led by my colleague Dr. Chen Yunsong, the research group searched cities involved in English literature in the past 300 years through big data in Google, so as to study the global influence of modern Chinese cities. The first peak of the curve of word frequency of Nanjing (so-called "hot words") appeared in 1912 after the 1911 revolution, when the nationalist government made Nanjing its capital. As the capital of the nationalist government, Nanjing's popularity peaked in 1937–1939 (second only to Beijing and Shanghai) and declined thereafter, never making it into the top five again. The top ten cities of contemporary international influence are Hong Kong, Beijing, Shanghai, Guangzhou, Shenzhen, Tianjin, Nanjing, Chengdu, Wuhan and Dalian. (This is the most recent data released in 2020). What is related to our discussion here is that, due to the Youth Olympic Games held in Nanjing in 2014, the word frequency of Nanjing in English literature has had a short "pulse" rise (Xu, 2014).

References

Ba, Jin, "My Childhood", in Jin, Ba (ed.), *Selected Works of Bajin*, Vol. 10, Chengdu: Sichuan People's Publishing House, 92–93, 1982.

Baudrillard, Jean, *The Consumer Society*, trans. by Liu, Chnegfu & Tong Zhigang, Nanjing: Nanjing University Press, 34, 2006.

Beijing Hantang Culture Development Co. LTD, *Decade (1986—1996): A Chronicle of Chinese Pop Music*, Beijing: China Film Press, 1997.

Berger, Bennett M., "On the Youthfulness of Youth Culture", in Clark, Shirley M. & John P. Clark (eds.), *Youth in Modern Society*, New York: Holt, Rinehart and Winston, 176, 1972.

Bian, Yanjie & Zhang Wenhong, "Economic Systems, Social Networks and Job Mobility", *Social Sciences in China*, 1, 77–89, 2001.

Bogardus, Emory S., "The Group Interview", *Journal of Applied Sociology*, 10, 372–382, 1926.

Bonnin, Michel, *The Case of the Lost Generation*, trans. by Ouyang Yin, Hong Kong: Hong Kong Chinese University Press, 2004.

Bourdieu, Pierre, "Youth Is Just a Word", in Bourdieu, P. (ed.), *Sociology in Question*, trans. by Richard Nice, London: Sage, 94–102, 1993.

Bourdieu, Pierre & Jean-Claude Passeron, *La reproduction: Éléments pour une théorie du système d'enseignement*, trans. by Tao Dongfeng, Shanghai: Shanghai Translation Publishing House, 2006.

Bronfenbrenner, Urie, *Two Worlds of Childhood: U. S. and U. S. S. R.*, New York: Russell Sage Foundation, 1970.

Cao, Jin & Zhuang Qianwei, "The World at Your Fingertips: Urban Preschoolers and Entertainment Invaded by Electronic Products", *Open Era*, 1, 179–198, 2013.

Cao, Lixin, "Media and Social Change: Communication Experiment in Ding County Experiment", *Journalism and Communication Studies*, 4, 48–53, 2005.

Carey, James W., "Harold Adams Innis and Marshall McLuhan", *Antioch Review*, 27, 1, 5–39, 1967.

Central Committee of the Communist Party of China, *Decision of the Chinese Central Committee on Several Major Issues Concerning Comprehensively Deepening Reform*, Beijing: People's Publishing House, 2013.

Chen, Duxiu, "To Inform Young People", *New Youth*, 1, 1, 1916.

Chen, Duxiu, "Politics in China Today", in Wang, Shudi (ed.), *Selected Articles by Chen Duxiu*, Beijing: Sanlian Bookstore, 271, 1984.

Chen, Jianhua, Zhang Yuan & Zhao Zhiping, "Consumerism and Beyond", *Guangxi Social Sciences*, 7, 88–91, 2009.

Chen, Lihui, "The Internet and the Reshaping of Social Organization: A Profound Social Transformation under Way", *Sociological Study*, 6, 13–31, 1998.

Chen, Subai, "Chinese Urban Family Media Contact and Attention to Advertising", *Modern Advertising*, 5, 20–27, 2005.

Chen, Xinyin, Chang Lei & He Yunfeng, "The Peer Group as a Context: Mediating and Moderation Effects on Relations between Academic Achievement and Social Functioning in Chinese Children", *Child Development*, 74, 3, 710–727, 2003.

Chen, Xulu, "The Countercurrent of Political Thought on the Eve of May Fourth: The Reactionary Restoration Thought in the Early Republic of China", *The Academic Issue*, `2, 53–56, 3, 70–73, 4, 73–76, 1959.

Chen, Xulu, "On Chinese Essence and Western Utility", *Historical Research*, 5, 39–55, 1982.

Chen, Zhou & Yu Lei, "The Change and Analysis of 2005 National Satellite TV Channel Coverage", *China's Advertising*, 1, 138–139, 2006.

Chiang, Zhongzhen, *The Fate of China*, Nanjing: Pingjin Branch Youth League Department, 1946.

CNKI, 2020. https://kns8.cnki.net/kns/defaultresult/index.

CNKI, 2020. https://kns8.cnki.net/kns/defaultresult/index.

CNNIC, (China Internet Network Information Center), Chinanews.com, "2019 Internet Development Report: 854 Million Internet Users Aged 20 to 29 Account for the Largest Proportion", 2019. https://news.znds.com/article/40425.html

CNNIC (China Internet Network Information Center), "Statistical Report on Internet Development in China", 25, 2010. https://wenku.baidu.com/view/29c8878da0116c175f0e4817.html.

CNNIC (China Internet Network Information Center), "Statistical Report on Internet Development in China", 35, 2015. https://wenku.baidu.com/view/be7c1fb067ec102 de2bd89a0.html?fr=search

Coleman, James S., "Peer Cultures and Education in Modern Society", in Newcomb, Theodore M. & Everett K. Wilson (eds.), *College Peer Group, Problems and Prospects for Research*, Chicago, IL: Aldine Publishing Company, 244–269, 1966.

Cooley, Charles H., *Human Nature and the Social Order*, NJ: Transaction Publishers, 1992.

Communist Youth League of China, *Constitution of the Communist Youth League of China*, Beijing: China Youth Publishing Group, 1, 2013.

Coser, Lewis A., "Maurice Halbwachs", in Halbwachs, Maurice (ed.), *On Collective Memory*, trans. by Bi Ran & Guo Jinhua, Shanghai: Shanghai People's Publishing House, 93–94, 2002.

CPC Central Committee, *Decision of the CPC Central Committee on Several Major Issues Concerning Comprehensively Deepening Reform*, Beijing: People's Publishing House, 2013.

Croteau, David & William Hoynes, *Media/Society: Industries, Images and Audiences*, trans. by Qiu Ling, Beijing: Beijing University Press, 2009.

Crowley, David & Paul Heyer, *Communication in History*, New York: Longman, 1991.

Cui, Shuqin, "Boundary Shifting: New Generation Filmmaking and Jia Zhangke's Films", in Zhu, Ying & Stanley Rosen (eds.), *Art, Politics, and Commerce in Chinese Cinema*, Hong Kong: Hong Kong University Press, 175–179, 2010.

Deng, Xiquan & Feng Xiaotian, "A Comparative Study on the Filial Attitude and Behavior of Urban Residents", *Chinese Youth Studies*, 3, 51–55, 2003.

Di, Long, *How to Create Ads*, trans. by Liu Yizhi, Beijing: China Friendship Publishing Company, 1991.

Donner, Jonathan, "The Social and Economic Implications of Mobile Telephone in Rwanda: An Ownership/Access Typology", in Glotz, Peter et al. (eds.), *Thumb Culture: The Meaning of Mobile Phones for Society*, London: Transaction Publishers, 37–52, 2005.

Eisenstadt, Shmuel Noah, "Archetypal Patterns of Youth", in Clark, Shirley M. & John P. Clark (eds.), *Youth in Modern Society*, New York: Holt, Rinehart and Winston, 1–16, 1972.

Elder, Glen. H., *Children of the Great Depression*, New York: Routledge, 2002.

Engels, Friedrich V., "The Condition of the Working Class in England", in Marx, Engels, Lenin and Stalin Works Compilation Bureau of the CPC Central Committee (ed.), *The Complete Works of Marx and Engels*, Vol. 2, Beijing: People's Publishing House, 269–587, 1957.

Ennett, Susan T. & Karl E. Bauman, "Adolescent Social Networks: Social, Demographic and Longitudinal Considerations", *Journal of Adolescent Research*, 11, 194–215, 1996.

Esarey, Ashley & Xiao Qiang, "Political Expression in the Chinese Blogosphere, below the Radar", *Asian Survey*, 48, 5, 752–772, 2008.

Fan, Peipei, "Evolution from Communication Technology to Production Tools: A Sociological Study of Mobile Phone Use among Low- and Middle-Income Groups", *Journalism and Communication Studies*, 2, 82–88, 2010.

Feng, Guifen, "Xiaobinlu Protests", in Zheng, Dahua (ed.), (revised) *Discussion on Adopting Western Learning: Collected Works of Feng Guifen and Ma Jianzhong*, Shenyang: Liaoning People's Publishing House, 84, 1994.

Feng, Jicai, "The Spiritual Journey of Old Red Guards", in Ding, Hui (ed.), *Secret Record of Red Guards*, Beijing: Tuanjie Publishing House, 235–237, 1993.

Feng, Xiaotian, "One-Child Families: A New Way of Life", *Social Sciences Journal*, 5, 28–32, 1994.

Firth, Raymond, *Man and Culture*, trans. by Fei, Xiaotong, Beijing: The Commercial Press, 78, 2009.

Foucault, Michel, *Discipline and Punish: The Birth of the Prison*, New York: Vintage, 2012.

Fraser, David, "Inventing Oasis: Luxury Housing Advertisements and Reconfiguring Domestic Space in Shanghai", in Davis, Deborah (ed.), *The Consumer Revolution in Urban China*, Berkeley, CA: University of California Press, 25–53, 2000.

Furstenberg, Frank F., "The Sociology of Adolescence and Youth in 1990s: A Critical Commentary", *Journal of Marriage and Family*, 62, 4, 896–910, 2000.

Gan, Yang, "Critique of the Concept of Civil Society", in Zhang, Jing (ed.), *State and Society*, Hangzhou: Zhejiang People's Publishing House, 28, 1998.

Gao, Hua, "The Birth of New People", in Gao, Hua (ed.), *Revolutionary Age*, Guangzhou: Guangdong People's Publishing House, 177–206, 2010.

Gao, Liang, "In 2018, the Number of Chinese Students Going Abroad and Returning Home Increased", *China Education News*, March 28, 2019.

Gibson, William & John Barlow, "Cyber Space", in Goffman, Ken (ed.), *Mondo 2000*, New York: HarperCollins, 78, 1992.

Grieder, Jerome B., *Intellectuals and the State in Modern China*, New York: Simon and Schuster, 1983.

Global Consulting Group, "The 2018 Hurun Financial Report is out! There are 3.87 million 'wealthy families' in China", 2018. https://www.baidu.com/link?url=43Uyc5pD-KoJxv-D084o69m-RjNkmd_jrP0u75onTYujvPEwQ_lRcMrnv-G1Q4ufv&wd=&eqid=dd8166c-b0010a92f000000055edaf8eb

Guo, Yuhua, "Infant Foods and Cultural Flow in a Transitional Society", *Social Studies*, 1, 39–49, 1998.

Guo, Yuhua, "The Concept of Fairness in Intergenerational Relations and Its Changes: An Analysis of the Old-Age Care Events in Rural Hebei", *Chinese Academic*, 4, 221–254, 2001.

Han, Yu, "On Teachers", in *Collected Works of Chang Li*, Shanghai: Shanghai Ancient Books Publishing House, 12, 2013.

He, Xuefeng, Yuan Song & Song Lina, *Study on Migrant Workers Returning Home*, Jinan: Shandong People's Publishing House, 2010.

Ho, David Y. F., "Filial Piety and Its Psychological Consequences", in Bond, Michael Harris (ed.), *The Handbook of Chinese Psychology*, New York: Oxford University Press, 155–165, 1996.

Huang, Jie, "Civil Society and Community Building", *Exploration*, 6, 52–55, 2002.

Huang, Shengmin & Chen Subai, "The Surface and Depth of Social Consciousness: An Investigation into the Advertising Attitude Consciousness of Chinese Audiences", *Modern Communication*, 2, 20–26, 2006.

Hutter, Mark, *The Changing Family*, New York: John Willis & Sons, 1981.

Hyman, Herbert Hiram, "The Psychology of Status", *Archives of Psychology*, 269, 5–28, 1942.

Inkeles, Alex & David H. Smith, "Becoming Modern: Individual Change in Six Developing Countries", *Ethos*, 3, 2, 323–342, 1975.

ITU (International Telecommunication Union), *Measuring the Information Society: The ICT Development Index*, Geneva, Switzerland: ITU, 2009.

Jiang, Naiqiang, "In 2009, Nearly 230,000 Chinese Students Studied Abroad", *China Education News*, March 12, 2010.

Jin, Yihong, "Mobile Patriarchy: The Transition of Mobile Farmer Families", *Social Sciences in China*, 4, 2010.

King, Ambrose, "Transformation of Modernity and Transitional Society", in Qin, Xiao (ed.), *The Question of Contemporary China: Modernization or Modernity*, Beijing: Social Sciences Academic Press, 30–33, 2009.

Kramarae, Cheris, "A Backstage Critique of Virtual Reality", in Jones, Steven G. (ed.), *Cyber Society, Computer-Mediated Communication and Community*, London: Sage, 36–56, 1995.

Larson, Reed W., "Adolescent's Daily Experience with Family and Friends: Contrasting Opportunity Systems", *Journal of Marriage and the Family*, 45, 739–750, 1983.

Larson, Reed W. & Suman Verma, "How Children and Adolescents Spend Time across the World: Work, Play, and Developmental Opportunities", *Psychological Bulletin*, 125, 6, 701, 1999.

Larson, Reed & Suzanne Wilson, "Adolescent across Place and Time: Globalization and the Changing Pathways to Adulthood", in Lerner, R. & L. Steinberg (eds.), *Handbook and Adolescent Psychology*, New York: Wiley, 299–361, 2004.

Latham, Michael E., *Modernization as Ideology*, trans. by Niu Ke, Beijing: Central Compilation and Translation Press, 2003.

LeVine, Robert A., "American Experience as a Socialization Process", in Newcomb, Theodore M. & Everett k. Wilson (eds.), *College Peer Groups*, Chicago, IL: Aldine Publishing Company, 116–121, 1966.

Li, Hui, "Listening to His Beautiful Story", in Ma, Guoliang (ed.), *A Pictorial and an Era*, Beijing: Sanlian Bookstore, 2, 2002.

Li, Oufan, *Shanghai Modern: A New Urban Culture in China (1930–1945)*, trans. by Mao, Jian, Beijing: Beijing University Press, 80, 2005.

Li, Peilin, "Modernity and the Chinese Experience", *Chinese Journal of Sociology*, 3, 1–6, 2008.

Li, Qiang, "T-Shaped Social Structure and Structural Stress", *Sociological Study*, 2, 55–73, 2005.

Li, Shi & Ding Sai, "The Long-Term Trend of the Rate of Return of Urban Education in China", *Social Sciences in China*, 6, 58–72, 2003.

Li, Wenhai & Liu Yangdong, "The Development of Filial Piety in Modern China", in Zhonghua Book Company, (ed.), *The Past and Present of Chinese Culture: Essays on the 80th Anniversary of the Founding of Zhonghua Book Company*, Beijing: Zhonghua Book Company, 212–231, 1992.

Li, Zhuojun & Chen Rong, "Network Culture: A New Media Culture", *Journal of Nanjing University of Posts and Telecommunications*, 1, 33–37, 2005.

Liu, Guili, "Why Do Tears Roll Down: An Analysis on the Tendency of Intergenerational Relations in Transitional Families", *Journal of Nanchang University*, 6, 1–8, 2005.

Liu, Jingming, "The Expansion of Higher Education and the Difference in Admission Opportunity: 1978–2003", *Society*, 3, 158–179, 2006.

Liu, Kexuan, "Qian Xuantong: One Should Be Shot at the Age of 40", *Literature and History Expo*, 10, 69, 2011.

Liu, Yaqiu, "Youth without Regret: A Process of Constructing Social Memory", *Sociological Study*, 2, 65–74, 2003.

Liu, Zaifu, "Finding One's Way in Pain: The Awakening of Three Major Consciousnesses in China over the Past Hundred Years and the Topic of Today", *Literature in Chinese Language*, 4, 41–49, 2011.

Lv, Xiaobo, "On the Rise of Political Press and the Breakthrough of Social Reform: A Case Study of *Current Affairs*", *Journal of Nanjing University*, 3, 164–165, 1994.

Ma, Licheng, *Thirty Years of Clash of Ideas: My Experience of the Four Major Debates on Reform and Opening Up*, Nanjing: Jiangsu People's Publishing House, 2008.

Madsen, Richard, "The Study of Chinese State and Social Relations by Five Generations of American Scholars", in Tu, Zhaoqing & Lin Yimin (eds.), *Reform and Opening Up and Chinese Society*, Hong Kong: Oxford University Press, 42, 1999.

Madsen, Richard, "Epilogue: The Second Liberation", in Davis, Deborah (ed.), *The Consumer Revolution in Urban China*, Berkeley, CA: California University Press, 15–16, 2000.

Mannheim, Karl, "The Problem of Generation", in Mannheim, K. (ed.), *Essays on the Sociology of Knowledge*, London: Routledge & Kegan Paul, 276–320, 1952.

Mao, Zedong, "The Investigation Report on Hunan Peasant Movement", in Theory Group of the Central Cultural Revolution (ed.), *Selected Works of Mao Zedong*, Beijing: People's Publishing House, 12–44, 1967a.

Mao, Zedong, "The Direction of the Youth Movement", in Theory Group of the Central Cultural Revolution (ed.), *Selected Works of Mao Zedong*, Beijing: People's Publishing House, 525–533, 1967b.

Mao, Zedong, "Absorbing a Large Number of Intellectuals", in Theory Group of the Central Cultural Revolution (ed.), *Selected Works of Mao Zedong*, Beijing: People's Publishing House, 581–583, 1967c.

Mao, Zedong, "Proposal to Carry Out Cremation", in Document Research Office of the CPC Central Committee (ed.), *Mao Zedong's Writings since the Founding of the People's Republic*, Vol. 6, Beijing: Central Academic Press, 110, 1992.

Mao, Zedong, "Establishment and Implementation of *Jianxuehui*", in Document Research Office of the CPC Central Committee (ed.), *Early Mao Zedong Manuscripts*, Changsha: Hunan Publishing House, 368, 1995.

Marx, Karl & Friedrich Engels, *Marx & Engels Collected Works*, Vol. 2, Beijing: People's Publishing House, 83, 1973.

McKinsey & Company, "China Luxury Report 2019: How Young Chinese Consumers are Reshaping Global Luxury", 2019. https://www.mckinsey.com/~/media/McKinsey/Featured Insights/China/How young Chinese consumers are reshaping global luxury/McKinsey-China-luxury-report-2019-How-young-Chinese-consumers-are-reshaping-global-luxury.ashx

McLuhan, Marshall, *Understanding Media: The Extensions of Man*, MA: MIT Press, 1994.

Meng, Ying, "On the Interactive Promotion of Media and Social Relations in Development", *Journal of Fudan University*, 4, 136–140, 2010.

Newcomb, Theodore M., "The General Nature of Peer Group Influence", in Newcomb, Theodore M. & Everett K. Wilson (eds.), *College Peer Group, Problems and Prospects for Research*, Chicago, IL: Aldine Publishing Company, 2–16, 1966.

Ngan, Raymond & Stephen Ma, "The Relationship of Mobile Telephone to Job in China's Pearl River Delta", *Knowledge, Technology, and Policy*, 21, 2, 55–63, 2008.

Ni, Tingting, "Non-Filial Piety and the Moral Plight of the 'May Fourth' Writers", *Literature Review*, 5, 28–34, 2004.

Odland, Jerry, "Television and Children", *Childhood Education*, 80, 4, 206B–206C, 2004.

Pareto, Vilfredo, *The Rise and Fall of the Elites: An Application of Theoretical Sociology*, Totowa, NJ: The Bedminster Press, 1968.

Parsons, Talcott, "Age and Sex in the Social Structure of the United States", *American Sociological Review*, 7, 5, 604–616, 1942.

Parsons, Talcott, "The School Class as a Social System: Some of Its Functions in American Society", in Parsons, Talcott (ed.), *Social Structure and Personality*, New York: Free Press, 129–154, 1964.

Peck, James, "The Roots of Rhetoric: The Professional Ideology of America's China Watchers", *Business of Concerned Asian Scholars*, 2, 1, 59–69, 1969.

Pei, Yiran, "The Constitution and Limitation of Yan'an Intellectual Circles", *Social Sciences*, 3, 147–156, 2013.

Phelan, Patricia, Ann Locke Davidson & Hanh Cao Yu, "Students' Multiple Worlds: Navigating the Borders of Family, Peer, and School Culture", in Phelan, P. & A. Davidson (eds.), *Renegotiating Cultural Diversity in America's Schools*, New York: Teachers College Press, 53, 1993.

Pye, Lucian, *The Spirit of Chinese Politics* (New Edition), Cambridge, MA: Harvard University Press, 113–114, 1992.

Qian, Xuantong, "The Future of Chinese Writing", *New Youth*, 4, 4, 350–354, 1918.

Qiu, Linchuan, "Labor Problems in the New Cyber Society", *Open Era*, 12, 127–139, 2009.

Qu, Zhe (dictated), "Struggle and Quest Have Always Been the Theme Song of This Generation", in Liu, Xiaomeng (ed.), *Oral History of Educated Youth in China*, Beijing: China Social Sciences Press, 123, 2002.

Reich, Charles A., *The Greening of America*, New York: Penguin Books, 1970.

Riesman, David, Nathan Glazer & Reuel Denney, *The Lonely Crowd: A Study of the Changing American Character*, New Haven, CT: Yale University Press, XV, 1961.

Riggs, Fred Warren, *The Ecology of Public Administration*, Bombay: Asia Publishing House, 1961.

Riggs, Fred Warren, *Administration in Developing Countries*, Boston, MA: Houghton Mifflin Company, 1964.

Rogers, Everett M., *A History of Communication Study: A Biological Approach*, New York: Free Press, 1994.

Savage, Jon, *Teenage: The Creation of Youth: 1875–1945*, London: Pimlico, 2007.

Scelenyi, Ivan, "Social Inequalities in State Socialist Redistributive Economies", *International Journal of Comparative Sociology*, 19, 1–2, 63–87, 1978.

Shen, Yifei, "China in the 'Post-patriarchal Era': Changes in Power Relations within Urban Families and Society", *Journal of Guangxi University for Nationalities*, 6, 43–50, 2009.

Sherif, Muzafer, O. J. Harvey, B. J. White, W. R. Hood & C. W. Sherif, *Intergroup Cooperation and Conflict: The Robbers Cave Experiment*, Norman, OK: University of Oklahoma Book Exchange, 1961.

Shi, Zhiyu, "Intellectual Ethics in Chinese Research Literature", in Wang, Ronghua (ed.), *China from Multiple Perspectives*, Shanghai: Xuelin Press, 14–46, 2006.

Song, Rongen, "Civilian Educator Yan Yangchu", in Feng, Keli (ed.), *Old Photos*, Jinan: Shandong Pictorial Publishing House, 85, 1–24, 2012.

Scott, Nigel, Garforth Christopher, Jain Rekha, Mascarenhas Ophelia & McKemey Kevin, "The Economic Impact of Telecommunications on Rural Livelihoods and Poverty Reduction: A Study of Rural Communities in India (Gujarat), Mozambique, and Tanzania", in *Commonwealth Telecommunications Organization for UK Department for International Development*, 2005.

State Council Information Office, A White Paper on the State of the Internet in China, 2010. http://politics.people.com.cn/GB/1026/11913615.html.

Steinberg, Laurence, *Age of Opportunity: Lessons from the New Science of Adolescence*, New York: Houghton Mifflin Harcourt, 2014.

Sun, Benwen, "Social Problems in Modern China", in Zhou, Xiaohong (ed.), *Sun Benwen Anthology*, Beijing: Scientific Literature Press, 6, 407, 7, 385, 2012.

Sun, Liping, "Social Transformation: New Issues in Developmental Sociology", *Sociological Studies*, 1, 1–24, 2005.

Sun, Zhongshan, "Speech in Europe", in Republic of China History Research Office, Institute of modern History Chinese Academy of Social Sciences (ed.), *Complete Works of Sun Yat-sen*, Vol. 1, Beijing: Zhonghua Bookstore, 560, 1981.

Supreme Council for National Defense, "The Program of General Mobilization of the National Spirit and the Measures for Its Implementation", *Education Magazine*, 9, 4, 15–39, 1939.

Szelenyi, Ivan, "Social Inequalities in State Socialist Redistributive Economies", *International Journal of Comparative Sociology*, 19, 1–2, 63–87, 1978.

Tajfel, Henri, M. G. Billig, R. P. Bundy & Claude Flament, "Social Categorization and Intergroup Behavior", *European Journal of Social Psychology*, 1, 2, 149–178, 1971.

Tan, Shen, "Family Strategy, or Individual Autonomy?" *Journal of Zhejiang*, 5, 210–214, 2004.

Tao, Dongfeng, "Advertising, Lies and Ideology", *Advertisement Panorama*, 5, 77–91, 2006.

The Ministry of Administration, "The Ministry of Administration Conveys to the Nationalist Government for Approving a Proposal of the Ministry of the Interior to Promote the Cultural Center of China as a Foundation for National Development", in The Second Historical Archives of China (ed.), *Compilation of Archival Materials on the History of the Republic of China*, Vol. 5, Nanjing: Jiangsu Ancient Books Publishing House, 41–46, 1994.

USAID (The United States Agency for International Development), A Mobile Voice: The Use of Mobile Phones in Citizen Media: An Exploration of Mobile Citizen Media Tools and Projects, 2008. www.Pactworld.org.

Van Loon, Hendrik Willem, 1925, *Tolerance*, trans. by Ze Wei & Jin Cuiwei, Beijing: Sanlian Bookstore, 1985.

Van Maanen, John James, M. Dabbs & Robert R. Faulkner, *Varieties of Qualitative Research*, Beverley Hills, CA: Sage, 1982.

Wang, Hansheng & Liu Yaqiu, "Social Memory and Its Construction: A Study on Collective Memory of Educated Youth", *Society*, 26, 3, 46–68, 2006.

Wang, Ji & Liu Xunfei, "Discussion on the Virtual Peer Group in the Network", *Frontier Economy and Culture*, 4, 110–111, 2006.

Wang, Xiaofang & Su Hong, "On the Influence of Advertising on Values in the Framework of Consumerism", *Journal of Xi'an Petroleum University*, 4, 85–89, 2006.

Wang, Xiaozhang, "Focusing on the 'Chinese Feeling' Is the Mission of Chinese Social Sciences", *Learning and Exploration*, 3, 35–37, 2012.

Weeden, Kim A., "Why Do Some Occupations Pay More than Others? Social Closure and Earning Inequality in the United States", *American Journal of Sociology*, 108, 1, 55–101, 2002.

Wen, Qing, Jia Zhen & Bao Yun (eds.), "Preparation for Adopting Western Practice", in *The Continuation of the Complete Library of Four Branches of Books*, Shanghai: Shanghai Ancient Books Publishing House (print version), 398, 2002.

Wu, Guozhong, "The Cover of *Good Friend* of the Republic of China and the Modern Construction of Female Body Space", *Journal of Hunan Normal University*, 5, 139–142, 2009.

Wu, Jianmin, "Knowing the World and Knowing Yourself", *Southern Window*, 19, 6, 2010.

Wu, Xiaoying, "Intergenerational Relationship", in Li, Peilin et al. (eds.), *Sociology and Chinese Society*, Beijing: Social Sciences Academic Press, 263, 2008.

Wu, Yue, "Wu Yue's Will", in Zhang, Binglin (ed.), *The Crusade of Heaven (A Supplement to Ming Bao)*, 7–8, 1907.

Xu, Fuguan, "The Formation and Evolution of Filial Piety in China and Its Problems in History", in Xu, Fuguan (ed.), *The History of Chinese Thought*, Taipei: Hsueh Sheng, 155–200, 1975.

Xu, Jie, "'Report on the Cultural Influence of Chinese Cities' Released by the School of Social Sciences of Nanjing University", *Chinese Sociology*, 2015. http://www.soci ology2010. cass.cn/xsdt/xsxx/xxzx/201501/t20150104_1977680.shtml.

Xue, Weixian & Liu Jun, "An Analysis of the Nature of the Digital Divide", *Information Theory and Practice*, 12, 41–46, 2010.

Xuncius, "Encouraging Learning", in Li, Yong & Fanf Bo (eds.), *Xuncius*, Shanghai: Zhonghua Book Company, 2, 2011.

Yan, Beiming, "Should We Still Talk about 'Filial Piety' Today?", *The Chinese Elderly*, 1, 15–16, 1983.

Yang, Bojun, *Translation and Annotation of Analects of Confucius*, Beijing: Zhonghua Book Company, 4, 1980.

Yang, Deguang, "The Development of Postgraduate Education in China", *University Education Science*, 4, 103–108, 2013.

Yang, Guobin, "The Co-Evolution of the Internet and Civil Society in China", *Asian Survey*, 43, 3, 405–422, 2003.

Yang, Xiao, "The Land of Aung San Suu Kyi", *Southern People Weekly*, 287, 38–47, 2012.

Yang, Zhongfang, "An Indigenous Framework for Studying the Chinese Character", *Chinese Social Psychology Review*, Beijing: Social Sciences Academic Press, 4, 223–251, 2008.

Yao, Jun & Zhang Li, "Network Peer Group and Adolescent Socialization", *Contemporary Youth Studies*, 4, 24–27, 2004.

Ye, Guanghui, "The Resolution Mode of the Dilemma of Filial Piety and Its Related Factors", *Journal of Institute of Ethnology, Academia Sinica*, 79, 87–118, 1995.

Yi, Qun, "Analysis on the Historical Changes and Characteristics of Postgraduate Education in the Early Years of the Founding of New China (1949–1966): A Case Study of the Early Education History Research Institute", *Journal of Education*, 1, 122–128, 2012.

Yin, Huanxia, "A Review of the Press during Social Change", *Journal of Chongqing Jiaotong University*, 6, 59, 2007.

Zhang, Yingduan & Zuo Bin, "Social Identity Theory and Its Development", *Advances in Psychological Science*, 3, 475–480, 2006.

Zhou, Li, "The Social Influence of Newspapers in Nineteenth Century America", *Journal of Zhejiang University of Communication*, 2, 27–29, 2006.

Zhou, Xiaohong, "The Influence of Mobility and Urban Experience on the Modernity of Chinese Peasants", *Sociological Study*, 5, 60–73, 1998.

Zhou, Xiaohong, "Cultural Reverse: Intergenerational Inheritance in a Transitional Society", *Social Studies*, 2, 1–66, 2000a.

Zhou, Xiaohong, "The Political Participation of Chinese Farmers from the Perspective of State and Social Relations", *Hong Kong Journal of Social Sciences*, 17, 117–150, 2000b.

Zhou, Xiaohong, "The Middle Class: What Is Possible and What Can Be Done", *Jiangsu Social Sciences*, 6, 37–46, 2002.

Zhou, Xiaohong, "1951–1958: Impetus for Collectivization of Agriculture in China", in Zhou, Xiaohong & Xie Shuguang (eds.), *China Studies*, Vol. 1, Beijing: Social Sciences Academic Press, 22–43, 2005.

Zhou, Xiaohong, "Filial Piety and Seniority: Intergenerational Relationship in Traditional Chinese Society", *Zhejiang Social Science*, 5, 77–82, 2008a.

Zhou, Xiaohong, "Identity Theory: An Analytical Approach to Sociology and Psychology", *Social Sciences*, 4, 46–53, 2008b.

Zhou, Xiaohong, "The Change of Chinese Social Mentality since the Reform and Opening Up: Another Interpretation of Chinese Experience", in Deng, Zhenglai (ed.), *Collective Works of Chinese Social Sciences*, Vol. 1, Shanghai: Fudan University Press, 1–11, 2009a.

Zhou, Xiaohong, "The Change and Development Trend of Chinese People's Social Mentality in the Past 60 Years", *Hebei Academic Journal*, 5, 1–6, 2009b.

Zhou, Xiaohong, "The Possible Position and Reconstruction of the Paradigm in China Studies", *Sociological Study*, 2, 1–29, 2010a.

Zhou, Xiaohong, "Globalization, Social Transformation and the Construction of the Middle Class", *Journal of Jiangsu School of Administration*, 1, 61–69, 2010b.

Zhou, Xiaohong, "Cultural Reverse and the Intergenerational Inheritance of Modern Utensil Civilization", *Social Sciences in China*, 6, 109–120, 2011a.

Zhou, Xiaohong, "Chinese Experience and Chinese Feeling: Understanding the Dual Vision of Social Change", *Tianjin Social Sciences*, 6, 12–19, 2011b.

Zhou, Xiaohong, "On Chinese Feeling: Connotation, Characteristics and Research Significance", *Sociological Review*, 1, 14–21, 2013.

Zhou, Xiaohong, "The Social Mentality of Contemporary Chinese", *Journal of Jiangsu School of Administration*, 5, 46–49, 6, 54–57, 2014.

Zhou, Xiaohong, "Social Transformation and the Historical Mission of Chinese Science", *Nanjing Social Science*, 1, 1–10, 2014a.

Zhou, Xiaohong, "Social Mentality and Chinese Experience in the Transition Era", *Sociological Study*, 4, 1–123, 2014b.

Zhou, Xiaohong, "Anxiety: A Symptom of the Times in the Context of Rapid Change", *Journal of Jiangsu School of Administration*, 6, 54–57, 2014c.

Zhou, Xiaohong & Qin Chen, "Exploring Chinese Experience and Chinese Feeling in the Context of Globalization: An Interview with Professor Zhou Xiaohong", *The Academic Issue*, 9, 155–160, 2010a.

Zhou, Xiaohong & Qin Chen, "Globalization, Social Transformation, and the Construction of China's Middle Class", in Lee, Cheng (ed.), *China's Emerging Middle Class*, Washington, DC: Brookings Press, 84–103, 2010b.

Zhou, Xiuming, "Anti-Urbanization Reinterpretation: Re-Understanding of the Phenomenon of the First Population Migration in New China", *Party History Highlights*, 10, 28–30, 2010.

Zhou, Xueguang & Hou Liren, "Children of the Cultural Revolution: The State and the Life Course in the People's Republic of China", *American Sociological Review*, 64, 1, 12–36, 1999.

Zhou, Yi, "Sociological Study of Generation Gap", *Sociological Study*, 4, 67–69, 1994.

Zhou, Yongming, "Living on the Cyber Border: Folk Political Writers in Chinese Cyberspace", *Current Anthropology*, 46, 5, 779–803, 2005.

Zhu, Hong, "Physical Capital and Urban Adaptation of Female Migrant Workers", *Society*, 6, 153–157, 2008.

Zhu, Hong, "From Communication Technology to Livelihood and Entertainment Tools: The Evolution of Mobile Social Functions from a Survey of Low- and Middle-Income Groups", *Journal of Nanjing University*, 3, 42–50, 2011.

Zhu, Huayou & Chen Ningning, "The Function Evolution of Village Ancestral Hall and Its Influence on the Construction of New Socialist Countryside", *China Rural Observation*, 2, 86–94, 2009.

Zhu, Rongji, "Government Work Report" (Report at the Third Session of the Ninth National People's Congress on March 5, 2000), in Literature Research Office of the CPC Central Committee (ed.), *An Anthology of Important Documents since the Fifteenth National Congress*, Beijing: People's Publishing House, 1174, 2001.

Index